Working Out

Jackie Sadek is 36. She has a first degree in philosophy and physics and a masters degree in business administration (MBA) from the University of East London. She has held a variety of management positions in the private, public and voluntary sectors, including five years heading up the public affairs function in an almost exclusively male environment of a large-scale property development company. She now runs her own business, Urban Strategy, a development consultancy. She lives in West London with her husband, James, and her children, Frances and Bruno. She was expecting her second child whilst writing this book.

Sheila Egan is 36. She was born and brought up in Dublin and took her first degree in psychology followed by a masters degree in clinical psychology at University College Dublin. She worked in Ireland, Germany and the United States of America before settling in London six years ago. She now lives and works in central London, where she runs her own business, Practical Resourcing, a research and training consultancy.

Both women have been active in many campaigns – both formal and informal – to improve the lot of women in the workplace, in society and in public life

WORKING
OUT

A WOMAN'S GUIDE TO
CAREER SUCCESS

Jackie Sadek

Sheila Egan

ARROW

Published by Arrow Books in 1995

1 3 5 7 9 10 8 6 4 2

© Jackie Sadek and Sheila Egan 1995

Jackie Sadek and Sheila Egan have asserted their right
under the Copyright, Designs and Patents Act, 1988 to be
identified as the authors of this work

First published in the United Kingdom by
Arrow Books Limited
20 Vauxhall Bridge Road, London, SW1V 2SA

Random House Australia (Pty) Limited
20 Alfred Street, Milsons Point, Sydney,
New South Wales 2061, Australia

Random House New Zealand Limited
18 Poland Road, Glenfield
Auckland 10, New Zealand

Random House South Africa (Pty) Limited
PO Box 337, Bergvlei, South Africa

Random House UK Limited Reg. No. 954009
ISBN 0 09 9468417

Printed and bound in the United Kingdom by
Cox & Wyman Ltd, Reading

FOR FIONA FERGUSON

'I have a profound conviction that if there were many more women in responsible jobs, it would help to bring about the peaceful revolution we all want… For in so far as women are different from men I believe that, perhaps by nature, perhaps by nurture, and certainly by life experience, they have the edge over men in caring more about people and less about personal power and status, and even about money.'

Mary Stott,
Before I Go (Virago Press)

Contents

Introduction   viii
Acknowledgements   xi

1 Firm Foundations   1
2 Your Career Strategy   29
3 Changing Your Job   55
4 Activating Support Systems   81
5 Your Training Strategy   100
6 Your Time: Your Choice   129
7 Effective Communications   148
8 Working Relationships   174
9 Resolving Conflict   199
10 HarnessingYour Stress   219
11 Managing Your Health   239
12 Dressing For Success   262
13 Home and Cash   287
14 Babies?   311

Further Reading and
Useful Contacts   337

Introduction

On a number of occasions we've been asked what makes us qualified to write this book. At first, we were bewildered by this question. Increasingly we became irritated.

Of course, the answer is: we're not *especially* qualified to write this book. We could name several dozen women (in our immediate acquaintance alone) who could have written it. The only thing that differentiates us from them is that we did, whereas they didn't (mainly because they were busy actually doing it rather than writing about it).

The only qualification that we have to write this book is that we've *been there*. We've made our mistakes. Although we don't regret too many of them, we often wish we'd known at twenty what we knew at thirty five.

In this spirit, we have collated the things that we wish we had known – the tough lessons we had to learn – for young women making their way in the world of work. Our book is written for women who are like we were, who need all the help they can get.

There are three basic beliefs that underpin this book.

The first – and most fundamental – of these, is that women can achieve anything they want to. It is incredible and sad that this truth is still not universally acknowledged. Our unshakeable belief in this fact goes right back to our experiences as little girls in Dublin and London, although we only began to articulate it, along with many other women, when we became involved in student politics in the late 1970s.

In common with most of our generation, we experienced something of a culture shock when we left the egalitarian student world and joined the workforce in the early 1980s. We hope that this book will help other women cope, at least a bit better than we did, with this inevitable culture shock.

The second of our basic beliefs is that collaboration – or skills sharing – is the most productive way of working (funnily enough, men don't seem to have got the hang of this). Collaboration is crucial and this book would never have happened without it. We didn't know about certain stuff so we asked. And people gave (even those who didn't know us terribly well). We were amazed and delighted by the amount that people were prepared to do for us; by the generosity of spirit. We have been immensely supported by a huge number of professional women and men, without whom we could not have delivered an holistic product.

The learning experience of collaboration is key. Our own career success would never have happened without it. Essential to it all is the fun and energy that you get from working this way. We cannot now deal with people on any other basis.

Our third basic belief is that there are no right and wrong answers. This book is about a *process*, not about a finished product. Success is only success if you've achieved it on your own terms. A fulfilling working life is not necessarily about 'reaching the top' and there are no ready-made solutions. Fulfilment comes from a willingness to *engage*.

What follows, therefore, is the collective experience of both of us, aided and abetted by a diverse range of wonderful working women. We wanted to produce something that would be a comprehensive guide for most areas of a typical working woman's life. Where it was inappropriate to explore a subject exhaustively, we have recommended further reading and sources of advice. We thought there should be *one* book for working women that would cover most topics, at least in outline, and that could refer women on to other sources if needs be.

We hope you enjoy our book and that it helps. We certainly enjoyed writing it (at least most of the time). Please write to us if you have any suggestions or if you think we got anything right or wrong. We'd love to hear from you.

Jackie Sadek and Sheila Egan
Working Woman Foundation
8 Cottons Gardens
London E2 8DN

Acknowledgements

Our grateful thanks to the following people for their invaluable assistance with specialist areas of this book:

Alison Brown, osteopath, and Sarah Williams, acupuncturist, for considered advice relating to the chapter on support systems; Sue Slipman, Director of the National Council for One Parent Families, for useful comments on her specialisms and on the tone; Karen Stevens, Managing Director of Pamela Stevens, largest independent chain of beauty therapists for sharing her skills in skin care and clothes; Charles Worthington (Hairdresser of the Year 1993) and Alan Peters of Worthingtons for their excellent advice on hair care for working women; Ann Pugh, at Fiona Price and Partners, for general advice on money and women; Elizabeth Sadek, Principal of Chiltern Nursery Training College, for comments relating to child care and to maintaining your relationship with your baby; Paul Shave of Federal Resources Europe (FRE) for advice on matters realting to job applications and CVs.

Also, thanks a million to the 'brainstorm group': Vicki Lennox, Sam Kenny, Sue Crampton, Karen Stevens and Sarah Williams. Sorry if it got a bit heavy in places, guys, but believe us, it really helped. Also thanks to Ziona Strelitz for her ideas and encouragement.

Thanks to those who gave us help with the mechanics of getting a book published (aside from Random House, who have been great): Claire, Ruth and Tanya Alboretti; Jane Conway-Gordon; Christopher Little; Billy McGrath; Erin Pizzey; and Cate Paterson.

There are a number of people who have been very supportive in various other ways. These are: Katherine Arnold, Briege Arthurs, Annette Bolger, David Chippendale, James Elworthy, Barbara Green, Jane Hyde, Stuart Lipton, Mary Stott, Liz Sayer, Kate Taylor and Linda Taylor. Thanks to you all.

Finally, and most important, our heartfelt thanks to the countless women whom we have met and enjoyed over the years, on whose anecdotes and experiences this book is based.

1 **Firm Foundations**

▶ ▶ ▶ ▶ ▶   SETTING REALISTIC GOALS • PERSONAL
COVENANTS • BEHAVING ASSERTIVELY • RISK
AND THE FEAR OF FAILURE • EXTERNAL AND
INTERNAL REWARDS OF WORK • TAKING
CHARGE OF YOUR CAREER.

INTRODUCTION

Work is everything – right? It's not just important, it is essential to your identity and well being – right? You need to be three times as good as the men – right? These are the only battles worth fighting – right?

Wrong.

Sorry if this seem like a strange way to open a book about work, written by and for those working women who have never done anything other than work and who have undergone years of hard labour in order to establish credibility in their chosen careers.

Sure, you need to prove yourself and you need to deliver your potential but a sense of real proportion about the world in which you live is essential if you are really going to succeed.

Reaching the top will be a hollow achievement if you have had to sacrifice everything to get there. In fact, the chances are that if you've had to sacrifice everything you won't get there anyway – people in top positions are not generally incomplete human beings. The grounding that you get from having a balanced life is the thing that supports you in what you want to achieve in your career.

Your career is only one dimension in your life and you neglect the others at your peril. Before you launch yourself back into the single track, take time out to appraise you priorities and to decide what rewards will make you happiest now and in the future. The complication, naturally, is that your choices will change with time, just as you do. Success means focusing on what you need to accomplish in your whole life. It is too easy to get caught up solely in your career, especially in the early, heady days.

This first chapter is about establishing some firm foundations in your career and in your life. It discusses some tools such as assertive behaviour and personal covenants which will enable you to take charge. It explains that we all need a balanced approach to our lives and that this becomes even more acute as traditional patterns of employment continue to break down all around us.

For almost all of us, the notion of a straightforward, step-by-step career progression is outdated. Unless you have chosen a profession which maintains a fairly standard career structure (such as medicine or ballet dancing), it is an odds-on certainty that your career path will resemble a series of crossroads rather than rungs on a ladder. In today's fluid labour market, you have to decide not only how to move forward but which way to go.

So, you are – largely – in control and can determine your own plan. But don't make the mistake of thinking of a career plan has to be completely prescriptive. Everyone makes mistakes and sometimes things don't work out as we expect them to do. Plans are made to be changed, modified and switched around.

Even if you thought there was no rhyme or reason to the series of jobs or training or qualifications that you underwent in your twenties, you may be surprised as to how coherent it becomes when you begin to consolidate your career in your thirties. Almost all women cobble their careers together using a variety of experiences and tools; essential amongst these are assertiveness and self-determination.

> *Long-term success can be an uncomfortable ride, fraught with the frustration of discrimination and the pain of tokenism. There are very few female role models, which makes it even more difficult, and the stress of balancing the desire to be perfect with the need to risk failure is immense.*

The key is to know what you want in your whole life, to go after it and to have the courage of your convictions. Be flexible enough to respond to change and brave enough to make mistakes. Have the courage to take risks and don't worry about what may appear like failure to others.

SETTING REALISTIC GOALS

Figuring out what you want to achieve is the first step towards achieving it.

> *I fell into the classic trap – I embraced the "family occupation" without even thinking about it. It was only after four years practising as a GP that I realised I had never even thought about what I wanted to do or where it all fitted in with my life. I realised that I didn't want to be a doctor and have finally managed to switch to teaching medicine, which I love.*

A goal is a dream with a deadline. Unfortunately, all too often the time frame gets distorted by the ever changing pattern of responsibilities leaving your precious dreams to fade under the duress of stress.

Setting realistic goals is the key to following your dream. Having goals will really focus your thinking, putting you in a future-orientated frame of mind in which you become concerned with results and developing strategies to get there.

Once you've developed the knack of setting realistic goals for yourself, they become great motivators, spurring you on to greater things and increasing your self-confidence as you hit the milestones along the way.

It's difficult to start. Many of us shy away from setting goals, finding the exercise intimidating and exposing us to potential failure. However, if you're prepared to grasp that nettle, you will find that, with practice, you can develop and fine tune your ability to set realistic goals for yourself. You may find the following checklist useful when you're setting new goals (or evaluating old ones):

▶ **Own your goals**. You need to believe in and be dedicated to your goals, otherwise your heart won't be in achieving them. There will, of course, be times when you share goals with another person – your partner, your manager or a friend, for example. When you decide to accept the goal of another person as your own, however, ask yourself whether it is consistent with what you want. Can you really commit yourself to it? If not, you are probably setting yourself up for failure.

> *I did a report for my manager which was over and above my area of responsibility but I knew he needed it done. And, although I hated the work, I thought it might stand me in good stead for my promotion interview; I accepted his goal in order to achieve my own.*

▶ **Be specific**. Goals are most useful when they are explicit, clear and written. Writing them down really helps clarify what you want and halts the decline of dreams into vague ideas that fade into the distance. Don't worry about whether they are long-term or short-term, large or small, simple or difficult. The idea is to get something, anything, down on paper. You can make them more specific later on.

▶ **Set measurement criteria**. Goals need to be measurable so that you can tell when you have achieved them. This is not always easy, as they are not always that tangible. Ask yourself, 'How will I know when I have accomplished my goal?' If you decide you want to improve your skills, how will you know when you have achieved that? Will it be when you have gained a qualification from a course, when you can give a presentation without faltering, when you can complete your tasks without working additional hours and days?

▶ **State a time**. Set yourself deadlines. They put pressure on you to achieve. Make deadlines reasonable, yet challenging. If you consistently underestimate the time it will take to accomplish a goal, you set yourself up for failure. If you give yourself too much time, you're likely to lose your enthusiasm. Pacing yourself effectively will increase your confidence in your ability to accomplish more challenging goals.

> *I had more ideas of what I want to do than anyone I know but it was always 'sometime in the future'. Then, my thirtieth birthday dawned and I realised that, if I didn't start to do something about them, I'd still be saying the same things when I was sixty. I didn't know where to start so I focused on an easy one – learning to speak French – and signed up for a course. I felt great – for the first time, I'd actually followed through on one of my ambitions.*

▶ **Set both short term and long term goals**. The aim of goals is to orientate yourself towards the future, giving you a framework to work within. If you have trouble setting long term goals, start with the shortest period you can handle. The point is to start somewhere! Once you form the habit of setting goals, you are likely to find that you can look further ahead.

PERSONAL COVENANT

If you are having difficulty establishing your goals, the following exercise may help. Many of the general guidelines for setting goals are evident in the exercise but it helps to systematise the habit for those of us who shy away from setting goals. It is a gentle way to gradually develop the method. A format is provided for writing a covenant which you can adapt to suit your own circumstances.

1 Set yourself a short term goal. Start with something that is not too threatening but is a target you are motivated to achieve. Examples could be getting to work earlier, eating a proper lunch each day, taking regular exercise.

2 Write down your goal. This forces you to be clear about what you want to achieve and helps you to take it seriously. Keep it in a place where you will see it every day – in your diary or the top drawer of your desk.

3 Write down as many benefits of fulfilling the covenant as you can think of, preferably on a daily basis. If you can't think of any benefits, you probably don't have a meaningful covenant.

4 Set the covenant for things you can see and measure so that you can readily assess whether you have been successful or

▶ **Be flexible**. Allow yourself the right to change your mind. As R.W. Emerson said, 'A foolish consistency is the hobgoblin of little minds.' Your priorities are likely to change over time; the goals you developed at the start of your career may no longer be relevant. Your personal goals will take precedence over your career goals at certain times in your life. Goals should never be seen as being cast in stone, to be followed at all cost.

not. An example of a woolly covenant would be 'to clear up the mess in my office'. A better way of approaching the same goal would be 'to eliminate one stack of stuff cluttering my office for each of the next ten days'.

5 Set yourself a challenge. An easily achieved target won't mean much to you; on the other hand, an aim that is too difficult may sabotage your efforts. Choose something that will require you to make a bit of effort but will not doom you to failure.

6 Limit the contract to a specific period of time. We suggest ten days but you can shorten or lengthen that. Think of the personal covenant as the first step towards something you want to achieve over a longer period of time. Breaking your long-term goal into a series of shorter-term ones will help keep you on track.

7 Write your contract in positive terms. Rather than writing that you won't stay in bed until 8.00 a.m., write that you will get up at 7.30 a.m., a half-hour earlier than usual.

8 Increase the stakes. As you become more confident in your ability to set goals and follow through, increase the challenge in the goals you set.

6 *I had done it all according to the book. I knew where I was aiming for in my career and, despite the few inevitable hiccups, my planning and perseverance paid off. Then I looked around and realised that, in my text book approach to my career, I had neglected to look at other aspects of my life. It was only when my social life began to be curtailed as more and more of my friends had childcare responsibilities,*

PERSONAL COVENANT

For the next _____ days I contract with myself to

The benefits I want to achieve are: _____
_____

Signed: _____ Date: _____

PROGRESS:

Day 1: _____
_____

Day 2: _____
_____

Day 3: _____
_____

Day 4: _____
_____

Day 5: _____
_____

Day 6: _____
_____

Day 7: _____
_____

Day 8: _____
_____

Day 9: _____
_____

Day 10: _____
_____

that I realised that I had never applied the same rigour to my personal life as I had to my career.

▶ **Stick with it**. Being flexible should not be used as a way of scrapping old goals. Be wary of abandoning old targets just because you haven't got there yet. Persistence and renewed enthusiasm may well be all that is needed. It's okay to falter along the way but that doesn't mean the goal is not still worth striving for. If it was worth aiming for in the first place, it may be worth sticking with now.

▶ **Take time out**. Detach yourself from all the hustle and bustle. Ask yourself: what are the good things in your life? Where are the frustrations? Is there a wider perspective? Look a little further. Where will you move next? When and in which direction? How far, how fast and who with?

It is essential that you re-examine your dreams regularly. There will be areas you wanted to pursue which you have forgotten about, and self-assessment will help to revitalise the excitement you feel for where you're going and what the next step is. As life circumstances change, goals and priorities will change too. One way of making sure that you re-examine your goals regularly is to make an appointment with yourself to review them each year, on your birthday for example.

Sooner or later, your goals will conflict. One goal may send you in one direction while another drags you in the opposite. Your career, personal, social and family goals may frequently conflict with one another. When this happens, you have to make some decisions about priorities and differentiate between those goals that you consider to be essential to achieving contentment in your life and those that would be 'nice but not necessary'.

 When I have a number of targets and hitting one precludes achieving another, I sit down with a piece of

paper and divide it into two. On one side I write down my 'main aims' and on the other my 'secondary aims'. If my secondary ones conflict with my main ones, I see if there's a way of changing tack to achieve both. If there isn't, I ditch the secondary ones – at least for the time being. You just have to be realistic and know that you can't have everything you want all at once. **,**

GETTING WHAT YOU WANT: BEHAVING ASSERTIVELY

If you want to exert control over your career, you have to learn to be assertive at work. Assertiveness skills will mark you out as someone who can be decisive and stand their ground without unnecessarily treading on colleagues' or bosses' toes.

Whereas men are expected to be assertive, women are not, and many feel unhappy being so. Made to choose between being thought pushy and being self-effacing, women frequently choose the latter.

Assertiveness is often viewed as masked aggression but it is anything but. Assertive people don't step on other people and they don't allow other people to step on them. Assertiveness is the act of standing up for your own rights without violating the basic rights of others.

There is a great tendency for women to act in a submissive manner. Submissive people typically see themselves as victims of unfairness and believe that their needs are less important than others'. Decisions are impossible and self pity is a constant theme. None of these traits are likely to be rewarded by organisations. Taking on the victim mantle will not serve you well in work or do your professional relationships any good. Passivity is often resented by colleagues and would-be supporters may well lose interest and avoid contact.

Assertiveness does not come naturally to many of us and few of us behave assertively all of the time. Our natural instincts of fight or flight frequently override the learned skills of assertiveness. Our responses will also vary depending on our self-esteem. If it is low, we will feel anxious when a conflict arises. We will feel insecure and threatened by the situation and the people in it.

Also, both aggressive and submissive behaviour have some advantages. Aggressive behaviour can be successful in getting us what we want, can give us a sense of power and help us to release feelings like anger and frustration. Submissive behaviour can defuse a conflict very quickly by avoiding it. It helps us to escape the anxiety of a confrontation. It also helps us to avoid feeling guilty about letting someone down or upsetting them. But there are many more benefits to assertiveness, the chief ones being:

▶ Better relations with others. Assertiveness tends to breed assertiveness, so people interact more effectively; working with rather than against each other. In this scenario, you are more likely to achieve your objectives.

▶ Greater confidence in yourself. Dealing assertively with work situations means they are more likely to have a successful outcome. This will increase your level of self esteem and confidence.

▶ Greater confidence in others. You develop a healthy regard for other people, seeing them in their own light rather than as superior or inferior.

▶ Increased self-responsibility. You take greater responsibility for yourself and your opinions and needs rather than blaming others or excusing yourself.

▶ Increased self control. You can channel your thoughts and feelings to produce the behaviour you want rather

DEVELOPING YOUR
ASSERTIVENESS SKILLS

Developing your assertiveness skills is easier said than done. There are no set phrases, trick techniques or magic words in assertive communication but the following guidelines will help.

▶ Show that you understand the speaker. This doesn't mean saying, 'I understand how you feel' when you don't. You have to show by how you listen and what you say that you really have understood. Assertive people are active listeners (see Chapter 7).

For example: saying 'You seem very angry and disappointed ...' gives the speaker a chance to agree that you've got it right or correct it if you haven't. 'I'm disappointed but not angry; more irritated because I've spoken about the same thing several times before.'

▶ Say what you think and feel. Decide what you want or feel and say so directly and specifically. Take responsibility for your feelings and be clear about what has given rise to them. Attribute your feelings to the event or behaviour – not the person.

For example: 'I feel really disappointed that you haven't helped with the report like you said you would.'

than being controlled by outside events or people or feeling you have to control them.

▶ Savings in time and energy. A lot of time is wasted worrying and scheming. If you are not worried about upsetting people or scheming how to put one over, you save yourself a lot of time and stress.

▶ Say specifically what you want to happen. Dropping hints doesn't always work! Being clear about what you want to happen increases the possibility that it will. Of course, it doesn't guarantee that you'll get what you want – you have to be prepared for the other person to say no or have a different point of view.

For example: *saying 'I think the presentation this morning would have been more successful if we'd had better slides' is far more constructive than saying 'The presentation this morning was bad.'*

▶ Take responsibility for what you say. Being assertive is about acknowledging that what you say is your opinion or feeling or idea rather than stating it as an accepted fact. There is a world of difference between the two, as the former allows for discussion, the latter leads to stalemate. Taking responsibility means saying 'I' and not trying to hide behind generalised statements.

For example: *saying 'I thought you talked too much at the meeting which meant that you lost impact on your sales pitch' makes for much more harmonious working relationships than saying 'You talk too much.'*

▶ An increased chance of everyone winning. Assertiveness increases the likelihood that all parties will have their needs met, their ideas and opinions heard and their abilities put to good use.

There are a number of excellent books available on developing assertiveness or you might prefer to attend one of the many assertiveness courses for women. The trick is to start experimenting with assertiveness in safe situations. Eventually, you will gain enough confidence and it will become a natural thing, like breathing. This is not to say that there is no conscious effort involved. As with most skills, you may feel uncomfortable acting in an assertive manner at the start but it will come more easily with practice. Eventually, these skills become part of you, your second nature.

> I know the whole assertiveness thing is seen as 'trendy' and all that but I learned an invaluable skill when I went on the course. As well as a general shift in how I thought about myself and my ability to control situations, I learned to say words that did not come easy but have stood me in good stead since. When I'm in potentially tense situations in work, the phrase 'I appreciate how you feel but ...' has helped to diffuse it and get to a solution. I smile to myself when I say it because I can remember my level of discomfort when I was rehearsing it on the course. Simply learning to say those words has kept me out of so many rows in work.

RISK AND THE FEAR OF FAILURE

People who achieve their goals are willing to take risks.

Many of us equate risk-taking with high levels of anxiety and avoid it at all costs. But you don't have to develop an ulcer to become an effective risk-taker. One of the key elements in becoming an effective risk-taker is knowing the amount of stress you can live with (see Chapter 10).

> The most crucial attribute a woman can bring to a career in any technology industry is an ability to face risk. You need a strong stomach for the ups and downs of the industry itself but a poker player's fortitude also comes in handy at the individual career level.

Risk-takers are not necessarily gamblers. Gamblers are basically helpless to control the situations on which they bet. Effective risk-taking is about taking calculated risks over which you can direct some influence. The effective risk-taker takes an active part in moderating risk, whereas the gambler waits passively for the results.

There are three basic attitudes to risk-taking: avoidance, neutrality and acceptance. Risk-avoiders won't take even a small chance for a possible high reward. Neutrals are basically objective about risk and will generally take a risk if it seems to have promise of high value over time. Risk-acceptors will take a chance on a high reward, even if there is only a small possibility of success.

Effective risk-taking is not synonymous with risk-accepting, and there is no one correct attitude towards risk. When you're thinking through a risk situation, ask yourself:

?
How likely am I to succeed?
How much will I gain if I am successful?
How likely am I to be unsuccessful?
How much will I lose if I am unsuccessful?
Can I live with the possible losses?

The last of these questions is the most critical. If you don't think you can live with the possible losses, avoiding risk-taking may be the most sensible approach in the situation. Frequently, however, our inability to live with the loss is driven more by anxiety than being actually unable to afford the loss itself.

> *I was so scared of losing face, that I panicked every time there was the slightest possibility of something going wrong. And the more I realised this, the worse I got. Then, one day, my manager said 'I really screwed up that presentation yesterday – we'll have to get some training and tighten up our act.' The relief. I suddenly*

realised that it was not the end of the world if
something didn't go right – it was OK to admit you'd
screwed up and that you were going
to do something about it. **'**

Each time a risk is taken there are consequences. Whether these consequences are positive or negative, they provide you with valuable feedback. If you want to improve your risk-taking skills, you can't afford to take a head-in-the-sand approach to feedback.

Of course, where there's risk, there's the chance of failure, and failure is one of the greatest terrors we ever have to face.

Women tend to be conditioned into thinking we're power-less in the face of our mistakes. Big failures, like losing a job, missing out on getting a job, screwing up an important report or giving a lousy presentation, shake our fundamental faith in ourselves. Failure makes us feel powerless and enormously vulnerable. We become unsure of ourselves, our abilities and our direction in life.

We are often more paralysed by fear of failure than men. In our efforts to compete successfully with men, we can set ourselves up as superwomen and demand perfectionism from ourselves at all times.

' *Women have got to be very careful not to fall head*
first into the 'I have to be ten times better than men'
syndrome. All too often, this stops us taking risks and
pushes our paranoia of failure to unacceptable levels.
We have to accept that nobody is born knowing how to
do everything right. This attitude can make women
afraid to ask for help when they're out of their depth or
embarrassed to admit when they're wrong
for fear of seeming less competent. **'**

Fear of failure can stop you from getting what you really want out of life. It can cripple the most promising career. Remember the old adage, 'nothing ventured, nothing gained'. In short, if we never put ourselves forward for fear of failing, we can't blame anyone but ourselves for not getting key positions or assignments.

> *The initial shock of not getting the promotion was immense but afterwards I actually felt a sense of relief. I realised I had to face up to what I really wanted and have the courage to go for it. If I failed – well, I'd been rejected once and it wasn't as bad as all that.*

You can develop your risk-taking ability with practice. Start with small risks. If small risks are successful, you get positive feedback about your ability to succeed. More important, if you are unsuccessful, you gain valuable experience in the less pleasant side of risk-taking, in a relatively non-threatening context.

If you fail, remember that failure can be an act of liberation.

Success in the eyes of others is overrated. It's not what anyone else thinks that counts. It's how you're doing inside that really matters. Failing can sometimes make you realise that you're looking for happiness in the wrong places and for the wrong reasons. Goals like wanting more money, a more prestigious job title or status to impress other people are frequently misleading markers of happiness.

Everyone can do far more than they think they can provided they are not afraid of something going wrong. It's only realistic to acknowledge that something, at some time, will go wrong.

> *Failure is always hurtful, humiliating, painful and embarrassing. But it's the price you pay for daring to get everything you want out of life.*

DEVELOPING YOUR
RISK-TAKING SKILLS

The following strategy for developing risk adopts a staged approach. There are four basic stages. If you are totally risk-averse, start at stage 1; if you have a more developed sense of risk-taking, start at a later stage in the process.

▶ Broaden your horizons. Begin with simple, trivial ways of doing something different. Do things that are positive or at least neutral, rather then threatening or negative. To start, explore unfamiliar surroundings – a museum, a park, a part of town, a shop – and allow yourself to be curious. Go to a place where people are different from you. Aim to increase your tolerance for unfamiliarity which will lower your level of discomfort with uncertainty – a key factor in risk-taking.

▶ Take no-lose risks. A no-lose risk situation is one in which you have nothing tangible to lose. Taking such a risk may make you feel anxious but this is usually because you have accepted certain expectations from others around you. Examples of no-lose risks would be to start talking to a stranger on the bus or in a shop, trying a new hairstyle or doing something on impulse just because you think it might be fun.

Try the following tactics for putting the process of failure into perspective:

▶ Accept failure. By the very act of accepting it, you will turn it into success.

▶ Remember, everybody is allowed to make mistakes. Promise yourself that if you make a mistake, you will learn from it and put it behind you immediately.

▶ Take minimum risks. This stage is about risking something, no matter how insignificant. Complain about something. If it makes you too anxious to complain in person, write a letter or phone. Bet on a game which is based at least partly on skill. If a work colleague is trying to take advantage of you, do not let them succeed but maintain a friendly stance. Deliberately resist a sales pitch. Go to a car showroom, listen to the sales pitch, ask questions, take a test drive but do not buy. Whatever small risk you decide to take, pay attention to your reactions to the situations and gradually increase the element of risk.

▶ Take moderate risks. This should come as a natural progression from taking small risks. Gradually increase the stakes as high as you can whilst still being able to live with the possible losses. You have to feel both that you can afford the loss and that it will not make you overly anxious to do so. An example of a moderate risk would be to take on a new work project. Moderate the risk by being sure that you have the skills and resources to achieve the task to deadline.

▶ Be honest with yourself and recognise that the most frightening thing about the possibility of failure is your anxiety about being judged by others. The fact is that other people are far less interested in your failure than you choose to imagine.

▶ Bear in mind that other people's judgements of you will rarely be as harsh as your own. Don't overemphasise the importance of your failures.

▶ Do not concentrate too much on those people or things you see as the winners in life. Remember, all winners are losers at times.

▶ Remind yourself that all of life is made up of successes and failures. When it comes to failure, you are more practised – and much more resilient – than you think.

▶ Be specific about your self-criticism. Instead of saying: 'I'm a useless presenter', just admit: 'I made some mistakes but I did the best I could at the time.'

▶ Accept the lessons of failure: if certain things you thought you wanted are not possible, ask yourself, what else is there? What else am I good at? Above all, what changes can I make that are going to make me really happy?

▶ Initially, it will feel like the end of the world. Tell yourself the intensity of the initial shock, terror, fear and humiliation will subside. You can help speed up your recovery by being objective.

> *Some women don't apply for new opportunities because they think that the more confidence they build up in themselves, the more they throw themselves into it, the greater will be their chances of success but the harder they will fall if they don't make it.*

It's nothing but superstition to think that because you messed up once, you'll mess up in exactly the same way next time. In fact, the opposite is true – failing gives you the impetus to try doing things differently.

Failure is one of the greatest catalysts for positive change. It makes us own up to our strengths and weaknesses realistically and encourages us to question not only the way we do things but also whether the path we're on is really the right route to personal happiness.

REWARDS FROM WORK

One way to determine the type of job you really want is to separate the outer and inner rewards of work. It might be helpful if you think of your job as a hazelnut. The outer shell includes your title, salary, perks, benefits, status, location and the current economic conditions in your organisation and sector. The inner kernel embodies what you actually do all day long and how you feel about it; the amount of variety, creativity, autonomy, challenge, excitement and feedback you experience; the ambience and morale of the office and how much you enjoy, and are stimulated by, the people you're in contact with.

Start by considering the more easily assessed outer shell. Ask yourself if your desires for external rewards have changed since the last time you thought about them. When women first enter the job market, high external rewards may seem like much ado about nothing. But after a few years on the job, many of us notice that the big expense allowance or grander title create a kind of halo of success around those who possess them.

> *When I was promoted to product manager from marketing assistant (in a large food manufacturer) I was offered the only available office, a tiny room off a back corridor with no window. My first inclination was to turn down the cupboard and remain in the open-plan office, which had a lot of natural light and where I enjoyed the bustle of working with my friends. Luckily, someone pointed out to me that as long as I stayed there, people would continue to think of me as an assistant. I took the minuscule office. I had begun to understand that silly little rewards are often major symbols in corporate life.*

When assessing the types of external rewards you want right now, take a look at how your contribution to the organisation has grown and whether the rewards have kept pace. Two years ago you may have struggled to prepare an oral presentation; today you can pull it off with great style and wit. Or perhaps you have developed an excellent network of contacts that keep you and your organisation informed of changes in your industry. Or you may have the job you've always wanted, only to find yourself restless at thirty-four and ready for new and bigger challenges and rewards. You may be worth a lot more money today and be ready for the power and prestige which go with the same position in a bigger organisation.

Above all, don't feel trapped by yesterday's choices. Changes in your personal goals can drastically affect your needs at work. External job rewards are like a vast buffet. It's impossible to get everything on to your plate at once. So choose carefully which benefits are most important to you at the moment. And keep in mind, you'll have future trips to the table and can select differently next time round.

Women who say, 'I love my work' are usually talking about the inner rather than the outer rewards. While they might not adore everything about their job, at least part of their daily routine gives them a thrill, helps their spirits soar and makes them feel that this is what they've been put on earth to do. Maybe their job dovetails exactly with their personal goals and priorities.

Those who are discontented with their jobs often have trouble putting their finger on exactly what is missing. It takes boldness and daring for a support staff person to admit that she longs for the challenge of a sales job where her individual accomplishments and failures are easily counted. Or for a field worker to confront the fact that she'd like to come in from the cold and work with a sympathetic, supportive team of people instead of facing dozens of rejections each week.

It is important to allow yourself to indulge in periods of self-exploration to find out which inner rewards you really want. Ask yourself, 'Who do I envy?' and analyse what it is these people have that you wish for. Is it their status in the organisation, or that they have an interesting job, or that they seem to have an integrated, contented life?

Examine what parts of your current or past jobs really satisfied you. Was it the time you were allowed to form your own team and complete a project without supervision? Perhaps you're yearning for more power and independence. Were you happiest during the last department emergency, when everyone was working round the clock? You might prefer a job with a heavier workload, faster pace and more team spirit. Do you miss having enough time to get on with the other priorities in your life?

Women who are prepared to address themselves to finding the answers to these questions are better placed to make informed choices about their futures.

However, many career consultants get a bit nervous when clients want to get out of their field altogether, fearing a 'grass is always greener' problem. Dreaming the impossible dream – the woman who was always poor at science but fantasises about medical school, or the one who's deep in debt but longs to buy a franchise – is sometimes a way to avoid thinking about the changes that *are* possible.

Unless you have a real pull towards something completely new, it's best to stay allied to your profession, where you can build on what you know and use your connections to find more suitable work.

I was really miserable in my first job with a large partnership of solicitors. I hated the pressurised atmosphere and spending forty hours a week doing research in the law library. I was seriously considering abandoning law altogether when somebody asked me whether there was anything at all I liked about the job. It was then that I realized that it was the few hours a week when I reported my findings to partners that gave

> *me my only buzz. I found their company intellectually bracing and felt more competent trading ideas with them than drudging in the library. After a lot of soul-searching I eventually found career happiness as a legal headhunter, where the bulk of my workday is spent chatting with and evaluating high-level lawyers.*

Finding the job you really want is not always a one-step achievement. You may not yet have the background and qualifications for the power, salary level and challenges you long for or your current personal commitments may mean that you have to temporarily put your timetable on hold.

Facing up to the question 'What is it that I really want next?' may feel like opening up a can of worms: you're not sure what subversive thought you will release into the world. Nonetheless, it's a question worth asking yourself at least every few years, even if you're rather proud of the job you have at the moment.

Your reassessment won't necessarily result in a drastic change of direction. Sometimes a shift in emphasis – such as incorporating more contact with the general public into your job, or transferring to a team of people you really respect and enjoy – is all that it may take to transform your current work into the job you really want. At other times a career overhaul is needed. One thing is for sure: fear of change is not a good reason to delay opening the can of worms. With all the time and energy you spend at work, being fulfilled from Monday to Friday is a large measure of how happy you are with your life as a whole.

> *People are living longer, and the chances are that when you reach "retiring" age patterns in the world of work will have shifted so much that you may not "retire" at all.*

TAKING CHARGE

Once you have a rough idea of the external and internal rewards most important to you, it's time to analyse how to wrest what you want from today's turbulent job market. To advance or even to merely survive, you will have to be prepared to be flexible and move around more than ever before.

Career development is a constant, active process. If you're not settling into a demanding new job, you're probably ready to gear up for new opportunities. The thing to avoid is standing still and waiting for something to happen – the 'good student' trap. It is not your boss's job to develop your career. She doesn't have a curriculum designed for you. She just wants her projects done. Neither your boss nor your organisation nor your contacts are likely to do anything to help you without a strong hint that you are thinking about a change. You have to create your own climate for career advancement.

Creating your own climate is directly linked to your attitude towards controlling events in your career. Natural self-starters have developed the quality of 'self determination' – belief in their ability to influence developments in their career (and elsewhere in their lives). They are prepared to take personal responsibility, plan, set goals and take risks. Achieving this is a tall order for most of us. But don't despair. Although few of us have an absolute sense of self-determination, we can develop our belief in our own ability to influence what happens to us.

Without any sense of self-determination, we are left to believe in control either by chance or by other powerful people. If you believe in control by chance, it is pretty debilitating: there is no reason to plan or make decisions, as chance is totally unpredictable and you can't do much about it. Belief in control by other powerful people is also debilitating as it leads to a resentful submission to authority and 'passing the buck'.

Although you can never totally determine all aspects of

SELF DETERMINATION CHECKLIST

To determine your attitude towards control in your life, quickly assess the following three groups of statements. Decide whether you agree or disagree with each.

Group One

1 If important people decided they didn't like me, I probably wouldn't get very far.
2 Getting what I want requires pleasing the people above me.
3 People like myself have little chance of protecting our personal needs when they conflict with strong vested interests.
4 Although I might have ability, I will not be given responsibility without appealing to those in positions of power.
5 I believe that what happens in my life will be mostly determined by powerful people.
6 To make my plans work, I make sure that they fit in with the desires of people in influential positions.

Group Two

1 It's not always wise for me to plan too far ahead because many things turn out to be a matter of fate.
2 Whether or not I get to be a leader depends on whether I'm in the right place at the right time.
3 When I get what I want it's usually because I'm lucky.

your career development (because some things *are* driven by chance and by influential people), it is possible to minimise outside influences. The key is to take an active rather than a passive approach: instead of letting things happen to you, you make things happen. The maxim is 'Don't solve problems – prevent them'.

4 To a great extent my life is controlled by accidental happenings.
5 I have often found that what is going to happen will happen.
6 There is often no chance of protecting my personal interests against bad luck.

Group Three

1 I largely determine what will happen in my life.
2 When I make plans I am almost certain to carry them through.
3 Whether or not I get to be a leader depends on my ability.
4 I am usually able to protect my personal interests.
5 When I get what I want, it's usually because I worked hard for it.
6 My life is determined by my own actions.

The more 'agrees' than 'disagrees' you scored in Group One, the greater is the extent to which you believe you and your life are controlled by other people.

If you scored more 'agrees' than 'disagrees' in Group Two then you have a powerful belief that your life is controlled by fate or chance.

The more 'agrees' than 'disagrees' you scored in Group Three, the stronger is your belief in your ability to control events in your life. More than three 'agrees' indicates a high degree of self determination.

The following guidelines may help you to develop a more self-reliant approach.

▶ Identify work situations which you believe are determined either by chance or by other people. If you find this difficult to do, list the work situations in which you believe you are in control. Now list all the other work situations – these are the ones you believe you cannot determine.

▶ Looking through the list, pick out two or three situations that occur most frequently.

▶ Think of as many ways as possible in which you could control the selected incidents. Put everything down, regardless of how crazy it may appear.

▶ Go through your list and pick out the strategies you think you could use at work. Ask yourself which one is likely to be the most effective given your organisation's culture and the personality of the people you work with.

▶ Make a conscious decision to implement this strategy next time the situation arises in work. If it helps, write down your strategy and carry it with you. For your first attempt, don't pick a particularly dramatic situation. Pick one that will not be too pressurised or significant. If you think that all of your work situations are too dramatic for your first attempt, pick a situation outside work.

▶ Take time out to review what happened. Were you successful in taking more control than usual? Did the exercise change your belief in your ability to influence situations? Were the results any different from usual? Write down what seemed to work well and evaluate why. Utilise the effective parts of the strategy to refine your approach even further for the next attempt.

Developing self determination takes time. Acquiring the skill is a gradual process. As you achieve success in influencing mundane, day-to-day situations, your self-reliance will increase and you can become bolder in your attempts to direct more significant situations. Remember, the aim is not to achieve absolute control but to increase the likelihood of forging your own dream.

2 Your Career Strategy

▶ ▶ ▶ ▶ ▶ STAGES IN YOUR CAREER • READY FOR
PROMOTION? • THE PLATEAU AND HOW TO
AVOID IT • COPING WITH THE PLATEAU •
UNEMPLOYMENT AND REDUNDANCY

The route to career satisfaction for women is still being mapped.

Very few women have a carefully laid career plan. Every step we take may appear like the final career move until something else unfolds and it's back to the drawing board. We owe it to ourselves to recognise this as an opportunity rather than a threat.

At the start of the eighties, when a prospective boss asked, 'What do you want to be doing in five years time?' the classic answer was 'I'd like to have your job.' Aspiring straight up the ladder was supposed to be the paradigm of ambition.

Things are different today. The idea of a prefabricated 'career ladder' is rather like the concept of the nuclear family – still honoured and revered in principle but an increasingly inaccurate description of reality. Successful career paths are more likely to resemble a rising zigzag than a vertical line.

> *Future career scenarios will be very different from the popular "upward and outward" view. People will need increasingly to take ownership of their careers and, in particular, of their own portfolio of skills. They will need to be more flexible in how they view their careers and think in terms of 'portability' rather than stability.*

Institute of Management

This is not to say that women cannot be successful in their chosen careers. They can, and there are increasing numbers of women breaking through the barriers. But don't expect promotion to be handed to you. More than ever, you need a strategy for moving on and meeting your targets.

An emerging phenomenon for the nineties is that, as women have moved up the management ladder, the throng crowding each rung has swelled, raising the competitive pressure to painful levels. This is a demographic and economic fact. It is therefore common to experience various periods of 'career plateau'. It is important to remember that this need not mean coming to a full stop. Likewise, redundancy and periods of unemployment may also form part of your career path. Managed carefully, these experiences – far from destroying your life – can represent real points for growth. You can develop strategies for coping and growing during difficult times, and you will be better equipped for the next challenge as a result.

Take heart. Women are far better suited than men - in almost every respect - for the flexible career patterns that will emerge in the 1990s and beyond.

STAGES IN YOUR CAREER

The reality of a career which comprises a series of upwardly mobile moves is fast becoming redundant in today's labour market. However, your career (especially if you work in corporate UK) will generally pass through three broad stages - foundation, consolidation and leadership.

The Foundation Stage of your career is a heady time. Your status is derived from your potential rather than your performance. It can be a time of meteoric rise, of quick job changes and rapid promotions. It's the skills acquisitions stage, a time for looking around, experimenting, making mistakes for which you aren't wholly accountable and learning the basic organisational ropes. Your organisation may shower attention on you, particularly if you were recruited via the 'milk round'.

Some of the characteristics of this early experience can be misleading and could allow you to develop unrealistic expectations for the future. Because the foundation level is the broadest sector in the hierarchy, it is often marked by frequent job hops. This means you run the risk of rising too high with too thin a veneer of experience. Over challenged and under prepared, the high flier may be judged incompetent by superiors looking for results and the outcome can be a massive wobble in confidence.

> *One of the biggest shortcomings in career development is not to spend time consolidating at certain stages so that the value of your actions can be built on and integrated. Those organizations with trainee schemes which move people every six or twelve months encourage this, because you never have to live with the consequences of what you do.*

For those of us not employed in corporates, the pattern is more erratic and less clear cut. With less opportunity for structured, linear development, you may have to switch organisations to get the breadth of experience required. The opportunities and risks, however, are the same.

Exercising judgement is as critical in the early years as it is later on. You will always face career trade-offs. Don't move just to move. Choose jobs that challenge your failings, not just your strengths. And don't mistake the early years as being anything but that – being able to profit from training and guidance that have practical value beyond any management course.

> *I'm so glad I didn't succumb to the job-hopping pressures of the late eighties. Many of my friends*

kept telling me that I would get left behind if I stayed more than two years in my job with a small company. But I was gaining experience in all aspects of the business and I could see it had huge management potential for me. I'm so glad I stuck with it, I'm now production manager.

The Consolidation Stage is more reflective. After five or ten years, the pace slows. You develop an expertise and you move into the second phase – implementation. This is the stage when you need to develop the skills of management; when people and communication skills become as important to your performance as technical ability.

In many organisations, middle management is the 'civil service corps', and there are many dead-end jobs at this level that may seem comfortable but offer little opportunity for real growth. To avoid getting stuck in a rut, you need clear cut ideas about what you want to get out of the job and how long you plan to stay in it. You also need to maintain an open and active communication channel with upper management to make sure your vision of the future matches their plans for you.

Your technical performance continues to be important but the test for future development lies in your ability to gain sophistication in people management, political aptitude, negotiation and tactical thinking. The jobs you choose in this phase, therefore, must develop these areas of executive talent if you are to forge ahead. Few positions will pack in all the lessons, though many can be broadened through your own initiative. Most likely, you will need to move through two or three different jobs to gain the variety and breadth of experience necessary to move up.

This implementation stage is one of the most difficult legs of the career journey. The management attention that you took for granted as an early recruit begins to fall off as you gain credibility and expertise. The autonomy may be refreshing but it can also feel like neglect, leaving you anxious about what your superiors have in mind for you or where you're headed next.

> *For the last year at least, I've been in a bit of a dilemma at work. It has become obvious that I'm not going to be one of those on the redundancy list (we had a lot of fall-out due to the recession) but I have really outgrown my role. Frankly, I can now do my job in my sleep. On the one hand, I'm delighted because it's giving me extra time to do my assignments for my part-time MBA. On the other hand, I feel quite undervalued and frustrated. Obviously I don't want to draw attention to my plight because of the risk of being made redundant and the difficulty of finding another job but my career is not progressing at all and I feel like I've been forgotten.*

The most emotionally taxing element of this phase, however, stems from the nature of the experiences you will encounter: managing crises, building a platform for yourself both inside and outside the organisation and learning patience and judg-. ment. These are hard lessons. At this stage, many women forgo corporate life in order to pursue a career in a small organisation or start their own business.

> *I'd been the model recruit. Performed well as a trainee and made it to the first rung of management. But, eventually, I saw the writing on the wall – I was sidelined to a support function and wasn't going to move much further. So, I took the plunge and went to work for a small organisation where there's no such thing as a 'support function'.*

The Leadership Stage is the final career stage. At this level, mastery in every area you are responsible for is no longer critical. Your remit is wide and your status in the organisation significant. You set the goals that your managers will work to realise. The top rung of this stage is the Chief Executive's office, though many high achievers decide that the advantages of that status are outweighed by the pressures and demands it imposes. Success, stopping short of being the big banana, can be very real; offering the rewards of excellent remuneration with less stress and the chance to fulfil other pursuits. The path does not end there, of course. It continues to broaden, if you exercise creativity and imagination.

Breadth, leadership, strategic (rather than tactical) thinking and vision are the important skills at this level. Having made it this far, you'll find that your ability to control the parameters of your future is considerably greater than in the implementation stage. The speed of advancement is less of a sticking point, since the growth potential of your job hinges on how effectively the organisation is growing.

Though there are a number of levels above general management, getting there is more a question of motivation than of building skills. For many people, pushing all the way to the summit is less appealing than savouring the rewards of success. Rather than being continually in the throes of an uphill climb, they want to continue as they are, commanding a high salary and a position of prestige and power while cutting down on stress and pressure.

> I made the board – which is more than I ever thought I would – and I'm happy. People (particularly my girlfriends) are always saying, "Why don't you go for the big one, become chief executive UK?" but I just know that I would have to make too many enemies to do that. I'm not prepared to be that ruthless – it just isn't worth it to me. I have such a great life. I have more than enough money and prestige. I do what I want when I want. I would have to give all that up to become chief executive. I've decided not to. It isn't a cop-out.

READY FOR PROMOTION?

Promotion patterns for women have never been the same as those for men.

Men tend to be promoted on potential, which makes for smoother, step-by-step career moves, whereas women tend to be promoted on performance, leading to rougher career shifts. Women more often have to make dramatic job or career changes to build their portfolio of skills. We don't automatically get the tough assignments that shape efficacy. When we want a challenge, we frequently have to discard the old and go cold into something new.

Of course, not everyone wants to be promoted. You may feel perfectly happy with the level you are at now, having decided that other aspects of your life are more of a priority. Don't let anyone make you feel that you are under achieving if you are content to remain where you are. The reality is that the further up an organisation you go, the more likely it is that your working life will encroach on your personal life.

If you are promoted, you may find that making the transition from one phase to the next is hard. Change is never easy and you do need to be able to face the idea of risk. Complacency can poison even the most promising career. By viewing jobs as different vehicles for learning, you can build skills with depth and test them from different vantage points. They will help propel you through the phases of your career, even as you confront the hard choices that are the inevitable consequences of doing anything worthwhile.

Despite expectations that fast track careers are built on an unwavering series of vertical moves, the disjointedness induced by rapid job switching is neither sustainable nor conducive to acquiring the full spectrum of necessary skills. To scale the organisational ladder you need functional expertise, which means staying in place long enough not only to learn the lessons but also to see the effect of your actions. You need the time to gain in-depth experience of more complicated, tougher assignments. Stepping into the slower-moving vehicles of middle management does not imply a career stall if the jobs you choose can teach you skills needed to move up. Not all jobs provide the same calibre of skill building, however, which makes the choosing critical.

How can you be sure whether you are ready to take on more responsibility? There's no cut-and-dried way, but here are some crucial questions to ask yourself before fostering any real expectation about being boosted to the next level.

Have I demonstrated ability?

Your organisation is unlikely to promote you if you are not already a solid performer. Such a decision would send mixed messages to your colleagues about how much the organisation values the quality of their work. If you are performing well, value your achievements and let others know about them without unnecessarily blowing your trumpet or stepping on your colleagues toes.

Am I ready to supervise?

If the promotion is to a first supervisory position, it entails a shift in philosophy and, often, in skills. Ask yourself if you are ready to learn how to manage others. You need the capability to join in with a different perspective – managing the work is not the same as doing it. For example, you may be great at selling and want to move into management of the sales force. Without the appropriate management skills, however, you may go along on sales calls with your subordinates and drive them crazy by interfering. You have to be prepared to relinquish (for the time being) the things that you are good at, in order to learn new skills.

Will I fit in with the managerial culture?

The culture at the individual level may be very different from that at the managerial level. Are you ready to move to a more sophisticated culture? For example, there's generally a different, less direct way of communicating. As you move up in the organisation, the messages are less clear, less easy to pick up on. Every organisation has its own management codes and culture – will you fit into yours?

Have I shown interest in moving up?

Have you volunteered for extra assignments because they may be learning experiences? Do you try to learn about your industry or field? Read annual reports, magazines and trade journals relevant to your organisation and show knowledge of what is going on. People who do, mark themselves down as ambitious. By volunteering for extra work or training courses (see Chapter 5), you identify yourself.

Can I communicate effectively?

Do you have the ability to communicate with others? It doesn't matter how brilliant you are if you can't communicate. It's not what you know, it's how you impart your ideas. People communication skills, in particular, are crucial for developing your career. You can demonstrate these on a daily basis by greeting people as you pass them, attending work functions, being effective in meetings.

Am I a good long-term investment?

If the new position is a training ground for higher positions in the organisation, it's especially important that you have the potential for further upward mobility. If you don't, the organisation will be wasting the chance to groom someone who does, thereby blocking the path upward.

Am I a good team player?

To advance in any organisation, the ability to support and lead a group is critical. More and more, team work has become a central part of organisational life. Think about how you work – do you exchange opinions, ideas, successes with colleagues? Even at top management level, an effective leader has also to be a good team player. Learning to be a team player is a lesson you can't learn early enough.

Would I make a good role model?

It's important to be aware of your own symbolic impact. A promotion is a statement of the values and priorities of your organisation. The recognition it confers will encourage other ambitious employees to imitate your behaviour. Are you the kind of role model they would want to have for the rest of the organisation?

Being the right role model is more difficult for women. Research has shown that managers (many of whom are white, middle-class men) display an innate tendency to hire and promote those who resemble themselves. Here lies the real reason for women's difficulty in climbing the organisational ladder.

If looking odd in positions of power is women's first big barrier to top jobs, feeling odd in them is the second. Women traditionally build networks and, when they surpass them, there's a tendency to feel very alone. The lack of a critical mass of women in the same position exaggerates these feelings of isolation. Senior managers' attitudes are changing more slowly than corporate image-makers would have you believe.

Tokenism abounds. When Sainsbury's appointed a female finance director, it was headline news. In general, such women directors as there are are disproportionately found to be running bits of organisations without profit-and-loss responsibility, such as personnel or public relations.

Women managers have an added burden of responsibility as their success and performance may well be used as the yardstick for the recruitment of women managers in the future. Women who have made it to the top, however, can take action to help other women on their way up.

> *I want to make certain that I'm the right kind of role model to other women in the business. I'm excited about that additional responsibility. One area in which it makes a difference is recommending promotions; occasionally I have been able to ask, "Have you considered so-and-so?" and it has helped a woman be selected where she might not even have been considered.*

THE PLATEAU

'Career plateau' describes the point at which managers find they can go no further in an organisation. It is quite commonplace; estimates suggest that in some large organisations, as many as half of all managers have plateaued.

Stripped of the incentive of promotion, people can easily become demotivated, experiencing not only a decline in performance but also a sharp fall in self-esteem. Alternatively, by refusing to accept that their careers have peaked, they may try to undermine the authority of those above them or develop the destructive characteristics of a workaholic. Yet, despite today's emphasis on self-development and career diagnosis, career plateauing remains a serious cause of frustration for many managers because neither they nor their organisations see the problem until it is acute.

The following behavioural characteristics are displayed by people who have reached a plateau in their career. Do any of these describe your own behaviour at work?

▶ Your work assignments have become routine.

▶ You prefer to be anywhere except in the office.

▶ Your performance has slipped and you are less concerned than you used to be about wastage at work and ensuring that tasks are completed on time.

▶ You are frequently late and often call in sick although you used to be very conscientious.

▶ You have not been promoted in the previous five years, or have been passed over more than once.

▶ You are considering looking elsewhere for a job because your loyalty to the organisation and your image of yourself within it has fallen.

Career plateauing is on the increase. A recent study showed that the proportion of upward moves by employees has declined markedly while the number of sideways moves has increased. The trend towards flatter, less hierarchical organisations suggests that in future there will be fewer opportunities for vertical promotion and that a growing number of women will hit the plateau earlier or on more than one occasion during their careers. Even the public sector is vulnerable, as previously sacred functions are opened to market forces and the monolithic bureaucracy is replaced by new, organic structures.

Plateauing, however, does not have to be a problem. It becomes a problem only when its symptoms are ignored. Your choice of jobs can also affect when, and if, you hit a plateau. Aim for growth jobs that meet the following criteria:

▶ The organisation is innovative and trusts its employees with responsibility.

▶ The area you move into is a mainstream activity for the organisation, such as a marketing job in a manufacturing company. Avoid a support function (unless as a temporary way of picking up valuable skills).

▶ The job offers an expansion in scope over your previous position, such as managing change, heading up a new project or turning a problem department around.

Getting jobs that fit these criteria may involve a lateral switch to another department in your organisation or to another employer altogether. Though this may fly in the face of fast-track conditioning, a lateral job hop can be as much a career advancer as any promotion.

> I moved in the height of the recession. Had it been two years earlier, I would have been very hung up on the fact that the job titles were equivalent. But I wanted the chance to balance the classical marketing lessons I'd learned at my first company with the entrepreneurial innovation of a consultancy.

Recognizing when and how to move is key to reaching the top of anything. It takes time and a variety of challenges to build up measurable accomplishments. In addition, you need sufficient stability and coherence in the jobs you hold to develop contacts and projects outside them. A pre-emptive strategy is to look ahead in your field, in order to acquire the training and/or education that could make you competitive.

COPING WITH THE PLATEAU

There are growing multitudes of professionals and mid-level executives in every line of work. What's surprising is why the long-standing, natural career stage of the plateau still comes as such a surprise.

> I am depressed at the prospect of spending the next eleven years (until I can consider retiring), in the same position. What's worse is that in my company, the positions above me are blocked by individuals who are not likely to relocate and who are all younger than me or approximately the same distance from retirement. Moving is out of the question because of family

responsibilities. How can you make work endurable
when you feel bored and unchallenged?

Many women in Britain are faced with the classic problem of structural plateauing. Whilst many of us understand why this situation is inevitable, we often cannot accept the realisation. We all know that not everyone can reach top management. There is usually only one top spot and immediately below are a handful of other almost-top senior management positions. At the bottom of the pile are multitudes of incoming aspirants aiming to climb the ladder. Whatever the size of the organisation, the odds of a single person reaching the top are probably akin to winning the pools. This fact of working life is nothing new. The identical slow-down has always existed in large institutions – whether in the public or private sector.

Individuals experience this progression unevenly. In the early years of a career, promotions come frequently or in small steps as the throngs of beginners are gradually sorted out. When people reach higher levels where jobs are more substantive, the rate of promotions slows down to accommodate years of experience in a single position. Traditionally it takes about twenty years to identify the few employees who are considered senior-management potential.

At this stage many unrelated factors enter the equation, especially the prevailing economic, social and political turmoil of the world. Expectations based on outdated assumptions are often responsible for plunges into depression. It is a common experience that simple seniority or longevity is replaced as a promotion criterion by greater education or training. Increasingly, senior management tends towards the belief that the changing needs of the organisation will require something more than lengthy experience in the 'old ways'.

I was passed over for a promotion about three years ago. The promotion went to someone with less

> *seniority and no experience but with better qualifications. I was really unhappy about it because I had considerable experience in the function and the previous policy had been to give heavy weight to seniority.*

The question is how to endure the next few years in a static, unchallenging position. It is largely a matter of attitude. Some people can make any job boring, while others find the most routine task interesting day after day. Sometimes it's a matter of choice, too. You have options to alter your situation, but these require personal risks. To start with, be honest and accept that you have plateaued. People who deny they are plateauing are setting themselves up for major problems. Equating self-worth with promotion is even more damaging. There is seldom a straightforward connection between plateauing and competence. You may not have plateaued because of your ability but because you got caught in a stultified organisation or in a slowing economy. A lack of promotion opportunities can too easily be confused with a lack of ability. This can have a very debilitating effect on your confidence and self-esteem.

> *Too few of us realise that we are plateauing. Since we are unlikely to receive any help from our employers, we have to develop ways of coping ourselves.*

If you find yourself on a plateau, do not despair. It's tough but it's not the end of the world. There are plenty of other things outside work that you can now give more attention to, whilst working on some of these strategies for coping with your plateaued job:

▶ Take the lead in redefining your role within the organisation. Reassess your career with a view to rediscovering skills that may have been forgotten and recognising the assets that experience bestows. Now is the time to take stock of your career in the context of the direction in which the organisation is moving.

▶ Take more control of your work by identifying projects that your experience equips you for, or by identifying ways in which your skills can be better used.

▶ Consider ways to make yourself more attractive to the organisation, for example, by upgrading your skills or adding to your qualifications.

▶ Work with your boss to find new challenges outside work, through horizontal transfer, or by secondment within or outwith the organisation.

▶ Check that you are being realistic about your career goals. Ask your boss to be frank about your promotion prospects and discuss your own aspirations. Perhaps you are too impatient for advancement, when you have really found a niche that suits you.

▶ Once you have evaluated your frustration in broader terms and you can begin to empathise with the rest of the people in your organisation who are similarly plateaued, it's possible that this small group could collaborate in finding ways to overcome your mutual immobility.

▶ Identify somebody in your group (could it be you?) who nurtures an optimistic view of the future and co-ordinate efforts to build long-term challenges. It takes a leader to initiate new approaches and to negotiate with peers or superiors to introduce change. That form of leadership does not depend on job level. It emerges from individuals who have enthusiasm and are eager to keep up to date.

The key lies in viewing this as an opportunity for personal development. Every so often, in any career, there comes a need to refocus on your individual professional development (see Chapter 1) and to reflect on how to achieve your redefined goals more effectively.

Fortunately, women do not generally shy away from the need to adapt to shifting circumstances and are practised in the art of change. Gaining control over the timing of change and setting goals less beholden to the organisational agenda are the real challenges of advancing an already successful career.

> *I talk to a number of women my age who have reached similar levels in their jobs, and I find we're all asking ourselves, "Where are we going?" I find myself thinking of alternative directions, such as being a teacher, working with children, working with animals.*

Handling the challenge of career success may involve taking a lesson from our fathers' generation, men who pursued politics or academia or community work once their careers reached a certain level. Capitalising on your position as an expert in your field can open a number of doors in alternative areas.

If, for example, you've always had a feeling that you'd like to teach, you may find that your local education/business partnership (contact your local Training and Enterprise Council) can find you a teaching placement for half a day a week. In this way, realising your ambition does not have to take the form of a job change; it can become a facet of your current job description, acting as a feather in your organisation's cap as you build an external reputation, while adding freshness and vitality to your daily routine. Serving on the boards of outside companies or health trusts, becoming a school governor, sitting on awards committees or on community councils fills a similar ticket. So does politics, since all parties are crying out for women leaders.

To make this work, however, the supplementary challenges you take on cannot be occasional pursuits that offer low-level responsibility or reward. Your job and the role you play outside the company should be compatible and roughly equal in stature if you are to gain the benefits of symbiosis between the two. Finding a substantive slot in community affairs or other external projects will probably require the same type of strategic decision-making that a career change does.

Juggling a full-time high-level job with serious outside activity does not mean that you must have superwoman capability. It means taking advantage of the benefits of success without getting hung up on the idea that the only measure of personal advancement is promotion and that self-definition can be gained only through career performance.

UNEMPLOYMENT AND REDUNDANCY

It is a hard fact that more and more of us will experience unemployment or redundancy during our working lives. Economic restructuring, investment in new technology and greater competition have created a contracting employment market. The days of the guaranteed job – no matter what your skills and competence – are on their way out.

The loss of a salary is usually the first shock. You may well feel that your whole lifestyle is crumbling before your very eyes. Try not to let the shock paralyse you. It is important to deal with your new financial situation at the start (see Chapter 13) and not let it get out of control. Confronting this problem immediately will in itself make you feel more in control of your life and better able to develop a coping strategy.

Facing the fact that you have been made redundant can still be very difficult, even if you have volunteered or have known for some time that it was likely to happen. But remember, being made redundant is not a reflection of your ability to do your job: the job has been made redundant, not the person. Redundancy exacts a high personal price, which has been likened to bereavement. The loss of earnings is a hard blow but more severe are the feelings of isolation and failure that it engenders. Many people feel worthless and obsolete and it can be difficult to accept that you are not alone and not to blame. British society, founded on the Protestant work ethic, retains a very negative image of people out of work.

> *It's not my fault that I'm unemployed. Much of the world out there thinks it is, because unemployment, to so many people, means shirking, sitting at home watching TV. There is a stigma – it's like economic AIDS. But it's not like that. I know I haven't changed – I'm still the same person I was when I was working. The thing is, though I used to think that I needed a thick skin to get on in my job; well, it's nothing compared to the sheer grit and determination you need to combat the negative stereotypes attached to being unemployed. They can really pull you down if you let them.*

It is a trap to take on the persona of being unemployed and fulfil all the negative stereotypes. To combat this, you need to keep your support network active and develop new networks to help you through. More than ever, you need to surround yourself with those people who will support you and keep your confidence going. At a time when your self-esteem may be at its lowest, you need to marshal all your confidence and belief in yourself.

▶ **Talk to your family and friends** as soon as possible about the practical implications of being out of work. Try not to let fear of rejection lead you to suffer alone. You'd be surprised how supportive most people will be. You need supportive but objective people around you to help you overcome the initial panic and inertia.

▶ **Review your support audit.** Chapter 4 contains an exercise for assessing your support audit. Review this in the light of your current situation. List all those people who can help you now. If you have gaps in your support network, think about how you could go about filling them.

▶ **Keep your old networks active.** Don't immediately fall into the trap of thinking that all your ex-colleagues won't want to see you. Suspend your fears. Think of those colleagues who have been genuinely supportive in the past. What reason have you to think that they will be any different now? Keeping in touch with ex-colleagues really helps lessen feelings of abandonment and bolsters your self esteem. It also means you won't be forgotten when jobs are being talked about.

▶ **Build new networks.** Seek out people who are in the same position as you. As well as sharing ideas and getting information on ways of getting back to work, this allows you to talk about your feelings and fears in a non-threatening atmosphere. Never forget that other unemployed people have their own networks and might be able to provide you with knowledge or a contact that could produce a result.

▶ **Exploit official support.** There is a wide range of support available for unemployed people. Some of it is through 'official' channels, some through more localised, community schemes. Although the value and quality of much of it may be questionable, there is bound to be some of it that will help you through this difficult time in your career.

❛ *Going to the Jobclub was a saviour for me. Not because of the official support you get – it's not that good – but because of the support and encouragement I got from the other members. I was totally sceptical and cynical when I first went but, by the second week, I'd met a bunch of great people who supported me, challenged me, gave me ideas – it was a whole new network for me. And we still meet once every fortnight. I've also learned to laugh again – something that was beginning to pass me by.* "

▶ **Be nice to yourself.** Take the time out for those activities that make you feel good. This is not always easy as it can be expensive to go to your homoeopath or hairdresser or whatever. But it is usually possible to get concessionary rates for many of these services. Shop around and you will be amazed what you can find.

" When I was working, I used to treat myself once a month to a day at a beauty salon – sauna, sunbed, facial. When I became unemployed, it was one of the things I really missed. Then this woman at the local community centre told me about the saunas and sunbeds at the local swimming pool. Because I'm unemployed, they only cost £4 so I go there once a month now and I can take all the time in the world. I've also found that the local college train beauty therapists and I'm a guinea pig once a month there as well. It's all about attitude and keeping your ear to the ground. "

The one asset you do have when you are unemployed is time. Typically, however, unemployed people view time as a burden rather than an opportunity. Research shows that unemployed people tend to withdraw more and more into their own homes. They spend an increasing amount of time on their own and less time going out for entertainment or leisure purposes. When you're unemployed, you no longer have the structure and routine of paid work and you may feel that there is nothing to replace them. Making effective use of your time is perhaps the most important skill you can have when you're unemployed. Having a regular routine, a sense of purpose to the day, interacting with other people are all important to our physical and mental well-being. The following tips may help you to get the most out of your time.

▶ **Activate your time management skills** (see Chapter 6) to set yourself a daily routine. There will be a number of job seeking tasks that you will have to complete every week and plan these in conjunction with pleasurable tasks to give yourself a break. Make sure to include your support activities as well.

▶ **Update your skills.** There are a number of ways you can do this. You might enrol at one of the training or work experience schemes that are open to you (contact your Jobcentre or TEC/LEC). Another really useful way to update or expand your skills is to do some voluntary work. The range of activities engaged in by the voluntary sector is enormous and most welcome the help of people who are enthusiastic, motivated and skilled.

   When I was out of work, I signed up as a volunteer in a local psychiatric hospital. At the back of my mind, I suppose I had always been interested in being a psychiatric nurse and I was intrigued to see what the work was actually like. After my first day as a volunteer, I was convinced. I just loved the work. I'm now in my second year of training and have not regretted it one bit.

▶ **Get out of the house every day.** It is important that you get involved in activities that get you out and about and put you in contact with other people. There is no end to the activities you can do – leisure, hobbies, community, campaigning. As well as giving you a sense of purpose, a feeling that you are doing something worth achieving, contact with other people lessens feelings of isolation and provides a sense of shared purpose. These sort of activities are important to maintaining your morale and a feeling of usefulness.

▶ **Keep yourself healthy.** Use your time to keep yourself physically fit. Exercise is always a great way to work out your frustrations and keep your stress in check. As an unemployed person, you are entitled to concessionary rates in all your local sports facilities. Make regular use of them.

▶ **Don't let your social life wither.** Unemployment does affect your social life. With reduced monies, you are no longer able to afford some of the more expensive social occasions you may have enjoyed in the past. But you don't have to become a recluse. Force yourself to maintain a social life. If, through your new network, you are in contact with other unemployed people, arrange to meet them at a set time each week, visiting each other's homes for coffee or maybe going to a local exhibition together.

With limited funds, it can be difficult to keep in touch with friends who are working. You feel embarrassed by not having enough money: always saying no when we're asked out. If, however, you take the initiative, you can in fact become the centre of your social circle. As you are the one with time, you can arrange outings. Plan a day's walk for a group of your friends or a visit to an exhibition. Have meals in – go to your local library and get a book on entertaining on a budget. At a time in your life when things are not going well, the warmth of human company and the joy of laughter should never be forgotten.

> ❝ I really have become the organiser amongst my friends now. We get together every two weeks for an "outing". I do all the research and plan the whole day. I've become an expert at foraging for free or cheap activities and, in fact, it's much more fun than just going

for a meal which is what we used to do because no one had the time to arrange anything else. We've been on walking tours of the city, exhibitions, free concerts, ice skating – all sorts of things we had never done before. My friends all wait anxiously to see what the next outing will be. And I feel an equal because of my time investment. **,**

Perhaps the most difficult thing to sustain when you're unemployed is motivation about your job-hunting. The longer you are unemployed, the more despondent you feel and the lower your self-esteem gets. There's no denying it's a tough time and you will need all your resolve to pull you through yet another rejection letter.

' *I thought that I would be back in work within a couple of months. I suppose I never considered myself as being unemployed – just taking some time out. I fully expected to go in to another job on at least the same salary and certainly with the same status. By the sixth month, reality began to dawn on me. I had to rethink all my values and ideas about work. When I let it be known that I was more flexible about what I was prepared to look at, I was offered a six-month contract with a supplier of my former firm. I am still with them but I would never have been there had I not awoken from the fantasy.* **,**

Here are some job-hunting tips that you might find useful:

▶ **View job-hunting as a job** If you take this approach to finding a job, it will be easier to set yourself targets and deadlines. Without the motivation of your work colleagues around you, you will need all your discipline to keep at it. Reinforce this by creating a 'work space' at home for your job search activities.

▶ **Stay informed** Force yourself to keep in touch with the world of work. Read newspapers, trade journals, sector reports. Become a regular visitor to your library and use all the facilities to build up your expertise and knowledge.

▶ **Keep in touch** Maintain contact with ex-colleagues and those in your work-related network. If you remove yourself totally, you are closing many doors to potential employment (it is estimated that as many as 40 per cent of jobs are accessed 'through the grapevine'). If you're not still in contact, how will you know about the opportunities?

▶ **Develop a strategy** Using your goal setting skills (Chapter 1), develop a back to work plan for yourself. You will need to re-evaluate your career goals but that does not mean you have to totally abandon your longer-term aims. You will, however, have to temporarily suspend some of your goals until such time as you are back on track. Use your strategy to set yourself weekly job-search targets. Hitting them will give you a sense of achievement and keep you going when things get tough. As always, be realistic with your targets.

▶ **Hone up your job-hunting skills** (See Chapter 3). There is a whole variety of job-search training and support available and you would be well advised to check this out. All the advice, however, can be overwhelming and, at the end of the day, you will need to develop an approach that best suits your skills, your ambitions, the type of job and sector you want to work in. Are there any personnel or senior management people in your network? Use them to give you feedback on your CV, your letters of application, your interview technique. Pick their brains about current recruitment trends.

▶ **Be selective** Don't be blinded by the sheer difficulty of finding a job into applying for everything. If you respond to too many opportunities, it will show. Difficult though it may be, your best ploy is to stick to your goals rather than end up in a job that you don't like and was never suitable in the first place.

▶ **Be flexible** Force yourself to look at alternatives to the nine-to-five. Would it be possible to do some part-time work while you are waiting for the right job to come along? Have you thought about working on a freelance basis? What about status and salary? Are you stopping yourself from getting back to work because you are stubbornly refusing to be flexible on these issues? Remember, it is far better to be able to say at an interview that you have been doing something, anything, no matter how temporary it may have been.

3 Changing Your Job

▶ ▶ ▶ ▶ ▶ CHANGING YOUR ROLE WITH YOUR CURRENT EMPLOYER • MOVING TO A NEW ORGANISATION • RECOGNISING YOUR 'BEST SELF' • WHERE TO FIND THE JOBS • WRITING EFFECTIVE CVs • GIVING EFFECTIVE INTERVIEWS • TURNING DOWN A JOB

Employment structures are changing. Our fathers may well have spent their entire working lives with one firm but it is different for our generation. Very few of us will go into a job from school or college and go up the career ladder within one organisation.

Estimates suggest that most of us will change jobs, on average, about once every five years. This could mean taking a different job within your existing employer, moving to a completely new organisation, periods of working for yourself or for two or more different organisations.

Whether the job you really want next involves upgrading or modifying your current job or making a major career shift, you'll need a job-hunting strategy as individualised as your personal needs and priorities. As with many things, time spent in preparation will help you avoid much heartache later. Changing your job is a major turning point in your career and needs to be thought through carefully.

CHANGING YOUR ROLE WITH
YOUR CURRENT EMPLOYER

If you're well thought of at your current employer, that's the place where you may be allowed to try a radical departure from your current role. This is not confined to promotions: your own company or organisation may provide you with the best chance of getting a 'sideways-move' job – switching from support to sales, for example, or from personnel to administration. In these times of 'staff rationalisation', organisations are trying to hire from within whenever possible and are looking more creatively at internal candidates than ever before. They know you, your boss can vouch for you, and they're less likely to ask you to take a pay cut because you're moving into unfamiliar territory.

Another advantage of an internal switch is that you can use the company grapevine to make sure the style and characters of your prospective boss and co-workers are a good match with your own. You may also be able to gauge whether a project or department is of key importance to your employer (and thus likely to be properly supported) or a backwater.

If you spot an intriguing job posted on the staff notice board, consider applying even if you don't have every single qualification required. It lets the organisation know you have aspirations. Asking for additional responsibility and higher-level jobs with your existing employer is a subtle way of delivering the message that you may be looking outside too. Seeking advice about training courses also marks you down as someone with ambition; this is not a bad message to give to your personnel department or line manager.

Similarly, if you're looking for flexible hours or part time work, try talking to your supervisor. She may be so panicked at the thought of losing you that she'll agree to almost any arrangement that enables her to keep you whilst getting the work done.

Go after types of assignments and projects rather than a particular job title. The process involves taking on new types of work and, at the same time, finding ways of gently unloading the parts of the job that no longer appeal to you.

Perhaps you have been longing to get a chance to escape from under a pile of administrative tasks, use your communications skills, and get noticed by top management.

You might approach your boss and say, 'I have an idea that will help save the department £5,000 and help me grow in my career. I think I can write a better proposal than the firm of consultants we usually hire. I know that you were pleased with the writing I did for the procedures manual. Since we don't have to make a commitment to the consultants for a few weeks, would you allow me to use some of my time so I can write a draft proposal and see what you think?' Your boss's reply is likely to be, 'I have no one else to do the job you're doing now' so part of your strategy must be to be ready with some concrete suggestions for how to handle the portions of your job you've been dying to get rid of. Perhaps your assistant is ready to take on more responsibility or some of the work can be discharged by someone hired on a temporary basis.

If you handle the proposal successfully, you can volunteer for more assignments of this kind, but be sure each time to shunt some of your current work aside. You don't want to be doing two jobs. When the time is right (after you've been highly praised or your boss has scored a big success), you can begin to negotiate for a title, a job description and a salary increase that reflect your new responsibilities.

If you're not sure how you'd like to re-create your current job, ask for an exploratory talk with your boss or use your appraisal system (if your organisation has one). Try asking where she wants the department or organisation to go in the next couple of years and how you can help her get there.

That's bound to get a much more positive response than if you simply tell her that you're bored with your job. Listen to where your boss thinks you could make an additional contribution. If it ties in at all with your own desires, you can enlist her help in creating steps and assignments to help you move forward. As we have said before, finding the job you really want is not always a one-step achievement.

MOVING TO A NEW ORGANISATION

The most obvious way of changing your job is to move to a new organisation. Developing the tools you will need to apply for a new opportunity is dealt with in the following sections, but before you embark on glossing up your CV, take a step backwards and evaluate *strategically* what sort of organisation would suit you best now. There are advantages and disadvantages to going to a larger or smaller employer.

Look to a larger employer if salary, perks and status are high on your list. Your best bet may be to try to find a position in one of the top organisations in your current field. The big-name places generally pay more. A move to a larger employer is also helpful for someone frustrated by an inability to do top-quality work in her current position. The big established organisations generally give their staff the time and resources to do a first-rate job, and they make more adequate budgets available for projects. They usually (although not always) have more professional personnel practices with more resources and commitment to training.

Securing a position with a leader in your profession may take some clever planning since these outfits are usually flooded with qualified applicants and many have been going through a series of staff cutbacks. One way to get noticed is to court executive search firms that specialise in recruitment in your field. If you're really clever, you may be able to find out which search firms your target employers use. You may wish to consider sending a CV to recruiters long before you actually need a new job. They are likely to call you up and offer you something inappropriate but that is your chance to describe the breadth of your current work and what you're looking for. If you have made yourself clear they may come back, even if it is months later, with something more suitable for you.

Getting to know people who work for market leaders is another tactic to help you get in the door and time your approach (a year after, not during, staff redundancies, for example, or just before recruitment announcements are made for a new division or project). Attending appropriate professional association meetings and running for office in relevant organisations are great ways to make contacts. And keeping up with the trade press is essential, since the leading organisations are often in the news.

Moving to a smaller employer is a good idea if you want to have more say in the real decision making, or work more autonomously. When there are fewer players it's easier to become a decision maker. There are fewer levels of bureaucracy to work through and usually lower staff levels. If the company grows rapidly, increasing your responsibilities and your title in just a few years is relatively easy.

Small organisations also provide a chance for more variety, hands-on work and broad experience. For example, you could get to see how every phase of production, sales and distribution works, because it's carried out right under your nose. The atmosphere at a small growing outfit still struggling for success can be bracing. Everything you do really matters in the overall success of the organisation and your experience of a bigger concern can be invaluable.

Department of Employment figures show that in some areas of the UK, as many as 90% of today's employers have fewer than twenty five employees. Yet small firms and organisations frequently don't advertise positions or use recruitment firms. They may have no personnel department to screen candidates and rely on trusted contacts and word-of-mouth. If you are considering a move to a smaller company, your research should include careful reading of the business pages of your local newspaper. Since bankruptcy is a greater risk among newly established companies, you'll want to know something about the company's prospects before you leap in. A newspaper article about a small company that has leased bigger headquarters to accommodate its expansion is one tip that jobs are in the offing at a firm with good prospects. News about contract awards and staff changes are other useful indicators.

RECOGNISING YOUR 'BEST SELF'

One thing you can be sure of – you are different from everyone else. Unless you have an identical twin, you look different; you act, think, talk, listen and lead differently. You have a unique set of friends, colleagues and relatives. You relate differently. You communicate in your own distinctive way. Your goals are different. In short, you are a unique individual.

These individual differences make you special. They define your unique way of functioning in the world and the unique set of abilities and experiences that you can bring to your career.

Before you embark on a career change, you need to undertake a robust appraisal of your particular strengths and weaknesses. The starting point is building a comprehensive list of all your abilities, which you can later customise when the time for application comes. The following guidelines may help:

▶ Focus on your best self. Ideally what kind of person are you? What skills, abilities and qualities do you have that are quite special to you (think about the kind of things that people who really like and admire you say about you). It might be that you are a very good problem solver or listener, or a good ideas person, or cheerful and great to be with, or an active person who will take risks and have a go. Maybe you're the person who really keeps the team going.

▶ Be creative. If you're having trouble getting the creative juices flowing, try a SWOT analysis (strengths, weaknesses, opportunities and threats). This is somewhat old hat but still valid management technique. Get a book out of the library if you're not familiar with it – it could prove useful to you in any number of scenarios.

▶ Include all your skills. Many of us are not aware of the full range of skills we possess. We may simply identify with our job title and recognise only skills we utilise in getting the immediate jobs done. But we all have a broad spectrum of skills with which we function in the world. Don't undersell yourself (women often do) and do include skills and achievements from outside the workplace – from leisure, social and domestic activities. We sometimes forget just how adaptable we can be.

> *There's a world of difference between saying, "I haven't worked for three years" and, "For the last three years I've run a home with two children, been treasurer of the local nursery and been a volunteer in the local hospital." Both of these statements are true but the second says, "I have skills; I can take responsibility; I can organise; I am a good communicator." The first one says, "I haven't done anything."*

▶ Categorise your skills. Categorising both your work and other skills will help you to identify transferable skills when it comes to applying for jobs.
People Skills are interpersonal skills of all sorts, skills used in helping, informing, teaching, persuading, supervising,

motivating, entertaining, selling – in short, every form of relating to other people.

Data Skills relate to skills required to record, communicate, evaluate, organise and dispense information. The information can be facts and figures but it can also be ideas and emotions.

Idea Skills include skills used in being creative, designing and experimenting. Having insight, seeking alternatives, developing others' ideas are all idea skills.

Physical Skills have to do with the physical manipulation of objects. Repairing, lifting, moving, making, typing and filing, for example, are all activities requiring physical skills.

▶ Check your list with someone who knows and respects you. Ask them to add anything that they think you might have missed out. All of this positive information will help you get to that crucial step – the interview.

This 'best self' is the person you want to take to the interview, this is the person that wants to get the job.

FINDING JOB OPPORTUNITIES

There are a number of ways to find a job and you will find that the mechanisms change as you move through the ranks. Generally, the more senior you are, the less hustling you will have to do (although this isn't a hard and fast rule). If you are serious about instigating a career change, you need to :

▶ **Target** appropriate companies, consultancies, agencies and job advertisements. Be clear about what type of job you want and what type of employer you want to work for. Sending your applications to any and every job that you think might be of interest will show. Your applications will be less focused, you will spend less time on them and the employer will know that they are part of little more than a mass mail-out.

> *There is a language to job applications and it varies from employer to employer. An application to a local authority, for example, is probably looking for very different things to a large blue chip company. You have to realise that and change the way you apply for a job, depending on the type of employer you are applying to. Applications have become much more sophisticated now and you really have to work at streamlining your application.*

▶ **Be prepared to invest your time.** Researching, targeting and following up companies and leads takes time. With consultancies and agencies, in particular, you will need to telephone, write and follow up regularly.

▶ **Get to know your way around the library.** Find a decent library and get to know the reference and business sections and the trade magazine rack. The reference section will have directories (Kompass, Sells, Extell and Kellys) which have a wealth of information on companies. Good business libraries will also have copies of major companies' annual reports.

▶ **Avidly read trade and professional journals** and the quality newspapers for potential leads on which companies are on the up. Articles on expansion plans, planning applications for new premises, new contracts won, product development are all useful pointers to companies who may be recruiting in the near future. If you can time your application with a staff need in an organisation, you have a much better chance of succeeding.

Trade journals will also have job advertisements. Fewer people respond to ads in trade journals than in the national press, so the competition is less severe.

▶ **Broaden your network.** Research has shown that a terrifying 80% of jobs in the City of London are filled through word of mouth. No wonder women are having such trouble breaking through. The message is clear though: you need to activate your network and let it be known that you are in the job market. Ensure that as many friends, contacts, relatives and colleagues as possible are told. One recruitment agency suggests that you get each person you tell to tell six more and to check back with them within a week to see who they have told. This is tough, but it will get results.

> *I got my job through meeting a woman at the local swimming pool. We used to meet once a week and began to go for a coffee after swimming. We got talking and I told her I was looking for work and what I'd done in the past. About two months after I'd met her, she told me about a credit controller's job that was going at her sister-in-law's firm. I rang that afternoon and had an interview the following day. By lunch time next day, I had the job. Never forget that by talking to one person, you are also talking to all their contacts.*

Spreading the word around more formal networks (Chapter 4) may also yield results. Obviously things are easiest if you have a direct contact within the prospective employer, but being a 'friend of a friend' is often good enough.

▶ **Get to know the job advertisement scene.** Job ads are the most visible and widely recognised way of accessing a job. Adverts appear in the local, trade and national press. You won't need to pick up much experience in the job market to know that, for example, marketing and media jobs appear in the *Guardian* on Monday. You will quickly discover where and when to look. Remember, be very selective about which job advertisements you respond to. Although it may be tough, keep your target market in mind at all times.

▶ **Sign up at a recruitment agency.** If you are in any sort of specialist field these are a good bet. These agencies make their living out of placing you so they put a lot of effort into supporting you in your job search. The drawback could be that they put undue pressure on you to accept a position you are not convinced of so that they can earn their commission. You have to handle agencies assertively and be prepared to say 'no' to the wrong job. You are running this show, not them.

▶ **Be visible.** Every woman's dream is to be headhunted for the plum position. This is a fairly rare occurrence – even if you're quite senior – and what a heady feeling it gives the chosen few. As headhunting methods are generally applied to only the top positions, it still happens more to men than to women. Having said that, there are ways of increasing the chances of it happening to you. Visibility is the key. Get word out on the network about your achievements. Enlist the support of your pals – particularly those with PR or marketing skills. Write articles and features for your trade journal. Speak at conferences. A good way of drawing attention to your availability is to find out who the principal headhunting agencies in your sector are and apply for any jobs which they advertise, even if they're not entirely appropriate.

▶ **Make speculative approaches**. On rare occasions these yield great results (we've all heard the apocryphal stories) but in the main they are pretty unrewarding. An unsolicited CV signals to an employer that the sender is probably unemployed and could be sending her details to every employer in town. However, if you think it's worth a shot, concentrate your efforts on truly targeting your CV and letter of introduction.

▶ **Regularly review** the success of your canvassing and modify future applications and letters accordingly. Most applications to vacancies are reviewed collectively around ten to fourteen days after advertising. Most invitations to interview are issued within seven days of this review and interviews held about ten days after invitation. Get a system going. Apply on day five. On day twelve, telephone to ensure that your application arrived and ask for the dates that interviews are likely to be held. Be pro-active and ready to market yourself further. In all, from seeing a recruitment advertisement to going to the initial interview can take thirty one days.

▶ **Don't confuse activity with action**. Invariably, a few well-thought-out and properly targeted job applications will yield more real results than sending your CV to a hundred organisations. Never underestimate the importance of targeting: you need a coherent plan of attack to help you find the job that is tailored to the external and internal rewards you want now. You must also be prepared to say 'no' if the job is not right for you. Keep your nerve and don't depart from your plan.

WRITING YOUR CURRICULUM VITAE

An effective curriculum vitae (CV) is a vital tool in getting the job you really want. The preparation involved in constructing your CV should help you to think through what you are aiming for next and which of your past achievements are relevant. A brilliant CV will not only open doors for you – it will give you the confidence to walk through them.

> *I think a lot of people are not aware of just how important your CV is. I went on a CV and interviewing course and I changed my CV totally after doing it. I don't put my age on the front page any more (I think being forty goes against me) – it's on the back. On the front, I have quite a lot of information about my current job and, if that interests them, they'll read on. I gave it to someone I know who is an employer and asked him to read it. He said that he only really reads the first page – he's not interested in volumes of information. When I went for an interview, they said I was selected (out of over eighty applicants), because my CV really stood out.*

Don't get your old CV out of your bottom drawer and just dust it down. You run the risk of being trapped in your image of yourself as you were five years ago. Think through from first principles how you want to present yourself and write a new CV from scratch. It will be much fresher as a result.

The following guidelines may prove helpful in drawing up your curriculum vitae:

► Be clear about what you are good at and what you are not so good at; what you want to do and what you do not want to do. Only if you understand these things can you communicate them to other people.

► Don't fall into the trap of using a generalised CV for all jobs. Never think of your CV as static, something to be photocopied for each job application. It is essential that your CV is shaped for the particular job you want. Use your best-self list (see pages 60–62) as the 'pool' from which you select items for your CV.

► Take the time and effort to tease out the skills and experience required for the job and match them with your own list, accentuating those that are most relevant. It's up to you to make it easy for the potential employer to identify your suitability.

▶ You are embarking on a marketing exercise and writing an advertisement for yourself. Think through how best to get a prospective employer to 'buy you'. Beware of 'over-selling', however – recruiters have a nose for blarney.

▶ The format of a CV is not cast in tablets of stone (although a fairly standard one is shown on page 70) and it is up to you to design a format that best suits you. The framework of a CV is fairly flexible and does allow for creativity. Lead on your strengths. If you have an excellent degree, put the education section on the first page. If your educational record is a bit lacklustre, put your education section after your experience and achievements.

▶ Concentrate on your achievements rather than your responsibilities. You'd be surprised how many people put a précis of their job description under 'experience'. This tells a prospective employer absolutely nothing about you. Your duties in your current (or last) job may have no relation to your experience and abilities.

▶ Make your CV succinct. It is designed to present your career profile at a glance. It is meant to be a summary. As a rough rule of thumb, about a page per decade of your life is a good guide. The first page should set you up and all additional pages should abet the story. For a college leaver in her twenties, two pages is optimum. For a mature manager in her fifties, it will take five pages to give the whole story.

▶ Detailed information should only be included where it relates to the actual position you are applying for. Remember, if your CV is good enough to meet the criteria of the job, you can also supply further information in the covering letter. This will be read in greater depth if you get called to interview.

You will be asked to supply references relating to either your character or your work reliability. If you are giving a current employer as a referee and do not want her approached until a job offer is made, state this clearly. Select people who will be able to give a realistic assessment of you and your abilities, whose standing in the community is recognisable. For example, Mary Brown of 15 Acacia Avenue is not obviously Mary Brown, human resources director of Dreamboat plc. It is important that your references are easily identified by the role or professional standing of those who provide them.

Remember to get referees, consent in advance; tell them the kind of job you have applied for and the kinds of things you are saying about yourself so that they can confirm these in their letters. Enlist their support. All too often, referees are surprised when they hear out of the blue that such and such a person has nominated them.

> *I applied for a job recently and gave two referees, thinking that I had plenty of time to alert them to what I'd done before they received the letter from my prospective employer. What I didn't realise was that very often in the private sector personnel officers just lift the phone and call people to assess your suitability before they invite you to interview. Well, I was caught on the hop a bit as I hadn't yet got to one of them. I think his surprise may have come over on the phone to the personnel guy. I don't know whether that was the reason I didn't get the job.*

In most instances, your CV will need to be accompanied by a letter of introduction or a statement in support of your application. Be sure to make it easy for the employer to identify your suitability. Your covering letter must contain all the appropriate facts and match the information to the relevant opportunity. A letter gives you the scope to explain more than

YOUR SKELETON CV

Name Print your name in bold type. No need to use your full or legal name. Use the name you wish to be addressed by at the interview

Address Directly beneath your name. Include your postcode.

Telephone Give the full dialling code number. Give your work and home numbers if you can.

Personal Put date of birth, not age. If you want to put marital status, use married or single – not divorced. Think carefully about declaring your children. Do it if it's relevant or if child care could act as a constraint but you may not wish to if these are not considerations.

Career Start with your present/most recent job and work backwards. Use bullet point style sentences – cut the waffle. Quantify when appropriate. Arouse curiosity. Do not use misleading job titles, jargon or buzz words. Use positive words such as 'success' and 'achievement'. Cut out irrelevant early jobs. Always state what you have achieved; do not simply give your job description.

Dates Put all dates on the left-hand side. Only put the years, exact dates are irrelevant and untidy. Do not leave years unaccounted for.

Education Omit examination failures. Give priority to the most relevant qualifications: if you have a degree there is no need to spell out each O Level or GCSE qualification. Be selective about training courses attended.

Key skills (Optional but desirable.) Be selective - no more than six key skills. Give priority to more important/relevant skills. Use action words to describe the skills. Do not include dates. Remember the importance of transferable skills

Interests (Optional but desirable.) Only include interests which are different, intriguing, or which indicate transferable skills, achievements or responsibilities. Assess the overall effect of your interests.

just who you are. It allows you to point out specifically why you would be an asset to that employer.

Until recently, covering letters were as important as CVs. This is not necessarily true today. With the onslaught of the recession and the fierce competition for jobs during the nineties, employers invariably use CVs as the frontline in screening out the no-hopers. So keep your CV as the pivotal part of your application.

GIVING EFFECTIVE INTERVIEWS

As with most things, the more you prepare for an interview, the better will be your performance. Never stint on your preparation. When preparing, remember that your goal is to give yourself the chance to prove that you are the right person for the job.

> You really need to spend time practising for an interview. A lot of us have habits – nothing drastic, but small habits that we aren't aware of. With me, I realised that I use hand gestures a lot – too much for an interview situation. I'm now very aware of that and control it during an interview. The more you practise, the better you are when you get to the real thing.

Find out everything you can about your prospective employer – its current position in the market or the field, the number of employees, the range of services or products it provides, its competitors and its culture. Before you go to the interview, visit the company's premises and look at the people who come and go. Are they like you? Would you look out of place unless you make some subtle changes?

This research will stand you in good stead, no matter what job you're going for. If you know next to nothing about the position being offered or indeed about the organisation itself, it will show up in the conversation and the interviewer will think that you're not really interested in the job.

Practise answering the kind of questions you might face at the interview The type of question you're asked will vary enormously. However, there are four that you can be fairly confident will come up in one form or another:

> Can you tell me a little bit about yourself?
> Why do you want to leave your current job?
> Why do you want this job?
> Is there anything you would like to ask us?

Think carefully about these questions in relation to the job you are going for. Formulate your answers in advance. Focus on the image you are trying to create and work on responses that will contribute to this. Don't undersell yourself (men hardly ever do) but present yourself in as positive a light as possible without unduly exaggerating your talents and attributes.

If you feel that something in your past or current work history may be a cause for concern (redundancy, for example), deal with it upfront. Practise an answer that lets you tell them before they ask you. Do not be drawn into recriminations. Stick to the twenty- second rule (no more, no less) and direct the conversation on to the next subject.

> *Anyone who bad-mouths their current organisation goes down badly with me as someone who is rather disloyal and untrustworthy. I'd far rather hear that someone wishes to advance their career with us than that they hate the people at their current employer.*

Also, if you're going to be asked to take any written or oral test, now is the time when you should be brushing up your specialist knowledge and thinking about ways of coping with the test situation.

Look your best. When you wake up on the day of the interview, spend some time getting yourself into the best possible frame of mind. Eat a decent, stamina-inducing breakfast, have a luxurious bath, wear your best suit – the one that makes you feel confident. Think about your 'best self' and bring that with you to the interview. In short, do whatever it is that will make you feel assured and able to deliver your best.

Don't leave things to the last minute – have your suit cleaned in time, polish your shoes, cancel any other appointments that might distract you or make you rushed. Allow plenty of time to pamper yourself, to build your confidence and to get to the interview on time.

You can expect the interview to proceed in stages. The divisions between each stage may be blurred and their order will change from one interview to the next but they are generally all there in some form.

▶ **Sizing up the Candidate.** You never get a second chance to make a first impression. For the first few minutes of the interview, both you and the interviewer will be trying to work out what makes the other tick. You can get off to a flying start at this stage just by looking your best (Chapter 12 may help). Research shows that something of the order of 80% of interviewers make up their minds about a candidate in the first ten minutes.

> ❝ I think that interviewers make up their minds almost straightaway about whether they want to employ you or not. If they give you an interview, it means that you have the skills they are looking for (they've decided that from your CV). The interview is more about 'Will you fit into the organisation?'; 'What type of personality do you have?' – all that sort of stuff. So, it's important they you walk in that door feeling confident, saying, "I can do this job really well." ❞

► **Your experience.** Don't just concentrate on your employment history. The interviewer will be keen to form a view of you as a whole, so tell her about your extracurricular activities as well as your work experience. This is the point in the proceedings where the interviewer can sit back and watch you in action and it's not only *what* you're saying that will make an impression.

Quietly take control of the 'business meeting'. You only have a short time to market yourself so make sure the interviewers learn all that you want them to know. Make sure that the skills and experience you are emphasising are relevant to the position for which you are being interviewed.

► **Over to you.** When the interviewer utters the classic phrase, 'Tell me a little bit about yourself', be careful. The question is far too open-ended and the chances are you'll waffle on forever and walk into all sorts of traps, especially if you're nervous.

Think positively. Have prepared a fairly brief statement which creates the image of a responsible, creative, friendly, conscientious individual. As soon as you can, steer the question back around to the interviewer by asking what aspect of your application attracted her and what she would like you to talk about in more detail. This puts you back in control.

► **On the spot.** By now you've given the interviewer some background about yourself and she will want to find out a bit more about what you have to offer. The best way to do that is for her to ask you questions about yourself, your experience, your interests and your qualifications. Unfortunately, interviewers are not usually detached and objective individuals who ask the right questions to elicit the right sort of information in the right way. You will need to be prepared to deal with a bad interviewer and with problem questions.

Ask yourself: what is she looking for at this stage? This will depend on the job. She will be trying to picture you in the role. Can she see you taking over from your potential manager if she became ill? Will you be able to cope with the pressure of the work? Will you fit easily into the existing team?

The specific questions the interviewer asks will vary from interview to interview. But you can still predict which type of questions are likely to come up. Remember that interviewers are unlikely to confine themselves to asking you questions about your work history and academic achievements. So be prepared to answer some more personal and sensitive questions, and to talk about feelings as well as facts.

At all times remember to be yourself and keep a sense of humour.

▶ **Anything you'd like to ask us?** Towards the end of their interview, interviewers generally ask candidates if they have any questions. Many people think that this is their chance to ask about salary, holidays and bonus payments. Try and find these things out before the interview, so that you can concentrate on asking the kind of positive questions that contribute to your main objective of selling yourself. Interviewers generally are not very impressed by candidates whose main interest seems to be what they're going to earn or how many weeks' holiday they're entitled to.

Make sure that you have a number of well-thought-out, intelligent questions to ask. Questions regarding the field of work or the market, about the impact of impending government legislation or demographic trends, about the company's expectations for the future. Do not be afraid to ask when the next interview will be and with whom. Always ask if it is possible to view the operation if you are being interviewed at the prospective employer's premises.

> *The way I psych myself up for an interview is to turn the tables – to view it as me interviewing the company to see if I want to work for them. This really helps me when it comes to asking questions at the end of the interview. It also means that I don't get so panicky about the interview.*

▶ **Let's talk turkey.** These days, standard employment practices are disintegrating. Things are far more flexible than they were and almost everything can be negotiated. The more senior you get, the more cards you hold in the negotiating game. Brush up on your negotiation skills and your assertiveness before you begin.

Negotiations may begin as early as the first interview. If this happens and you are in doubt, say nothing or give a holding response in order to buy yourself time to think about it. If an interviewer asks you what salary you expect, have the answer ready but keep it in reserve.

Put the ball back in her court: tell her that you have some ideas but that it would depend on what else was included in the package, and ask her how much she thinks you are worth to the organisation. Keep your cool. If you name a figure that is too high, you may price yourself out of the job. If you name a figure that is too low, the employer may decide you aren't competent to hold the job. If after this, the interviewer names a figure which is too low, you should first stress that you very much want to work for the organisation and then explain why that salary is too low. Stick to your guns.

> *I did a trade off between salary and vacation at interview. They'd advertised at £25,000. I knew cash was tight, I said I'd do a forty week year for £20,000 and*

was confident of meeting the terms of reference in the research programme. It was a both-sides-win scenario. **,**

▶ **After the Interview.** Very few interviewed candidates bother to write a thank-you letter to the interviewer. If you do, it will make you stand out from the crowd, give you an opportunity to add any additional information they may have missed at the interview and show appreciation for the time given. You can also use it as an opportunity to confirm your interest.

Remember, there will be a lull while you wait for the outcome of the interview. It is tempting to relax, especially if you think it has gone well. Don't relax. Continue marketing and researching. Expect a second or third interview and prepare accordingly.

Being unsuccessful at an interview can be very demoralising but try to view the experience in a positive light. Getting to the interview stage is a success in itself. It means that your skills are in demand and your CV is effective. Also, the value of real-life interview practice should never be underestimated – it makes each successive one less of a stressful experience. You cannot expect to get every job you apply for. If you do, you may not be stretching yourself enough or aiming high enough.

Failure doesn't matter if you use it to build success. Review the interview and see what you can learn from it. Was the job right for you? Did the job or the company meet your expectations and was it suitable to your skills and aspirations? Did you prepare properly for the interview, finding out as much as you could about the company beforehand, practising your techniques. Did you sell yourself well, emphasising all the points you wanted to?

Turn your disappointment into a learning experience. Get feedback from your interviewer about your performance.

Find out what your strong points were and what areas you could improve on. Most interviewers are only too happy to give you constructive feedback on your performance: they do not like rejecting candidates and welcome any opportunity to turn a negative result into a positive one.

> **'** I think it's very important to get feedback from employers when you do an interview. Sometimes you do an interview and you come out thinking that you did very well but you don't get the job. And you're left with no idea as to why. The last interview I went for, I got feedback from the employer and it really was useful. It really helped me to polish my interview skills but, more importantly, it's much more positive and doesn't leave you feeling so demoralised. She told me that she had interviewed eight people and one of them had been outstanding and she got the job. But she was very helpful to me – she told me I talked much too fast, didn't take my time answering questions and didn't take the opportunity to sell myself as well as I could have. I felt so much better about the whole thing after she spoke to me. She genuinely wished me well in my search for work. **'**

TURNING DOWN AN INAPPROPRIATE JOB

One of the things that you must be prepared for is to turn down a job if it is wrong for you. Women sometimes have real difficulty saying no to people. Try to remember you were interviewing them as much as they were interviewing you. You owe it to yourself and to your self-esteem to stick to your goals, and there are gentle ways of letting people know.

Of course, you must be upfront: job candidates who turn down positions without explanation risk giving an impression of unprofessionalism that will not be forgotten, whether they're from inside or outside the organisation. Almost all employers invest a lot of senior staff time in job interviews, and that's money.

The way you reject a job offer shouldn't slam the door on other opportunities. Although you may not like the position you've been offered this time, you want the prospective employer to keep you in mind for a future opening. So how do you strike the necessary balance of candour and tact in declining?

First, avoid leaving the suitor with the impression that she was being strung along. You should get back to the employer within forty-eight hours. Nothing riles a prospective employer more than the person who asks for two weeks to think about it.

Before you call, rehearse your reasons for refusing. In the view of a number of personnel officers, the following are acceptable excuses:

► I'm eager to work for the organisation, but after thinking about it, I feel the position doesn't fit my career objectives.

► I've realised I'd rather work in a more inner-city area.

► Although I do have the skills in operations I believe my abilities are better used in the sales area.

► The company is on the brink of exciting times but I'm looking for an employer operating in a more mature business market.

► Some family issues have come up that I have to resolve. In another year or two I will be able to relocate but right now I feel I have to stay near my ageing parent.

► The offer you've made is excellent but the opportunity for promotion doesn't seem as great as where I am. As it stands now, I'll be up for general manager within a year.

And the bad reasons? Anything that hints of game-playing or a personality conflict. Personnel practitioners hate it when a candidate says, 'I took this to my company and they matched the offer.' That may be a lose-lose game since you could have bought your own organisation time to replace you.

If you think you're incompatible with your potential boss, don't state this as the reason for rejecting the opportunity. There is no point in alienating people unnecessarily. Find another excuse to turn down the offer.

Even after you've declined the offer by phone or in person, your campaign isn't complete. Write to each person you dealt with and say how much you appreciated their time. A prospective employer won't see it as a total loss if you say that you are grateful for the way you've been treated and that you hope to meet again.

Large organisations do keep files of past prospects and will call back those who left an impression of courtesy and sincerity. Even if you are certain you would never want to sign on with a particular organisation that has made you an offer, a little diplomacy is a wise investment since you may be surprised to discover who you'll be working for tomorrow.

4 Activating support systems

▶ ▶ ▶ ▶ ▶   GETTING HELP: YOUR SUPPORT AUDIT • FAMILY
AND FRIENDS • NETWORKS AND NETWORKING •
FIND A MENTOR • WHEN TO PAY FOR SUPPORT –
PSYCHOTHERAPY • OTHER TYPES OF THERAPY

You can't do it all on your own. Nobody can.

The over-arching theme of this book is that all of us, to a very large extent, write our own life script and hold the key to our own success. Using that key to unlock real doors, however, takes more than just the skills we have painstakingly developed, it takes sustainable confidence in our ability to apply those skills and the self-esteem to know that we deserve to succeed. For a number of reasons, many working women lack this all-important level of confidence and self-esteem, although men seem to take it for granted. These are the qualities that we must obtain from our support systems.

Of course, there are still going to be circumstances around you which will be beyond your control but, for the main part, the better your support system, the better your ability to develop the power to take control of your life and your destiny.

If you are to survive as a working woman, you will need a realistic assessment of who the people are that you can genuinely count upon for support, together with a plan for developing new support systems to bridge any gaps.

Who Can You Count
on for Support?

▶ **Colleague:** someone who understands your work situation.

NAME(S): _____

▶ **Problem-Solver:** someone who can look at your problem and advise what could be done.

NAME(S): _____

▶ **Fun-Lover:** someone who will make you laugh and feel better for having spent time with them.

NAME(S): _____

▶ **Good Listener:** someone who can listen without passing judgement.

NAME(S): _____

▶ **Sharer:** someone with whom you can take time off and relax.

NAME(S): _____

Like everything else in life, good support systems need to be worked at. You can't always rely solely on your partner or your best friend. The person who knows you best is not always the best person to speak to. Relying on one person to fulfil all your needs is almost always bound to cause disappointment.

There are enormous difficulties associated with being a fledgling female pioneer and you must never underestimate how invaluable role models, mentors or just other women to talk to are.

▶ **Just-Like-Me:** someone who is like yourself, who understands you.

NAME(S): _____

▶ **Mentor:** someone who has your interests at heart and who will give you the benefit of their wisdom.

NAME(S): _____

▶ **Nurturer:** someone who is there for you, who looks after you, who will give you a cuddle if you need it.

NAME(S): _____

▶ **Other Categories:** any other types of people you may feel you need in the context of your own particular circumstances.

NAME(S): _____

And, important if appropriate:

▶ **Carer:** someone who will take the children or your elderly mother off your hands, even if it's only for an hour or two.

NAME(S): _____

GETTING HELP: YOUR SUPPORT AUDIT

Before you do any work on developing new support systems, it is important that you have a realistic idea of who you can count on already.

You will need different people at different times in your life for different types of support. When you want to sound off about a problem at work, a colleague may be the best person to listen and to offer constructive advice. On other occasions you may need a shoulder to cry on; practical support with writing a report; the acknowledgement of someone who has been through it all before; objective advice on how to handle your boss. Or you may find that you need someone who can offer two or more of these types of support at once.

Likewise, you may often find that a colleague is looking to you to support her through any or all of these typical situations. If you can help, you should be more than happy to do so: support systems only work if they cut both ways.

It is important to know exactly what strengths and weaknesses there are in your support portfolio. The exercise on page 82–83 should help you to do that. Be absolutely honest: fill in the categories of supporter with the names of those you can rely on. If you cannot think of anyone who fills that category, then leave it blank rather than putting in someone who you cannot really depend on.

Keep your support list in mind as you read through the rest of this chapter. As you develop your own support systems you will find that it becomes easier to fill those categories which are important to your life.

FAMILY AND FRIENDS

Some of us still live in extended families where support may be available in spades (although often at a price). Extended families are great for bringing up kids (in fact this is what they're best at) but they are not always totally sympathetic to the new needs of working women.

Society is changing and the vast majority of working women in Britain today live either as single adults (with or without children) or with their partners in small family units. Many of us live in the inner city or in the suburbs, miles from our parents, in streets where the neighbours keep much to themselves. In this new society, friendships have taken on a greater importance in our lives. Friends have become the new families. More than families, sometimes.

> My friendships are almost more important than anything. I'm single, I'm an only child and someday my parents won't be around any more. I know that no matter what happens to me there are a couple of friends I will always have.

What changed to elevate friendship to its new status?

Basically, everything. The extended family – and even the nuclear family – are no longer the norm. Many of us left our homes and parents in order to go to college and never returned. In our new environment, we found ourselves dealing with different concerns, from writing job applications to writing annual reports, from living with men to living alone, from campaigning on abortion rights to coping with working motherhood. When we want to talk about these things, we can't (except in rare cases) talk to our mothers. We naturally turn to our friends.

A lot of women still have great relationships with their parents and can and do lean on them for support, particularly with childcare. But for many of us, coming of age during a time of rapid social and political change has meant that we often can only connect with friends on some of the issues concerning our day-to-day lives. If you really want to be understood, talk with ease and openness and make sense of what's going on in your life, it generally has to be with a contemporary. In any case, many of us don't see our mothers from one Christmas to the next.

> My mother belonged to a baby-sitting and coffee morning circle known as the "Housebound Wives" when my sister and I were small in the early sixties. None of the women worked but the conversation was pretty highbrow just the same – most of them were college

> *graduates. It meant that we children had a very wide*
> *circle of friends too but the husbands were nowhere.*
> *Well I can't conceive of belonging to such a group now*
> *that I'm a (working) mother. For a start I just don't have*
> *the time. Secondly who could join anything*
> *called the "Housebound Wives"?.*

Friendships today are not dependent on whether your family would approve. Typically, our friendships will be entirely separate from our families. We now pick our own diverse groups of friends who reflect the various aspects of our lives and fulfil different roles: old friends, new friends, work friends, college friends, male friends, and so on.

> *One of my pals describes these various kinds of*
> *friendships as a sort of tapestry. The threads remain*
> *individual and separate offering their own distinct*
> *quality. It's only when they're woven together*
> *into the tapestry that a total picture emerges.*

We tend to divide friends into other, more personal kinds of categories too: friends who are great for talking to about romance or the personal side of life; friends who are always ready with a sympathetic ear and good advice in times of trouble; friends who are alter egos at work; friends who are just plain good for a laugh.

Once forged, these female friendships tend to remain important through moves, partner changes, career changes, children.

> *I was living with someone for six years and tended*
> *to exclude friends because it was easier to go*
> *home and just be with my boyfriend. When we broke*
> *up, I was devastated but the one good thing was that I*
> *see my friends more (although I had lost quite a few*
> *through neglect). If I got into a serious relationship,*
> *I'd work harder to stay close to my friends.*

As we are all now (hopefully) living so much longer, it is good news that women (unlike men) continue to make friends, have new experiences and maintain support networks throughout their lives. This is because men's friendships are task-orientated and therefore revolve around activities, whereas women's friendships usually focus on talking about feelings and personal matters.

> My friends and I joke about starting a colony for retired humanities teachers on a Greek island. We're going to sit in the taverna and have boozy lunches from eleven to three and cocktails starting at three-thirty. It sounds like fun but it's also a little scary.

These friendships are investments for our future: research has shown that women in old age who have one good friend are in better psychological health than women who have twelve grandchildren. Remember, you can never rely on your kids (or their kids) to look after you in your old age.

NETWORKS AND NETWORKING

> Men who are my counterparts don't know half as many people as I do. I have much more access to that power than they do and when they need to hire someone to do something, they ask me if I know anybody.

The term 'network' when applied in a women's context has come to mean a positive process of mutual support. Working women ignore the potential of networks at their peril: it is the practice of extending your contacts to give you greater access to ideas, people, support and opportunities, all of which is extremely positive and influential. Networking is not just about getting names to put in your personal organiser – it's about feeling free to use them.

Your own network is simply everyone you know. If you extend that again to everyone that they know, your network multiplies many times. Most of us get to know other people either haphazardly or through association. Your network, therefore, could include people at work, fellow professionals, people in other organisations, members of professional institutes, people you've met on courses, your family, your neighbours, people you know from college, your hobby interest groups, members of women's groups. You can use your network as a basis for building your contacts, whether formal or informal.

> *We host a lunch club of local businesswomen in our restaurant once every two months. The group has been meeting for some time now and the conversation is very high-spirited and self-confident – the sort of shop talk one would expect from women in expensive suits handling multi-million budgets (although I don't know what any of them actually do). Over poached salmon and Chablis they exchange success stories and follow the mini-dramas of one another's offices the way my mum follows Coronation Street.*

The more people you know, the greater your flexibility to achieve your goals. You do not have to be friends with everyone within your network, indeed you do not even have to like them (although it generally helps) but the more people you know, the broader your horizons.

Who are your contacts at the moment? Ask yourself these questions:

▶ Are they up-to-date or do they go back a long way? Or a bit of both?

▶ Are they work people?

▶ Are they spread around all the departments at work?

▶ Do you network with people away from work?

▶ Do you ever meet people who are totally different from you?

▶ In which areas do you want to build up your contacts?

▶ Do you have any contacts who can help you do that?

▶ Do you regularly add new contacts to your list?

▶ What do you do to keep in touch with all these people? Is it enough?

▶ Are you tending to network with all the same sort of people?

There are also increasing numbers of networks within organisations, some of which are quite informal and not registered anywhere (so you will have to do some asking around) and many of which have been formed after a training course or conference. A few large organisations have formal networks, such as Women in BP or Women in ICL.

> *Women who are involved in networks based on professional and personal connections agree that they have become so strong that they can outstrip the old-boy networks they were formed to compensate for.*

Obviously, only you can decide whether you should join a formal institution to have access to what is essentially an informal process. As with most things, go with what is right for you, but don't put off joining a formal network just because you're scared: that's the worst reason for not trying something.

> *There's no strong serious female lobby consulted for reactions to major events the way a CBI spokesman is always sought for an opinion. We could become that lobby. We could influence developments,*

> *sponsor research projects and become a voice to influence change in the nineties – to shape things in a way that makes sense for us. We're still struggling with rigid corporate structures but there are massive demographic changes on the horizon – we could make it impossible to push us around.* **'**

FIND A MENTOR

Whether consciously or not, most of us will, at some stage, suffer from a feeling of isolation at work and our natural practice is to make career choices without talking to others. This is never a good idea. Acting blindly can derail a career.

> **'** *Nobody told me I was being groomed for promotion. When I was given a really difficult project on which to prove myself, I decided it was too hard for too little reward and I jumped ship. I went to what was a better job in the short term. Several months later someone told me that the chief executive had had great plans for me. Now I've lost ground in my career development since the change required acclimatisation to establish familiarity and a track record, whereas I had already proved my credentials in my old borough. I wish I'd taken some advice.* **'**

This is where a mentor becomes invaluable.

A mentor is someone who believes in you more than you believe in yourself. They challenge, support, advise, motivate and encourage you. They understand your work and believe in your potential. They are not, however, your social worker, psychotherapist, substitute parent or teacher. A mentor will provide a safe harbour – a space to ask questions, think out loud, make mistakes without feeling embarrassed. They view you objectively and give you constructive feedback whilst guiding you in the path of your career. They can also be great fun.

Each mentoring arrangement is a delicate balance. In any relationship, it is important to outline the expectations and limits of both parties. This is particularly true of mentoring. Those involved in mentoring suggest that you write down what you and your mentor expect of each other and, perhaps, more importantly, what your mentor can offer. This 'agreement' will, obviously, change as your circumstances do. Ideally, a mentoring relationship is a long term one.

In recognition of the value of a mentor and in an attempt to formalise the process, some organisations have begun in-house mentoring programmes. Among their objectives might be gaining greater employee loyalty, developing a stronger managerial base for succession planning or ending gender and racial inequalities. Some go as far as expecting executives to recruit and develop their own replacements as they move up the career ladder.

When your mentor is also your boss, it becomes more complicated. You may work ten times harder than anyone else for the unwritten promise that you will glean wisdom and experience under your boss's guidance, but beware: when one employee is singled out for a favoured role, both mentor and protégé may incur the ill will of others who feel overlooked.

When consciously looking for a mentor, single out a kindred soul. You will only get on with someone whose ethics, values and *modus operandi* mesh with your own. There needs to be a foundation of mutual respect. The ideal mentor is a good role model, a great listener, a sounding board and a cheerleader combined. This is worth bearing in mind, no matter which side of the mentoring arrangement you find yourself on. Ideally, your mentor should not be a friend first as true friends are rarely objective enough about you.

> *I suppose I fell into my mentoring relationship. My mentor is a friend of my aunt and I went to work for her company during the school holidays. We just got on straight away and she's always taken an interest in my career. It was she who really challenged me when I wanted to drop out of college. But she does more than challenge me, she really supports me in my decisions and following them through. She has also given me access to her network, to people I would never otherwise have met.*

If your organisation doesn't have a mentoring scheme and if fate hasn't seated you across the room from your mentor, there are ways to initiate your own mentor search:

▶ Decide what kind of help you want. For example, is it to learn managerial skills, or are you looking for feedback on your personal progress?

▶ Analyse who are the most influential people within your organisation or field, then narrow that list to those who could help you meet your objectives. Research those individuals jobs and special interests – also whether they have mentored others.

▶ When you have a potential mentor in mind, volunteer to work on projects with her/him – even if it means working overtime. Your enthusiasm and hard work are bound to be recognised and rewarded.

▶ Go slow on formalising the relationship. Some people may balk at the idea of having demands put upon them.

▶ Recognise that it takes time and communication to establish rapport. But considering that this relationship is an investment in your career, it is well worth the effort.

WHEN TO PAY FOR SUPPORT – PSYCHOTHERAPY

Some of us feel that our problems are quite deep-seated and that we are unable to obtain enough sustained support from our friends, families and colleagues to deal with them. As with most tough things, recognising you have a problem and being willing to confront it is half the battle won.

Many working women are now turning to various forms of psychotherapy to guide them through problems in their personal lives that could be affecting their careers. It's okay to pay for support.

The psychotherapeutic process can help you make inroads towards tackling behavioural problems – classic examples being perpetual lateness, procrastination, unwillingness to confront the boss and so forth, which many women find really debilitating in their careers. There are the sorts of problems that go away once you understand the root cause. They are the sorts of problems that could stand between you being a moderate achiever and a stunning success.

> I started seeing a psychotherapist when I was twenty-nine. I had had a bad relationship with my father, a series of useless relationships with men and I was drinking too much. Within six months I had re-defined my relationship with my dad and had really cut down on my drinking. I found I was spending most of the sessions discussing problems related to my work. It has turned out to be quite the most useful tool in my career. Kate (my therapist) helps me to unpick the problem and begin to identify solutions. In addition, I find I have a much-enhanced capacity to learn new things. In the last two years, I've had two promotions and become fluent in Italian. It may sound extreme, but I would recommend it to any woman, even if she

*doesn't feel that she has emotional problems. It's a
tough world for working women –
we need all the help we can get.*

You need to really think about the type of therapy that will most benefit you. Most women choose individual psychotherapy where you consult your therapist in a one-to-one situation at a set time each week for what is generally termed the 'fifty-minute hour'. It is common to visit your therapist once or twice a week, depending on what you can afford and how quickly you want results. The regularity of the appointments and the commitment to the process that this entails is all part of the treatment. If you embark on a course of psychotherapy, it is as well to understand from the outset that it has to be taken seriously. After all, you are taking up another woman's professional time and space and, in any case, you will be charged for missed appointments.

Psychoanalysis is a more intensive form of therapy which involves visiting your therapist five times a week. This is generally advised if you are severely emotionally disturbed (it could be part of the rehabilitation process after a violent attack or a bereavement, for example). Group therapy is when you attend with a number of other people (usually there are seven of you in total) at a set time or times each week. The session is moderated by a psychotherapist who ensures that the group works properly and that members behave responsibly both towards themselves and to the other members.

There are several forms of psychotherapeutic process(es) and, as with everything else, it is important that you do the research necessary to find out what works best for you. There are a number of books and sources of advice that will help you with this (see pages 340–341). Referral from friends is also a valuable starting point.

Psychotherapy, however, is not a panacea. There are a number of fundamental things that you should be appraised of before you consider embarking on it:

► It is important to understand that it is both you and the therapist who do the work. Unless you are totally committed, you are wasting your time and money. Just because you are paying a therapist, it doesn't mean that you don't have to work at it. Therapy is not a passive service whereby you lie back and reap the dividends.

► Don't expect a quick fix or any miracles. It is a slow, difficult and sometimes painful process. Like most things that are worth doing in life, the harder you work at it, the more you will benefit.

► It's expensive. A session can cost £15–£60, depending on where you live and how experienced your therapist is. It is only in exceptional cases that counselling can be had through the NHS. View the cost as an investment in yourself. You may find it expensive to embark on this process but can you afford *not* to?

► It takes up time and energy. Most therapists will be sympathetic to the needs of the working woman and will, whenever possible, fit you in at the beginning or end of the day or at lunchtime. There is a limit to flexibility, however, and once you've agreed the times, then you must stick to them each week. There may also be travelling time to consider.

► This isn't America and it isn't fashionable to have a 'shrink' here. The British have long maintained a stiff upper lip and people may view your activities with enormous suspicion, as psycho-mumbo-jumbo or as a self-indulgent display of weakness. Think very carefully about whether you want your boss, your colleagues, your family or your friends to know, and on what terms.

► A lot depends on whether you have confidence in your therapist. Unfortunately, you have no real way of finding out whether she's any good until after you have invested some weeks in engaging in the process. Take heart: rogue therapists are rare and if you proceed methodically, you are unlikely to find one. If, however, you end up with a therapist who is not working for you, treat it as a learning experience and use the knowledge to find one who is right for you. Don't feel hemmed in by your first choice.

▶ Finally, you will need to be brave. Tackling your problems is tough and you are very courageous to be contemplating it at all. If it works for you, it may mean some short-term discomfort, but rest assured, if you persevere you will find that you stand to reap huge rewards.

We only get one shot at this game and there's no point in wasting your precious life being unhappy. If you find you're not happy, seek help now rather than later. You'll never know whether it could work for you unless you give it a try.

OTHER TYPES OF THERAPY

The boom in alternative medicine which began in the early eighties was due, in large part, to women seeking a more holistic approach to their own well being than that generally on offer from their GPs. There was a renewed belief in the concept of treating the whole person rather than merely treating the symptoms of any illness; alternative therapists will not generally hold out any promise of treating individual symptoms but will give a more radical commitment to treating you.

Since women are naturally much more inclined than men to put themselves in touch with the needs of their own bodies, many of us have turned to alternative therapists to sustain our physical well-being. In the process, we have discovered that they can meet some of our emotional and mental needs also. Many professional women consciously equip themselves with a network of alternative therapists, whom they use as an additional source of support in their busy lives.

The type of in-depth consultation that alternative practitioners offer is not generally available through the National Health Service. Since you may spend an hour or more on each visit, it is fairly labour intensive and therefore expensive (anything from £10 to £60, depending on the type of therapy involved, geographical location and so on). However, many of us find we are willing to invest in therapy if it liberates more time and energy elsewhere in our lives.

> *I will never know whether acupuncture works in the scientific sense. Actually, I don't care any more. What I do know is that it works for me.*

There are a wide range of alternative therapies available. Those that working women find most useful include:

Acupuncture, used in its most thorough application, is a system of balancing the body, mind and emotional well-being. Very fine needles are used on certain defined points on the body to restore the balance of chi energy which is perceived as essential to good health.

Learning **Alexander Technique** can help you see how you are reacting unconsciously to the demands life makes on you and give you the self-knowledge you need in order to change the pattern of your response. It aims to treat and prevent a range of disorders by what is essentially a system of postural changes. It is a re-education of your body's mechanisms.

Aromatherapy is a particular form of treatment in which essential oils or aromatic essences are rubbed into the skin or used as inhalants or in baths or footbaths. More people are beginning to use aromatic inhalants in their office as a way of coping with stress or dealing with a cold, for example.

Chiropractic is a therapy which specialises in the diagnosis and treatment of mechanical disorders of the joints, particularly those of the spine.

Homoeopathy is based on the principle that symptoms are often the consequence of the body's resistance mechanism working to repel an attack and that, far from seeking to suppress symptoms, it may be desirable to take some form of treatment calculated to help the resistance. There can be few of us who haven't tried a homoeopathic remedy at some stage in our lives.

> ❛ I am a total convert to homoeopathy. Not just because it cured my stomach problem which I'd been suffering from for years but because I find it such an empowering process. It's such a luxury to be allocated an hour for diagnosis and treatment and my homoeopath is a wonderful, warm woman whom I see as a friend more than anything. ❜

Osteopathy is concerned with the establishment and maintenance of the normal structural integrity of the body. This is done primarily through manipulation of joints in order to restore them to their normal positions and mobility, thereby relieving abnormal tensions in muscles and ligaments. The greater part of an osteopath's work relates to the spinal column, not merely because its integrity is basic to the whole bone and muscle system but because it houses the spinal column through which the nervous system operates. Highly recommended for keyboard operators.

Reflexology is based on the premise that all organs of the body are mirrored in the feet. The therapist will stimulate areas of the sole of your foot in order to perform a set of functions to remove waste deposits, congestion and blockages in the energy pathways, improving blood circulation and gland function and relaxing the whole system, including the mind.

Of course, this is by no means an exhaustive list and your friends may tell of good (or bad) experiences they've had with crystal therapy, shiatsu, herbalists, colour therapy or whatever. As the old adage goes, don't knock it till you've tried it. If it works for you, you should get on and do it and not worry about what anyone thinks. Many women build up a supportive relationship with their homoeopath, chiropractor or reflexologist over several years and find that these therapists are far more sympathetic to what makes them tick than some of their colleagues or friends. It can be much more therapeutic to spend a lunchtime with your aromatherapist than having a drink in a smoky pub. In addition, being prepared to do things for yourself – even if it costs a bit – does wonders for your self esteem.

> *I've been visiting my osteopath about every six weeks for over six years. I really look forward to it each time. I first consulted her because my neck had seized up due to stress but she soon sorted that and I carried on seeing her regularly. I was a childhood asthmatic and am given to stiffness in the muscles in my back due to a learned compensation for my rather inefficient lungs. In the days after I've seen her I always have more physical energy and feel tons better. She re-aligns my body and puts me back in balance. In the process, she seems to treat more of me than just my physique. She has also become a friend.*

Women who are interested in trying an alternative therapist will find some useful addresses at the end of the book. As with most services, though, ask your friends and colleagues where they go, since personal recommendation is the safest and easiest way of finding a therapist.

5 Your Training Strategy

▶ ▶ ▶ ▶ ▶ LIFELONG LEARNING • LEARNING APPROACH •
DEVISING YOUR TRAINING PLAN • ADVICE AND
INFORMATION • FLEXIBLE APPROACHES TO
LEARNING • COPING WITH PART TIME STUDY •
RETURNING TO FULL TIME STUDY • FINANCING
YOUR TRAINING • THE MBA QUALIFICATION

Training is a vital part of career development.

If you really want to make a change in your career, the decision is likely to involve some element of training. Your dream is more likely to become a reality if it is backed up by knowledge, skill and qualification.

The status and need for training has changed. In today's ever-shifting labour market, the need to keep your skills up to date is crucial. One of the great advantages that women have is that we can cope with diversity much more readily than men. This means that we stand to capitalise in the fluid environment of the British workplace. Training – both formal and informal – and the willingness to train and retrain at various stages in our careers are crucial ingredients in our success.

The days when training was seen as a sign of failure and incompetence are, thankfully, on the way out. As Rosabeth Moss Kanter said, 'If security no longer comes from being employed, then it must come from being employable.' Women stand to benefit greatly from this shift in emphasis.

The acquisition of skills acts like a credit facility at the bank: although you may not need those skills right now, you never know when you might have to call upon them. Even if a particular new area of expertise doesn't immediately impact directly on your career, it is usually the case that the personal growth and the increased confidence that come with it will be a payoff in themselves.

The best way to get out of a rut, to add to your expertise, to prepare for promotion or just to learn something new for pleasure is to undertake some training. You don't have to do this by formal course work – sometimes working with an experienced practitioner is just as good. Often, it is better.

Some of us benefit most from taking a theoretical approach to learning by attending courses, for others it is more beneficial to throw ourselves in at the deep end and learn by doing. Most of us have adopted both approaches at some stage in our careers. Of course; there is no right or wrong way to learn. You will do what is best for you in each circumstance but the ability to be flexible, to be receptive to acquiring new skills whenever necessary and to keep an open mind to new developments will mark you out to succeed in a rapidly changing labour market.

LIFELONG LEARNING

Training used to be regarded by managers almost as a punishment, a signal that they were considered not to be quite up to scratch in some aspect of their job. Now it is seen more as a reward or incentive and a sign that we are being groomed for higher things. There is now a recognition (tacit or otherwise) that in an information-based, post-feudal workplace, the level and up-to-dateness of your knowledge is the most traceable asset you have.

Successful careers will be built on a commitment to lifelong learning, and growth opportunities through learning exist at all levels in the workplace. They may take a bit of finding, however, and sometimes you have to create some of these opportunities yourself – but there is no doubt that they exist.

> *Every year that I am here, I know more about what I am doing and I am better at it. You have a duty to your organisation to grow. Most of all, you have a duty to yourself.*

Lifelong learning does not necessarily mean long-term formal education. For some aspiring women, an MBA is certainly an asset, whereas for others the most important training credential is the one that working in a high-tech environment will provide. The secret is to always retain an open and enquiring mind. This is particularly true for women who have not been encouraged to follow a technical track in school or college.

> *Having never studied science or engineering in my life, I found it was crucial not to be afraid to ask questions since my role is to support the technical staff. I need the capacity to understand the process and the systems at a general level but not necessarily at the most technical level.*

The need to update skills never ceases, even for senior managers, because there is a de-skilling aspect to management itself. Knee-deep in strategy, your practical skills can begin to vanish over the horizon as you move further away from the requirement to 'do' on a daily basis. Keeping your skills up to date and widening their range is an absolutely crucial aspect of your career management.

The challenge of lifelong learning can be off-putting for many of us. We enjoy the comfort of having done our time and feel that, having mastered the core skills and expertise, we can sit back and enjoy the fruits of that labour. There is no doubt that the junior stage of our careers is the most heady in terms of the learning curve, but resting on your laurels may well lead you to a premature plateau (see Chapter 2).

Embarking on a process of acquiring new skills and expertise can be intimidating, particularly as we grow older and feel distant from the formal learning process.

> *When my boss suggested that I attend a management development programme, I made excuses for about three months. I was terrified at the thought of attending, feeling that I would come over as stupid in front of everyone else on the course whom I assumed would be much better than me. In the end, I went under duress. Once I got over my initial panic, I just loved the feeling of learning again and it did wonders for my confidence.*

Lifelong learning is all about attitude: not being afraid of exposure to new experiences and challenges; being prepared to suspend our old ideas and ways of working. To adopt a positive attitude to lifelong learning:

▷ Accept that **you are never too old to learn**.

▷ **Don't be afraid to admit that you find learning difficult:** everyone has problems. Even if your experience of formal learning in the past was negative, think of all the things you have learned at home, at work, or in your hobbies or leisure activities.

▶ **Seek clarification when you don't understand.** Don't be afraid to ask questions of your work mates, more experienced practitioners, your tutor.

▶ **Take things in stages.** Don't tackle too much at once. Make sure you have really mastered what you have just learned before you go on to something new. It's important to get plenty of practice.

▶ **Relate learning to your own experiences.** When you are trying to understand something, compare and contrast it with things you know.

▶ **Keep an open mind.** Be prepared for some of your old ideas to be challenged by the new methods or systems. Accept that for some learning you will initially have to accept ideas without proof because the proof may be beyond your current level of knowledge.

▶ **Realise that learning needs to be worked at**. Although you may not be studying for a formal qualification, all learning involves effort and concentration.

LEARNING APPROACH

Learning is partly determined by our learning style. There are four basic learning types – Activists, Reflectors, Pragmatists, and Theorists. Although all of us have learning styles that combine elements of the four approaches, one of them tends to predominate. Your personality, formal learning history, career path and occupation will have influenced your approach to learning. The key features of the four learning styles are:

Activists involve themselves fully and without bias in new experiences. They enjoy the here and now, are happy to be dominated by immediate experiences and are open-minded and enthusiastic about anything new. Their philosophy is 'I'll try anything once.' They rush in where angels fear to tread and revel in short-term crisis fire-fighting. As soon as the excitement from one activity has died down, however, they are busy looking for the next. They tend to thrive on the challenge of new experiences but are bored with implementation and longer-term consolidation. They are gregarious people constantly involving themselves with others but in doing so they hog the limelight.

Reflectors like to stand back to ponder experiences and observe them from many different perspectives. They collect data, both first-hand and from others, and prefer to chew it over thoroughly before coming to any conclusions. Their philosophy is to be cautious, to leave no stone unturned, and they tend to postpone reaching definite conclusions for as long as possible: 'Look before you leap.' They prefer to take a back seat in meetings and discussions and enjoy observing other people in action. They listen to others and get the drift of the discussion before making their own points. They tend to adopt a low profile and have a slightly distant, tolerant, unruffled air about them.

Pragmatists are keen on trying out ideas, theories and techniques to see if they work in practice. They seize the first opportunity to experiment with new applications. They are the sort of people who return from management courses brimming with new ideas that they want to try out. They don't like beating around the bush and tend to be impatient with ruminating and open-ended discussion. They are down-to-earth people who like making practical decisions and solving problems. They respond to problems and opportunities as challenges. Their philosophies are: 'There is always a better way', and 'If it works it's good.'

Theorists adapt and integrate observations into complex theories and think problems through in a step-by-step, logical way. They tend to be perfectionists who won't rest easy until things are tidy and fit into their rational scheme. They like to analyse and synthesise and are keen on principles, theories and models. 'If it's logical it's good.' They tend to be detached, analytical and dedicated to rational objectivity rather then anything subjective or ambiguous. They prefer to maximise certainty and feel uncomfortable with subjective judgements, lateral thinking and anything flippant.

Over the years you have probably developed learning habits of your own. Since you are probably unaware of this, the exercise on pages 106–109 will help you pinpoint your learning preferences so that you are in a better position to adapt your learning approach or to select experiences that best suit it.

Learning Approach Checklist

Be honest. The accuracy of the analysis depends on it. There are no right or wrong answers. If you agree more than you disagree with a statement put a tick by it. If you disagree more than you agree put a cross by it. Be sure to mark each item with either a tick or cross.

☐ **1** I have strong beliefs about what is right and wrong, good and bad.

☐ **2** I often throw caution to the wind.

☐ **3** I tend to solve problems using a step-by-step approach, avoiding any flights of fancy.

☐ **4** I believe that formal procedures and policies cramp people's style.

☐ **5** I have a reputation for a no-nonsense, call-a spade-a-spade style.

☐ **6** I often find that actions based on gut feel are as sound as those based on careful thought and analysis.

☐ **7** I like the sort of work where I have time to leave no stone unturned.

☐ **8** I regularly question people about their basic assumptions.

☐ **9** What matters most is whether something works in practice.

□ **10** I actively seek out new experiences.

□ **11** When I hear about a new idea or approach I immediately start working out how to apply it in practice.

□ **12** I am keen on self-discipline, such as watching my diet, taking regular exercise, sticking to a fixed routine.

□ **13** I take pride in doing a thorough job.

□ **14** I get on best with logical, analytical people and less well with spontaneous, irrational people.

□ **15** I take care over the interpretation of data and avoid jumping to conclusions.

□ **16** I like to reach a decision carefully after weighing up many alternatives.

□ **17** I'm attracted more to novel, unusual ideas than to practical ones.

□ **18** I don't like loose ends. I prefer to fit things into a coherent pattern.

□ **19** I accept and stick to procedures and policies so long as I regard them as an efficient way of getting the job done.

□ **20** I like to relate my actions to a general principle.

□ **21** In discussions I like to get straight to the point.

□ **22** I tend to have distant, rather formal relationships with people at work.

☐ **23** I thrive on the challenge of tackling something new and different.

☐ **24** I enjoy fun-loving, spontaneous people.

☐ **25** I pay meticulous attention to detail before coming to a conclusion.

☐ **26** I find it difficult to come up with wild, off-the-top-of-my-head ideas.

☐ **27** I don't believe in beating around the bush.

☐ **28** I am careful not to jump to conclusions too quickly.

☐ **29** I prefer to have as many sources of information as possible – the more data to mull over the better.

☐ **30** Flippant people who don't take things seriously enough irritate me.

☐ **31** I listen to other people's point of view before putting my own forward.

☐ **32** I tend to be open about how I'm feeling.

☐ **33** In discussions I enjoy watching the antics of the other participants.

☐ **34** I prefer to respond to events spontaneously rather than plan things out in advance.

☐ **35** I tend to be attracted to techniques such as network analysis, flow charts, contingency planning.

☐ **36** I don't like it if I have to rush out a piece of work to meet a tight deadline.

☐ **37** I tend to judge people's ideas on their practical merits.

☐ **38** Quiet, thoughtful people usually make me feel uneasy.

☐ **39** In meetings I put forward practical, realistic ideas.

☐ **40** I can often see better, more practical ways to get things done.

SCORING THE LEARNING APPROACH CHECKLIST

The checklist is scored by awarding one point for each ticked item. There are no points for crossed items. Looking at your questionnaire, add up your points by awarding one to each ticked item under the following headings:

	Activist	Reflector	Theorist	Pragmatist
	2	7	1	5
	4	13	3	9
	6	15	8	11
	10	16	12	19
	17	25	14	21
	23	28	18	27
	24	29	20	35
	32	31	22	37
	34	33	26	39
	38	36	30	40
Totals	**5**	**7**	**7**	**7**

The score for the four different learning styles give you a general indication of your strongest tendency. If your score coincides or exceeds the highest score for one of the learning styles, this indicates a strong preference for that particular learning style. Keep this in mind if you decide to pursue further training and aim for approaches that best suit your own style.

DEVISING YOUR TRAINING PLAN

Having the right attitude to the world of learning is half the battle. The other half is finding the right training programme for you at this stage in your career. This requires a certain amount of strategic analysis and, as with many things, time spent in planning your next move will save you much grief and aggravation later.

There are thousands of options in terms of courses and other ways to learn new skills and knowledge which women at work (or, for that matter, at home) can pursue. Even at a cursory glance the choice is bewildering, so you owe it to yourself to think through the what, why and how of your training programme in a structured way. Satisfy yourself on each of the following points:

THE PRELIMINARIES

▶ **What do I want more training in?**
Spend some time clarifying your subject area. Do you want to expand your current skill and knowledge base or undertake training in a new area? The identification of your training need should come from a more measured approach to your long-term goals (see Chapter 1) and assist you in achieving those rather than being based on some whimsical notion.

▶ Why do I want to undertake the training?

What are you expecting the gains of the training to be – career advancement or personal development? Don't be afraid to admit that, as yet, you really don't know exactly what training you want to do but you have a real desire to undertake learning again. If you're in this position, the best thing may well be to start off on a short personal development course to get you back into the swing of learning and allow you the space to make clear, long-term training plans.

▶ How important are qualifications?

Is accreditation important? Many courses simply offer a certificate which may be all you require. But if you intend to pursue training over a long period, check that the qualifications you are achieving along the way are compatible and you can build up credits to a recognised qualification.

▶ How important is track record?

You may want to consider the status of the courses you are considering. Given the unbelievable number of courses on offer, this criteria can be key in determining which one to select.

▶ What level of training do I want to undertake?

Do you want to embark on a degree or postgraduate-level training, or is a short, sharp input on a particular skill area important? Whatever level you select, be sure that it stretches you. Avoid the temptation to pitch yourself at a level that will not be particularly challenging.

THE PRACTICALITIES

▶ How much time can I spend on training?

Be realistic about this. Keep in mind your other commitments and priorities for the future not just in terms of work but also in your social, personal, home and leisure activities. Are you prepared to sacrifice time devoted to some of these activities?

> *I had to drop out of the course after six months. It was dreadful. I assumed that once I had won the battle in work to have one day a week off, time would not be a problem. How wrong I was. I ended up working longer days and hung on to my weekend activities, which left me little time for course work. I fell more and more behind. I just hadn't really thought through the time commitment.*

▶ Which courses am I eligible for?
If qualifications are a barrier, don't be disheartened. You can talk to the course tutor about your skills and work experience which are increasingly taken in lieu of qualifications. Greater flexibility has put university education within reach of many women who would have been excluded because they stepped off the educational ladder too early. Alternatively, an access course (which provides a route into higher education for those who do not have the necessary qualifications) may be the answer. Ask about 'credit accumulation and transfer' (CAT) schemes. CATs award students credit for previous study and even for work experience, and many of the universities operate the scheme. You may, for example, be able to go directly into the second year of a course.

▶ Which courses can I afford?
Be realistic about what you can afford before you start. Remember that course fees are frequently only the start of the cost of training, particularly if it is long-term. You also have to take account of the cost of books and materials, travelling and eating. If you have children, you may also incur additional childcare costs.

▶ Which type of leaning method should I consider?

Don't be rigid in your idea of training. There is a whole array of open – and distance – learning approaches which are available. Take the time to check these out. Think about how you learn best. Are you an academic learner? Do you work well in a group? Are you disciplined enough to work on your own from home? Do you really need formal training? Could work colleagues, friends or family pass on any of the skills you want to learn?

▶ Where am I going to study?

You will need a quiet space with good light and a desk or table. Make sure you can achieve this without disrupting or imposing on your day-to-day life or the people you live with. Make sure also that they agree not to disturb you.

THE IMPLEMENTATION

▶ What can I do over the next year?

Once you have decided the type of training you want to undertake, you will need to plan for its introduction into your life and the impact it will have on both your finances and your time. You can't afford to sit and wait. You may lose your enthusiasm or, worse, your goal. You may also need to apply for courses some time in advance. Many full-time courses that begin in September or October often start recruiting students in January or February.

▶ Should I ease myself in gradually?

Would it be worthwhile to undertake a short course to ease yourself back into formal learning again? The content of the course is not necessarily relevant; the practice of studying is. Maybe you could ease yourself into the course by requesting a basic book list from the tutor well in advance of the start date and beginning to familiarise yourself with the subject area.

> ❛ I had decided two years previously that I was going to do a postgraduate degree. Then a promotion came along and I knew I couldn't afford the time until things had settled down in the job. But I promised myself that I would stick to that goal so I started doing evening courses – French, pottery, car maintenance. Then, six months before I was due to start, I got the book list from the tutor and bought the three 'bibles' which I read before the course started. Doing this kept me on track for my goal and increased my enthusiasm for learning. ❜

▶ Can I build up a support network?

Talk to friends, colleagues, family about what you are going to do. There will be times when the process is difficult and will interfere with other, more pleasurable things you would like to be doing. In these times, it is important to have support around you to cajole, encourage, comfort and most of all, make sure you start.

TRAINING ADVICE AND INFORMATION

Whatever type of training you decide to embark on, you will need to obtain reliable information and advice to ensure that you end up on the right course for you. This is easier said than done and you may find that you have to invest almost as much time in finding a suitable course as you did in reaching the decision in the first place. The bewildering array of agencies offering advice and information on training opportunities can be confusing and intimidating.

Don't be put off and don't take the first course that comes along. Shop around. There is nothing worse than investing your time, effort and money in a course that is not really suited to your needs. It is worth sticking with the search until you are satisfied that the course fulfils your expectations in terms of timing, cost, accreditation, level, track record and relevance to your occupation. You may have to consult many of the following before you find the right course for you.

▶ Most towns have an educational advisory service for adults, offering information on careers and training at both local and national level. Local libraries also have reference books, leaflets and addresses. The *UK Directory of Educational Guidance Services for Adults (UDACE)* is a very useful guide to your local services and can be found in most libraries. There may also be a special information service attached to the main library. Advice centres, job centres, social services and education departments also have information on grants, training allowances and other financial help.

▶ Your personnel department may be able to help you with advice about courses. Seeking guidance from this source also carries the advantage of marking you down as someone who is willing to develop their skills and who might be worth watching for future promotion. Ask them if there is anyone else in the organisation who has attended a training course similar to the one you have in mind. If there is, have a chat with them about their experiences.

▶ See if your area has a Training Access Point (TAP), a service which is available in over thirty areas in Britain, with computer back-up in job centres, public libraries, adult guidance units and other high street locations. This offers a wide range of information on education and training for all kinds of skills at every level and provides support in putting together a learning programme which meets individual or employer needs.

▶ There is a plethora of courses for women seeking to return to the labour market after a break for childcare. The

Women Returners Handbook lists over 150 courses around the country.

▶ If you are interested in investigating what the government can offer, contact your local Training and Enterprise Council (TEC) (or Local Enterprise Council (LEC) in Scotland). TECs are responsible for the local organisation and delivery of the two main government-funded training programmes whose primary focus is the unemployed, although there are also courses on offer for those in employment.

▶ If you are considering returning to formal, third-level education, a visit to a university careers library may be useful. Not only will they have details of the various courses available, they also have information on grants and bursaries and how to apply for these.

▶ Your professional or trade association should be able to tell you about the relevance and status of different courses for your particular career. The trade press frequently carries advertisements for courses which are more likely to be relevant to your career or occupational sector.

▶ Use your network. Ask senior colleagues about the types of training they would recommend and which courses are most appropriate at your particular career stage. Tell colleagues what you are considering doing and ask them to put you in contact with anyone in their network whom they think might be useful. At the end of the day, such informal advice may prove to be the most beneficial in helping you select the right course.

> *I had decided I wanted to do an M.Sc in social research and had a list of four potential courses. As I was paying for the course myself, I was determined to make sure I ended up on the right one so I contacted my professional association. They put me in touch with a*

research director who met me for lunch and talked me through the strengths and weaknesses of the various courses. I knew when I left which one was for me. I also made a very useful contact.

Don't narrow your choice of course until you have compared quality. The best way to do this is to ask the trainer to put you in contact with two people who have attended the course in the past. Contact them and ask them about their experience and impressions of the course. Don't be afraid to do this – feedback from past participants is the most reliable source you can have on the general quality of the course.

I won't go on a course unless the trainer will put me in touch with past participants. If they won't do it, I don't trust the course.

Don't forget that all colleges are selling training as a product and all will tell you that their particular course is the best on offer. Seek as much independent advice as you can before you finally decide.

FLEXIBLE APPROACHES TO LEARNING

There has been a rapid growth in flexible approaches to learning and even mainstream university courses are incorporating open-learning systems into their courses. Open-learning approaches can be particularly suitable for working women as the system is very flexible and allows students to fit in studying around the other activities in their lives. If such an approach is suited to you, you need to look at one of the following:

CORRESPONDENCE COURSES

These have long been a popular and successful method for people studying on their own and are a particularly useful for people who cannot easily get to a college. Traditionally, correspondence colleges mainly offer courses leading to qualifications such as GCSE and A level, though some colleges are more specialist, for example, the College of Estate Management. In recent years, study by correspondence has also been incorporated by many higher-education colleges. Students are assigned a personal tutor and are usually provided with a basic programme – an individual timetable, complete sets of notes, information, written assignments marked by the tutor, self-assessment tests and specimen answers. The cost of correspondence courses varies a lot, so you need to shop around.

OPEN LEARNING

Open learning covers a wide variety of flexible learning schemes that enable students to study in their own time and at their own pace. They are known by names such as distance learning, open learning, directed study or learning by appointment, and incorporate a variety of learning methods.

The Open University (OU) still leads the field in home-based study and has built up a formidable reputation for the quality of its tutorial support and study materials. It offers a wide range of degree, non-degree and vocational courses. Learning is mainly carried out through correspondence, radio and television broadcasts and some face-to-face tuition, mostly on a part-time basis. There are no minimum entry requirements, and courses can be spread over several years.

The main courses of study provided by the Open University are in the sciences and humanities (up to degree level) and a range of courses for professionals. Student fees range from a few pounds for a simpler personal interest study pack to several hundred pounds for a professional course. An undergraduate course will cost £200 to £400 per year for tuition and other fees. On longer courses the fees can usually be paid in instalments.

Set up in 1987, the Open College provides open learning courses which emphasise retraining and updating vocational skills, particularly in new technology. Each course takes on average thirty hours but an individual can take longer if appropriate. Teaching is carried out through a variety of methods, including workbooks, videos, computer software, assignments and some face-to-face tuition, though this varies in amount. Tutors are based at Open Access Centres which are usually situated in colleges of further education. The cost of the courses ranges from about £25 for a basic course to £120 for an advanced course.

The Open College of the Arts operates on the same principal but with an obvious focus on art subjects. The National Extension College also provides a variety of open-learning courses and resources.

Learning by Appointment is a scheme which enables students to come into colleges and teach themselves, using materials and equipment supplied by the college. The written material allows for independent study, and covers a wide range of subjects, for example, exam courses and basic computer studies.

COPING WITH PART TIME STUDY

You may find it strange to return to studying if you haven't done it for a while. In addition, you have to cope with the conflicting demands of your job and your course and your home/social life.

Time management (see Chapter 6) becomes essential: you will need a realistic plan which covers the times of college lectures or seminars and adequate time to travel to college and back, if you are taking a course outside the home. You may also need to include times of radio or TV broadcasts, if these are relevant to your course.

Many women find they can do a certain amount of studying at work. Most bosses do not mind this, particularly if the course is going to benefit your work, provided that you still manage to deal competently with your normal work-load.

You will, however, still have to do a lot of studying at home where you could make a virtue out of doing alternate academic and domestic work. Many writers and creative artists say they like to do manual work, such as gardening or woodwork, to relieve the strain of constant mental activity. You, too, could learn to turn from problem-solving or essay-writing to household chores – and without necessarily turning off your thought processes completely. Let your academic work and housework dovetail, and you will find that they harmonise better than you might expect.

Make a realistic timetable that you can stick to. Don't budget every minute of every day to useful purposes because it just won't work. Keep in mind which are the most important tasks you need to do in a particular day, and keep flexible periods for use as you please. If you allow for distractions such as phone calls, dealing with odd visitors or chatting with a friend, you won't find yourself falling behind schedule all the time.

You may find the following points helpful when you are planning your course work:

▶ Whenever possible, give private study priority over other domestic activities.

▶ Try not to do more than eight hours academic work in any one day. On the other hand, make sure you allocate usable periods for study of about one to two hours at a time. Periods of less than an hour are not much use except for sorting out notes, checking a booklist, reading the odd review. Don't study for more than three hours at a time.

▶ Dole out your private study hours to give roughly the same amount of time to each course you are taking; don't skimp on the time you spend on courses you don't like as much.

▶ Bear in mind that study hours are best if they come early in the day, when your concentration and attention are at their peak. So don't start your day with your household chores which can be done later in the day when your brain is too tired to study further and your body needs a change.

▶ If you are an early riser, consider getting up well before you need to leave for work and doing one to two hours study. Set your alarm for 6.00 and start reading as soon as you have made a cup of coffee or tea. Don't say you can't do this until you have tried to make it a regular part of your life. You could break from your studies to eat breakfast and then go off to work. If you are not an early riser, could you work for an extra couple of hours most evenings, after work? If this makes for a disturbed night's sleep, however, scrap the idea.

▶ Allow time for relaxation between bouts of study. Time spent in rest and quiet is not wasted, because you get real benefit from it and will work better afterwards.

> *I always tell my part-time students to allow twice as much time for home study as they spend at college each week. This is a realistic assessment of how much time you'll need to fulfil your obligations to your course.*

RETURNING TO FULL TIME STUDY

You may have screwed up first time around; dropped out of college in your first year or flunked your finals due to a failed relationship. You may never have had the opportunity to get a degree or professional qualification in the first place. Or you may wish to go abroad to study for your masters degree. For whatever reason, you may now wish to take a career break and return to full-time education.

Colleges are increasingly more sympathetic towards mature candidates, particularly if they have had a family or other caring responsibility and/or can offer a breadth of work and life experience alongside a serious commitment to learning or retraining. In some cases, they will waive the formal entry qualifications and, in many cases (particularly if you didn't use up your entitlement in your late teens), you may be eligible for a full grant.

Changing career direction and returning to academic study after years of working demands strength. It is not an easy path to follow.

> *I started my first degree at the age of thirty two. I hadn't bothered with school much and had spent the previous ten years as a legal secretary – something I had just drifted into. Eventually I was so bored that I took three A levels part-time and was accepted for a place at Nottingham. I was terrified – probably more so than many of the eighteen year olds who had left home for the first time. But it was OK, you know. I liked most of the people on the course (despite the age difference) and I discovered that there were a whole lot of mature students just like me throughout the university.*

When considering whether to undertake a full-time course, many women may be contemplating a complete career change. Try not to allow your age to enter into your deliberations in a destructive fashion. You may think you're too old at forty-four to, say, read for the Bar, but you sure as hell aren't getting any younger and you may as well grasp the nettle of your life's ambition.

New 'quickie' degrees look like being popular with mature candidates as they offer a fast-track route to career change. They take two years to complete, working forty-five weeks a year (instead of the usual thirty), and students are awarded bigger grants. These innovative courses, which started in the summer of 1992, are available in a growing number of universities and colleges of higher education. Your local education advisory service or careers service will be able to give you further information on which colleges offer these degrees.

Change is scary – and it carries its own set of risks – but recognise that the skills which you have already developed to confront challenges in the workplace don't disappear whilst you are acquiring new skills for new challenges. Be ready to deal positively with the ambivalence that can surface whilst taking a study leave.

FINANCING YOUR TRAINING

When you're used to earning your own way there can be a certain loss of freedom – and self-respect – from no longer getting that regular pay cheque. For women with partners it can make them feel suddenly and uncomfortably dependent. For women who take leave to go back to college, that sense of dependency can be compounded by the feeling that they've lost their adult status. All the more important to get as much help with financing your training as possible. Some of the following may be applicable:

LOCAL AUTHORITY GRANTS

If you are returning to full-time study and you live in England, Wales or Northern Ireland, you can apply to your local education authority (LEA) for information about grants. You will find their address and phone number in your local phone book. LEA grants cover most full-time degree courses and some courses in further and higher education. You apply to the LEA in which your home is located, which may or may not be the one in which your prospective college is located. If you live in Scotland you should apply directly to the Scottish Education Department.

CAREER DEVELOPMENT LOANS

Career Development Loans (CDLs) are available to people wanting to undertake vocational education but who are unable to raise sufficient funds to do so. To be eligible, you must be over eighteen years of age, a UK resident and prepared to pay 20% of the cost of the course. The training can be full- or part-time, college-based or distance learning and last anything from one week to one year. The loan can be between £200 and £5,000 and the government pays the interest on the loan during and for up to three months after the course. From that point on it is up to the individual to pay back the loan. The CDL scheme is set to expand and does offer a real option to women to grow in their careers in an increasingly competitive market.

EMPLOYER SPONSORSHIP

Your employer, particularly if you work for an enlightened organisation, may have a training policy which will support you through your chosen further education or training course. Arrange to have a chat with your personnel manager, training manager or company secretary.

Training policies vary widely from employer to employer. Whilst some organisations are more than happy to pay all your tuition and expenses and give you day release to study, others do not have any formal strategy. Other companies will provide part funding and offer interest-free loans to staff for the remainder of the fees – you could be surprised what you can negotiate with your own company. Large firms, however, do tend to have a better track record and small businesses may have trouble sparing you at all.

> ❝ I work for a small business. Well, it's a medium-sized business now but when I joined there were only twenty-three of us. When I wanted to do my

masters degree part-time my boss was very supportive but there was no personnel function or any training policy in the company. So we invented it ourselves. Basically we agreed that the company would foot the bill for all my tuition and books but, if I failed, I would repay the lot. I don't know how that compares to other employers but it seemed quite enlightened to me and there was an extra incentive to make the grade. The procedure later became the company policy, which was very good news for my work colleagues.

If your employer does not have a formal policy it is well worth you suggesting they form one. The General Institute of Personnel Management (GIPM) or your local TEC/LEC should be able to assist you. Remember that any financial cost to the employer can be offset against tax.

TEC/LEC FUNDING

Although the bias of government funding for training is towards the unemployed, there is support available for businesses through the network of Training and Enterprise Councils (TECs) and Local Enterprise Councils (LECs). It is generally offered to a company rather than an individual and applications are usually made on that basis.

I was recently promoted to manager in our company and wanted to undertake some formal training. When we got the brochures in, the cost of training seemed astronomical to a small company like ours. Someone suggested that I contact our local TEC and I am now attending an eight-week part-time course which is being subsidised by 50%.

TECs and LECs provide grants and subsidised training to businesses to improve their staff training and development practices. The cost of consultancy services to identify training needs in the company and part payment for staff training can be paid for by the grants. The criteria for eligibility vary and you need to contact your local TEC to find out more.

THE MBA

This year alone, more than 5,000 new MBA graduates will spill out of British universities clutching a piece of paper that used to be an instant passport to a top salary.

The MBA is the much-hyped masters degree and something of an obsession with some major organisations. Working women should, however, beware of viewing the MBA as a career panacea: no matter what your dreams and motivation, the real world isn't going to change as soon as you have achieved MBA status.

By definition, the MBA attracts people who are very self-confident, with strong personalities and sense of direction. It is designed to be as daunting, as difficult, as demanding a course of study and self-improvement as one is likely to find. The hope is that the MBA graduate will be capable of earning high salaries and be respected and revered by colleagues. It was typically seen as the stepping stone to high-flyer promotion at a young age, guaranteeing to double or triple incomes. There is a catch within the small print of this guarantee, however, as the MBA also necessitates a heavy investment of time and money at a stage when an aspiring working woman would normally be earning well, in line for salary raises and promotions.

In the early 1980s, it did seem that gaining an MBA brought about fairly instant financial and career rewards. However, as MBAs have become less of a rarity, the attitude towards them is changing. The value of an MBA in today's job market increasingly depends on where and when it was awarded. Furthermore, not all employers can now afford the luxury of 'buying' the intellectual qualities that an MBA course fosters.

> ❝ I felt so insecure about my ability to manage that before I even thought of applying for promotion I felt I had to get my MBA. Thinking about it now, I realize that none of the boys had these inhibitions. Anyway, having pulled myself through three gruelling years of hard work and little social life, I discovered that the MBA wasn't going to teach me how to manage at all. True, it gave me some fascinating insights into comparative managerial techniques but the plain fact of the matter is that you can only learn to manage by working alongside a decent manager before taking the plunge and doing it yourself. Some things you can only learn by doing. ❞

The reality is that an MBA is of limited value in isolation. It has to be part of a wider career plan, otherwise it can easily lead those who possess it in the wrong direction. Embarking on an MBA, however, can be an effective way to bring about a career change (a recent study suggests that as many as 90% of today's MBA graduates undertake the course to change their career path). If, as a young woman you were directed into 'soft' or typically female types of undergraduate degrees or first jobs – such as nursing or social work – you may have reached the point when you have decided that this is not sufficiently challenging to sustain your interest for the rest of your life. The MBA may be a passport for a major change: promoting you from a passive, dependent role to a fully-fledged managerial one.

> ❝ I was a thirty-four-year-old ward sister with fourteen years of bedpans behind me when I decided I needed a change. I wanted to branch into management and embarked on the MBA. I am now a customer relations manager for a power company and I would never have had that opportunity had I not done the MBA. ❞

There are upwards of a hundred different MBA courses on offer in Britain today, varying from the prestigious course at the London Business School to those at the bigger universities and former polytechnics, the Open University, various American colleges based in London, as well as in-house courses offered by some major corporations. Would-be graduates from the UK can also apply to influential colleges in other countries, whether it is INSEAD in France, or Harvard in America. This may give you the extra dimension (or burden) of learning a foreign language. Research well before you decide.

Despite the lowering of the status of MBAs, they remain an important vehicle for promoting women in management in British business and, at least on paper, give us equality with our male counterparts when competing for work.

6 Your Time, Your Choice

▶ ▶ ▶ ▶ ▶ UTILISING THE ENERGY CYCLES OF YOUR WEEK •
UTILISING YOUR OWN ENERGY CYCLES • THE
POWER OF PLANNING • KEEPING FORMAL
MEETINGS TO A MINIMUM • KEEPING INFORMAL
MEETINGS TO A MINIMUM • DEALING WITH
VISITORS • HOW TO STOP PROCRASTINATING •
EFFECTIVE USE OF SUPPORT STAFF

Given the conflicting demands placed on most of us, the discipline of time management is even more essential for women than it is for men. Time management is concerned with being properly focused and able to accomplish your highest priorities.

Even if you feel that you currently manage your time pretty well, it is important to re-examine the use of your time every so often, especially if your circumstances change. As your career develops, the demands on your time make effective time management more and more of a challenge: the departmental head needs your evaluation and analysis; your clients need your service; your colleagues need your input and encouragement. The number of meetings, visits and telephone calls multiply until you never seem to be alone in your office any more. Only during the evenings and weekends do you seem to have time to get the core of your work done, and this doesn't begin to tackle the issue of how to make enough space for your home life, your social life or yourself.

Nothing about our work gets us as panicky as the feeling that we are running out of time. As the sense of panic grips us, we start thrashing about in the time-management equivalent of hyperventilation. We then do an increasingly poor job of coping with the tasks at hand. As a result, they begin to take up more time. That leaves less time for planning future operations which sets the stage for further hyperventilation and the whole vicious cycle repeats itself all over again.

If this is you, you need to learn how to break out of such cycles. Being more selective in the work you take on, or adding strict regularity to your schedule, requires a great deal of that elusive quality of self discipline. *Now* is the time to take back control of your day, your time and your life. You must learn to be disciplined enough in your work to be able to reduce excess meetings and visits to bare-bones operations, so that you can attend to your most vital priorities.

There are any number of excellent books that will give you the basics of good time management, and buying one of these is a wise investment. It is better still if you can convince your organisation to send you on a course. The earlier on in your career that you can begin to use these skills, the greater the benefit will be to your effectiveness in the longer term.

What follows in this chapter will not cover the same ground as a straightforward time-management course but is intended to complement what you will learn elsewhere. We can find effective ways of saving time (and energy) by working with the behaviour of the people around us. We have the strength of being more sensitive than men to the behaviour of both ourselves and others and of using this sensitivity to make the best use of the resources at our disposal – one of these key resources being the finite quantity of time available.

We concentrate here on beating the time-eaters, the habits we picked up when we first started working, when it seemed as if we had all the time in the world, but which do not enhance our productivity and which we really cannot afford any more.

UTILISING THE ENERGY CYCLES
OF YOUR WEEK

One way of getting more out of your schedule is to work out the efficiency patterns of the week in your organisation and tailor your own workload accordingly.

Every job and every workplace is different but with a little shrewd observation on your part you can match key tasks to each day to get a productivity increase from your week. You need to be sufficiently aware of the behaviour of the people around you to be able to time your own interaction with them for the best result.

Here are some general pointers that work in most office-based situations:

Monday: Don't bother to try to fix up appointments or meetings. The likelihood is that neither external nor internal colleagues will be in full gear yet. It is a far better use of your time to deal with your in-tray, work on reports and plan for the week that lies ahead.

Tuesday: This is a good day for strategic meetings with selected individuals, either from the home team or from outside. Since most people will be working on this day (it is unlikely to be a bank holiday or to clash with anyone's long weekend) you have a better chance of connecting with your key contacts.

Wednesday: This is the day to make your most difficult calls or approaches to people, since most are into their week's agenda by now and are more apt to be receptive to new ideas. It is the day to fix up appointments and meetings for forthcoming weeks. It is also a good day for team meetings, for monitoring projects' progress mid-course (and deflecting potential problems) and for a strategic review of what remains for the rest of the week.

Thursday: Try to approach the key decision-maker in your work, whether it is your immediate boss or your most difficult customer, for decisions that are pending. If you leave it until Friday, they'll say anything to get rid of you and then change their mind on Monday morning.

Friday: Get as much work as you can off your desk. Try to schedule two clear hours (or however much you need) to sign off your work for this week and plan for what's ahead. If you are really disciplined about this then you'll find that you'll enjoy your weekends much more.

UTILISING YOUR OWN ENERGY CYCLES

Your own internal energy cycles are as important in effectively managing time as your organisation's schedules.

We all have our own particular energy rhythms. You might be someone who is energetic in the morning but loses momentum in the afternoon. Alternatively, you might be a night person, who finds it difficult to function in the morning. Taking advantage of your personal rhythms can enable you to use your time more effectively.

A common mistake is to use high-energy times to take care of routine work which, although it has to be done, requires little or no creativity or concentration. If you tend to tell yourself 'Once I get all of these things out of the way, I can start on the important project', you may be falling into a trap. The result can be that you spend your high energy time in a flurry of activity, then feel tired or uninspired when it comes to the more challenging or creative tasks.

> *Every night before I leave the office and at the time when my brain is fully in gear I write a list of the things I have to do tomorrow. The next day I look at the*

*list and do the most difficult task first. This gives me the
necessary impetus to knock off the
rest of the list quite easily.* **"**

There are obvious limitations to exactly matching your personal energy cycles to organisational patterns and schedules. If, however, you work in an organisation that operates a flexi-time scheme, make use of that to tailor the hours you work more to your own energy cycles. Even without the advantage of flexi-time systems, most of us can exercise considerable control over when we undertake routine work.

The trick is to acknowledge your high-energy cycles and aim to use them for the more important and creative tasks. Set aside your low-ebb times in the day for the more mundane tasks – filing and administration, for example. If you have routine weekly update meetings, don't schedule them during your high-energy cycle. Timetable any energising activity for when you are likely to be at a personal low.

Aim to create a balance between your own energy cycles and those of your organisation rather than setting them in competition.

" *I went on a time management course and as a result
tried writing a "To Do" list each morning. I soon
became frustrated because I couldn't think of items to
put on my list. I discovered the problem was that I was
alert at night and lethargic in the morning. So, I tried
making my list before going to bed, and this worked.
Now I do my planning when my thoughts are clear and
my list is waiting to help me function
when I'm feeling fuzzy in the morning.* **"**

THE POWER OF PLANNING

" *My department's responsibilities have grown more
rapidly than its staffing. We are all flogging*

ourselves to death just to get the reports out. As a result, most of my time is spent in crises management. I never have time for planning and I don't accomplish as much as I might. I end up trying to do everything more or less at the same time. Even as I work harder, I fall more behind. Then I start taking short cuts and the quality of my work suffers; so I have to redo things, which further compounds the situation. And so it goes on. **9**

Planning is the single most important factor in saving time in your job.

Most of us have had the dreadful experience of being busy all day but getting very little accomplished. If this happens frequently to you, you may believe that you have no time to plan. You must conquer this belief: once you have mastered a few techniques and developed some discipline in applying them, you will discover that you can't afford not to plan. The time you take to organise yourself will pay off in more stream-lined work, fewer forgotten tasks, and a more relaxed approach.

Before you can begin to plan, you must realistically assess the constraints:

▶ Some things must be scheduled during fixed periods. Work with suppliers, customers and so forth will have to be completed during business hours.

▶ Peak hours, such as peak computer-use times, post offices at five o'clock and supermarkets on Saturday mornings, should be avoided.

▶ Some tasks require certain environmental conditions in order to be completed effectively. If you are trying to do work that requires concentration, find a time and place where you won't be interrupted.

▶ Certain tasks will require the use of equipment which is only available at set hours, which will limit the time periods in which you can do this work.

▶ Understand your own rhythm and work patterns; as you become better at planning your time this will come more naturally.

Planning techniques will only work for you if you develop your own. As a starting point you might consider adopting some of the following techniques:

▶ Establish a regular planning appointment with yourself. This could be a once-a-week session (last thing on Friday or first thing on Monday), or a shorter daily session, or a combination of these.

▶ Don't overorganise. The best systems of time management are simple. Don't make the mistake of assuming that because some planning is good, then twice as much is twice as good.

▶ Take a pocket diary/notebook or organiser everywhere you go. If something occurs to you that you need to do, write it down immediately. If you have small bits of time (between appointments, waiting for a bus), you can use this otherwise wasted time for planning. Use a dictaphone if you are the type of person who ends up with loads of bits of paper.

> *The most invaluable piece of equipment to my working life is my dictaphone. I carry it with me everywhere and use it immediately I think of something I have to do or if I get an idea. Unlike with paper, I never lose the tape and I can get the thing out of my head immediately by putting it on the dictaphone.*

▶ Schedule similar tasks together. If you have a number of letters to write or a number of telephone calls to make, try doing them all during the same time period.

▶ If follow-up action is needed for a task you have completed, make a note of it in your organiser. For example, if you expect a reply to a letter in, say, two weeks, write 'Follow up with Janet on ...' in your diary two weeks from today. If your follow-up will be by telephone and you have the number handy, write that down as well.

▶ Use the principle of divide and conquer. It is easy to put off starting a complex task simply because it seems overwhelming. Divide such tasks into less intimidating parts. If you still have trouble getting started, try doing the smallest task possible in order to get yourself going and involved.

▶ Create a favourable working environment for yourself. This can help you to streamline routine tasks and to complete projects requiring concentration. A few simple measures can make a big difference. Anticipate the things you will need and have them within reach. Every time you break your concentration to find something else, you must spend time getting back into the rhythm of the work.

▶ Establish a regular quiet time. Let other people know that you do not wish to be interrupted during specific times. Schedule your quiet time to coincide with your high-energy periods.

▶ Eliminate distractions from your field of vision. One executive accomplished this simply by moving her desk. When her desk faced the door, she was distracted every time she saw colleagues passing by. Remove your in-tray from your desk. It can constantly distract you from the task at hand by reminding you of other things you have to do.

▶ Know when to stop. When you become so tired that you begin to make a lot of mistakes or have difficulty comprehending what you are reading, further efforts are likely to be a waste of your time. Drop the task you are doing, take time to relax and come back to it later.

Start by working on one or two small things. If you try to rearrange your whole life in one stroke, you are likely to become frustrated and discouraged. Your current ways of handling time have evolved over a long period and developing new habits takes time. By starting with something small, you establish success experiences, which will encourage you to continue your efforts. Also, don't expect a single system of organising your time to be effective forever. As your responsibilities change or the nature of your work shifts, your time-management system may need to be adjusted.

> *When I first started I went a bit overboard. I found myself making lists and organising lists, then photocopying lists and even listing lists! I got quite carried away. I understand now that planning is a means to an end and it never should be allowed to become an end in itself.*

Don't insist on perfection in your planning. A system which has flaws will still be worth using. Work gradually with your faults. Give yourself the benefit of the doubt if you find you are backsliding. Although effective time management can help you to simplify your life, nobody said it was going to be easy. Above all, respect your own ways of doing things Techniques you adopt should be adjusted to fit your own personal style, otherwise they just won't work.

KEEPING FORMAL MEETINGS
TO A MINIMUM

Millions of business meetings take place in this country every day. Unfortunately many are totally unnecessary and even more are abysmally conducted. Chapter 7 will give you some pointers to enable you to be more effective during meetings but here we deal with the time management of your meetings. There are several tactics that you can use to cut back your time spent at formal meetings, without impairing your effectiveness. Obviously the tactics will vary depending on whether you have any control over the meeting.

If you are chairing the meeting (or act as secretary or clerk or in any other official capacity which exercises some control over the conduct) the following ideas may help you to reduce meeting time.

▶ **Double your preparation time** in order to cut your meeting time in half. Preparing effectively is the best way to save time. Define the topics or problems as clearly as you can, then put them in writing. Work up the possible solutions for each of them ahead of time and ask attenders to do the same. That way, all you'll need to do during the meeting is present the ideas, not formulate them from scratch.

▶ **Give a time limit for each agenda item** and make sure you stick to it.

▶ **Limit verbosity.** When you start a meeting, ask for everyone's co-operation in sticking to the agenda and speaking as directly as possible. This can take care of those who use a hundred words to say what could be said just as well in fifty or ten (or not at all), as well as those who have issues they feel so strongly about that they air their views at a meeting, whether those views are relevant or not.

▶ **Commit to times for starting and finishing.** Do not follow the standard behaviour of those meetings where half a dozen people are expected, but you and the person who convened the meeting are the only ones there on time. When this happens the chairperson usually says, 'Let's wait for the others.' What that really means is, 'I'm going to punish you for being on time by making you wait. I'm going to reward the latecomers by waiting for them to arrive.' Or else the chairperson starts the meeting, but when latecomers arrive, she reviews everything that's been discussed so far. Punctuality should be rewarded, not punished. If everyone in your circle of possible meeting attenders sees that you're committed to starting and ending meetings on time, they'll become committed too.

> *I had a mad boss who always stood by the door before a meeting. When it was time to start, all empty chairs were removed from the room. Anyone who came late was forced to remain standing, facing the group. People in our department soon learned to arrive on time.*

▶ **Summarise the action points and deadlines** for action when you are ready to close the meeting. These give a clear signal that proceedings are at an end and that you are efficient and mean business.

If you are attending a meeting called by someone else, you are a bit more constrained but you still can control the amount of time you spend there. You shouldn't feel compelled to stay at a meeting that isn't valuable to you. Early exits – without embarrassment for either you or the meeting chairperson – are possible. Warn the convenor well ahead of the meeting about your time constraints and possible early departure so that she won't be offended or unsettled when you leave. Here are some ways to make exits easier or to spend unavoidable meeting time wisely:

▶ **Gracefully ask if your presence is still needed.** You can say, 'Excuse me, Kay. I believe that my area has already been fully covered. Is there any further contribution I can make to this meeting?, If the answer is no, the convenor will excuse you. If it is yes, your sense your urgency will be appreciated anyway and perhaps she will accommodate you by moving any relevant topic further up the agenda.

▶ **Sit at the back of the room.** Slip out when the meeting no longer is productive for you.

▶ **Ask to be excused from the meeting.** Simple and to the point.

▶ **Open your diary or organiser.** If you don't want to or just can't leave early, you can make the most of your time by doing your own planning or jotting down mental reminders. An open diary is not conspicuous in a meeting where you're discussing plans for the next few months. If you're going to stay, make the most of your time there but keep a mental note of what is being discussed. Be careful not to be accused of being preoccupied or uninterested.

If your working day is crammed with regularly scheduled meetings, there is a danger that you may lose track or forget things you were asked to do throughout the day. If you find this is happening to you, then you must create spaces in your working day during which you can catch your breath. They may be very brief but they should take place after each meeting. Sit down at your desk or in the corner of the meeting room and jot down in your notebook what you need to do as a result of that meeting. Write down these tasks clearly, so you'll be able to follow your notes even after another meeting has shifted your attention elsewhere. This practice may not create time for you but it will help maintain your sanity and effectiveness.

KEEPING INFORMAL MEETINGS
TO A MINIMUM

Women, especially, prefer to operate an open-door policy.
We start this in our first job out of college and continue the
practice through the years, as our colleagues seem to like it.
We all like to think we are flexible and approachable. However, as time goes on and more responsibilities are assumed,
the paperwork begins to pile up.

An open-door policy is a good one because it demon-
strates that dealing with issues as they come to your attention
is a major part of your job. However, as you become more
senior you will need to channel your interaction with
your colleagues into a more disciplined form so you can
maintain the rest of your time for other matters, like your
paperwork.

The following suggestions may give you some scope for
stopping people from abusing your open door policy and cutting back the time spent on informal meetings:

▶ **Establish regular times** for the people who tend to come
  barging in with questions and concerns. These meetings
  will not eliminate interruptions but they will help to
  reduce them. If your colleagues know that there is a
  'surgery' at your office every Tuesday and Thursday afternoon they may feel compelled to hold their questions
  until then. An office hour is another alternative. Hang a
  sign on your door that says, 'I am writing a report. Please
  don't interrupt me until 4.00 p.m. unless it really can't
  wait.' If you do this, make sure that at four o'clock your
  door is open and you are receptive to anybody who wants
  to see you.

▶ **Pass information to others in memos** rather than in
  meetings. If all you have to do is disseminate information,

put it down in as few words as possible and distribute it in a note. You're not increasing paperwork by much but you're decreasing the time it takes by a lot; it's much faster to write a short memo than to attend a meeting. Even if the organisational style leans towards informal meetings rather than formal memos, you can follow the style by writing informal memos which save you time and better serve your purpose.

▶ **Conduct the encounter standing up.** If someone comes into your office, stand up to greet her and remain standing, indirectly asking her to do the same. Listen to what she has to say. If it's something that can be discussed or resolved quickly, remain standing. Sometimes it's good to hold that informal stand-up meeting in the corridor, where there are no chairs.

▶ **Visit the other person's office** or hold the meeting in the corridor where it is easier for you to end it, because you're the person who exits. Define the purpose of your meeting at the very beginning; say what you have to say as succinctly as possible, then leave.

▶ **Try to formulate an agenda** with the people present when the meeting begins, if there is more than one person at an impromptu informal meeting. Write it down on the board or on paper as you formulate it.

▶ **Avoid informal meetings altogether.** You won't be able to eliminate all meetings (and this isn't desirable anyway) but you can eliminate many. One manager who had been holding hour-long staff meetings every weekday morning with ten subordinates (fifty five staff hours a week) was able to reduce it to one forty-five minute session on Wednesdays, saving more than forty-six hours each week.

DEALING WITH VISITORS

Many people enjoy socialising at work and will indulge in lengthy office visits and telephone conversations. An informal meeting may turn into a friendly but lengthy chat; business discussions turn into unnecessary digressions. We sometimes don't know how to end a long visit without hurting the other person's feelings. And we may feel uncomfortable making up an excuse to stop talking. Here's how to cut down on a visitor's overly long stay politely and gracefully:

▶ **Set a time limit.** At the very beginning of the visit, select as precise a time as possible, preferably one that no one is used to hearing such as, 'Let's meet for twenty-five minutes' or, 'I have four minutes.' This creates a greater sense of urgency. Even if during the visit you both decide you need more time, sensitivity to the minutes passed will encourage you to take only what's necessary.

▶ **Maintain a business-like stance** and a formal tone. By remaining quick and alert, sitting at the edge of your seat, you ensure that both you and your visitor will concentrate on the issue at hand and stop any potential side topics from straying in.

▶ **Do not allow interruptions**, particularly when visits are planned (unless, of course, it's vital and urgent).

▶ **Refer to a clock** placed where only you can see it. Try keeping a stop watch in a partially opened drawer, glance at it from time to time, allowing yourself two minutes to summarise and bring the meeting to a close.

▶ **Stand up**, when the time comes for the visit to end. You don't need to interrupt your visitor, but when it's your turn to speak, take the liberty of standing up and walking over to her. By the time you arrive, she is standing too. If she isn't, gently take hold of her elbow, help her up and escort her to her office, the lift or her car. She will appreciate the personal attention, and you are now in a good position to get on with your work.

▶ **Use body language.** You may want to close your diary or organiser, shuffle some papers slightly and move further out on the edge of your seat. Give a summary for action. Try saying, 'Considering what we have discussed, there are two actions to be taken.' Briefly list them and then say, 'That's it then, thank you for coming in.' Or you may prefer, 'Well, that just about sums it up' or 'I certainly appreciate your dropping in.'

Remember: if a visitor is late for a meeting, do not sit and fume over the time lost to you. Get on with something productive: return some outstanding calls; fill in your expenses claim; plan your activities for the forthcoming week. It is your fault if you do not utilise this interlude for something constructive that will save you precious time elsewhere.

HOW TO STOP PROCRASTINATING

A procrastination habit is the most common explanation for paperwork getting out of control. It is also a habit which is inordinately hard to break. If you suffer from this behaviour trait try the following tactics:

▶ **Do something right after the task is given to you** or when an idea strikes you. Take some immediate action, even if you'll be going off half-cocked. Such instant action may break the spell of procrastination. You may have to refine your work later but, having started the task, you'll find it easier to return to it promptly.

▶ **Try to handle each piece of paper only once.** Make a decision about the destination of each memo, letter or circular the first time you see it. If it's an invitation, check whether you're free and if you're not, put it straight in the bin. If you can't decide whether you want to go, put it straight in the bin anyway – you obviously don't really want to. Deal with as much as you can by simply writing a response across the top.

▶ **Understand your behaviour.** Procrastination is learned response. Clinical psychologists have found that children often use procrastination to feel they have more control. A child who can't control what she's eating for dinner learns that she can control how long it takes her to eat. So she takes forever to finish. This response can resurface in the workplace.

▶ **Take back control and responsibility.** You are controlling when you begin work on an assignment to make up for a lack of control in what you do or how you do it. Regain your sense of self-control – take as many 'what' and 'how' decisions as possible yourself. If a project has to be completed in different stages, *you* decide which stage you want to work on first. If there are a number of ways to go about doing the assignment, choose your own agenda.

▶ **Remove sources of frustration.** If you have to spend time tracking resources and gathering additional information before fulfilling an assignment, you're more likely to delay doing it. Gathering information makes the project seem more burdensome than it is. Try to get it in proportion: understand clearly all personnel and budgetary support available to you and where supplies and equipment can be found. Do not be afraid to request additional resources, supplies or guidance if you need them.

▶ **Rethink your time constraints.** Procrastinators have a flawed sense of time. You probably have trouble estimating how much time different tasks take and how much time you have left before your deadline. Since you perceive time to be less available than it is, you become frustrated and put off starting the task. Before you begin a project, make an estimate of how long key tasks take. Remember that adequate time is probably available. Try saying to yourself, 'We have enough time to do this, if the work is organised.' If you don't think you have enough time, discuss it immediately with your boss. Maybe he or she can delete a phase or reorder the tasks.

▶ **Look deeper if the problem persists.** Your procrastination may stem from your dissatisfaction with some aspect of the job. You may be bored with your work, fed up with your boss or dissatisfied with your salary. Try working out what it is that's really bothering you and then work on a strategy to raise your satisfaction level.

EFFECTIVE USE OF SUPPORT STAFF

I was promoted last year and was given an assistant. I'd never had one before and wanted to start out the right way. But I was just so embarrassed to ask a bright professional woman to take on the mundane jobs I was used to doing for myself. I didn't know how to begin to enable my secretary to help me most. I didn't know how much to empower her.

If you are fortunate enough to have a secretary or an assistant (or a share in one), you are way ahead in your struggle with time. A secretary will not only take over certain tasks but can also help you to maintain self-discipline and avoid panicking. Before a secretary can do this for you, however, you need to spend a certain amount of time together negotiating workable systems. And – here is the catch – this is another burden on your time at first. However, investing time in training your secretary will pay off. Focus the training specifically on the contents of your job. If your secretary understands what you do and why, then she (or he!) will do things in a way that's consistent with how you would do them yourself.

▶ Take the routine tasks of your office, such as setting up meetings or handling your incoming phone calls, and talk through them. Ask your secretary to keep a record of what you have covered; this will create a handy reference for later use.

▶ Arrange to have her meet some of the individuals with whom you have frequent contact; a fifteen-minute meeting, conducted without pressing matters hanging over the participants, will build a good foundation for future dealings.

▶ Don't stop with just a basic familiarisation. Set up weekly one-on-one meetings with your secretary in which you spend half an hour reviewing the events of the past week and those of the upcoming week. These sessions will fine-tune your secretary's knowledge of the job and enable her to help you more and more.

Investing time in your assistant or secretary may be the best investment you ever make. It will be repaid with dividends in the form of time saved, but you do need to learn how to delegate to – not dump on – this very valuable asset. Chapter 7 may also help you with some suggestions on sensitive delegation techniques.

Don't expect your assistant to always make the coffee or to collect your dry-cleaning for you. Men have been doing this to their (female) secretaries for generations and it is demeaning. Take your turn fetching the hot drinks and picking up the sandwiches. If you're popping out to the shops, ask if there's anything you can get for her while you're there. In short, treat her with respect and in the spirit of friendship. Treat her as you would wish to be treated.

7 Effective Communications

▶ ▶ ▶ EFFECTIVE VERBAL EXCHANGE • NON-VERBAL
COMMUNICATION • HEARD IT THROUGH THE
GRAPEVINE? • MAKING PRESENTATIONS • MAKING THE
MOST OF VISUAL AIDS • USING THE PHONE • WRITING
EFFECTIVE MEMOS AND REPORTS • THE DOS AND
DON'TS OF CORPORATE WRITING

Most of us take communication for granted, yet an essential part of human relations is the ability to make ourselves understood and to understand others. Sharing ideas, giving opinions, finding out what you need to know, explaining what you want, working out differences with someone are all crucial elements to being able to relate to and work with other people. Being an effective communicator is one of the key aspects that will mark you out for promotion potential.

We begin to communicate from the day we are born. This doesn't mean, however, that communication skills cannot be learned.

Some people are more skilled at communicating than others and some of us have developed habits which reduce our effectiveness as communicators. Often the source of a problem at work is a minor misunderstanding that has got out of hand. Time and time again poor communication causes difficulty in the workplace.

Some people exert power by withholding information. They think they're stronger when they know something no one else knows. This sort of retentiveness will rarely work for you. Poor communications create problems: try to be sure you're part of the solution, not part of the problem.

Good communication skills are so essential to career success that we devote a chapter to them. How good you are at verbal, non-verbal and written communication will determine how others perceive you and how effectively you can operate.

> *Almost any successful senior executive will tell you that the most important aspect of management is communication: making expectations clear, making people feel important, making sure the staff knows that the boss's eyes and ears are open.*

EFFECTIVE VERBAL EXCHANGE

Being a master of verbal communication is even more important for women than it is for men. It is now well known that within mixed groups, even highly qualified women put their views less forcefully than men and listen much more than they talk. Strident counter-examples, such as Margaret Thatcher, leap to mind just because they are so rare.

In a study of university faculty meetings, with one exception, the men taking part spoke more often and at greater length than their female colleagues. Men's contributions ranged from eleven to seventeen seconds; women's from just three to ten seconds. At an academic conference, women (who made up nearly half the audience) contributed only a quarter of the questions. At the prestigious French management school, INSEAD, female students are grouped in pairs within study groups because instructors found that lone women seldom get a word in edgeways.

When we advance our viewpoint, we preface our remarks with deferential clauses such as 'Don't you think?' and 'Isn't it?' far more often than men do. This deferential behaviour may be fine at a cocktail party but it isn't much use in the boardroom. Working women, at whatever level, must arm themselves with the skills to combat their diffidence and do themselves justice.

Because communication takes place between people, the atmosphere greatly influences the clarity of communication. If the atmosphere is friendly and open, the message will be picked up loud and clear; if it is antagonistic or cloudy, the message will be distorted. In a positive climate, mistakes can be made in communication but the situation is recoverable, whereas if the climate is negative, mistakes only increase the negativity and make communication even more difficult.

> *I worked in an organisation once where there was absolutely no sense of trust – you had to watch your back all the time. On one occasion, a quite innocent remark I made became a major incident. By the time I left, I was afraid to open my mouth. Saying nothing seemed to be the most effective way of dealing with the sheer destructiveness in the place. It took me quite a while to trust people in my new job enough to feel secure when I communicated.*

There are two roles in communication – that of talking and that of listening – and each has a set of skills. Most of us have a tendency to be more effective in one aspect of communication but we ignore the other at our peril. You can be an excellent speaker but if you can't also listen, you won't mark yourself out for greater things. Similarly, great listeners who can really assimilate ideas but who can't communicate will find themselves left behind when promotions are being considered.

What we say and how and when we say it gives out strong messages to our employer and colleagues about the type of person we are. It can single us out as a positive, capable force in the company, a potential promotion prospect or it can consign us to a plateau in our career.

> **6** I have a colleague who is constantly negative –
> about everything. She never has a good word to say
> about work and she argues all the time. What really
> amazes me is her righteous indignation when she gets
> passed over (again) for promotion. Can't she see it? Her
> whole way of communicating is negative – what
> employer would reward that? Of course, it just gives her
> more to complain about. We all avoid **9**
> her like the plague.

It's easy to talk but talking is not communicating. You can
talk for hours with someone and still not communicate.
Although most of us are usually quick to complain about the
lack of communication from others (if we feel we are being
talked at or to), we can be slow to see our own communication pitfalls. The following guidelines may help you to give
more effective messages.

▶ **Know what you want to say.** Be clear about what you want
to say and avoid being pulled into talking about red her-
rings. Develop the habit of ignoring these and biding your
time until it is appropriate to say your piece. If you're dealing with a difficult situation, plan what you want to say.

▶ **Decide when is the appropriate time to speak.** Pick a
time when you are most likely to be heard, not a time
when your listener is preoccupied with something else.
Confronting a colleague about a problem when she is
up to her eyes trying to meet a deadline is not effective
communication.

▶ **Decide where is the best place** to say it. Pick a place that
is conducive to being heard. Telling someone off in front
of other people, for example, will not assist your communication. If it's better that you chat out of the office, invite
your colleague for a coffee around the corner.

▶ **Be a positive communicator.** Effective communication is as much about attitude as it is about content. There is always something positive in every situation – find it and articulate it. Be aware of your listeners and their sensitivities and needs. Avoid words that will immediately create resentment and put up barriers.

▶ **Keep your message simple.** Avoid the tendency to use complex or long-winded language or jargon. This can confuse your audience and lose your point.

▶ **Be concrete.** Nothing irritates more than someone who loves the sound of their own voice – it does not mark you out as someone who can get things done. Rather, it signals procrastination tendencies. Avoid being vague and make sure that your meaning is understood.

▶ **Check that your message is understood.** Resist the temptation to impose your idea without allowing others to contribute and take an active part in the discussion.

Communication experts have one golden rule for effective speaking: **the 3S Sentence** – simple, short and specific. Remember, you do need to operate particular communication skills in the workplace. You can interrupt, talk at length, waffle, mumble with close friends and partners and get away with it, but at work, aim for a minimalist approach.

Most of us take listening for granted and see it as a passive activity. But effective listening is much more than hearing; it means giving the speaker our full attention and letting them know that we are. This is easier said than done, however. Our level of interest, our own emotional and mental state, our preoccupations can mean that we hear but don't really listen. Think about how it feels when you're talking to someone who isn't listening – it doesn't make for harmonious working relationships.

It's not always necessary to invest our energy in concentrated listening, but it really can pay dividends, particularly in tricky or important work situations. By really listening, you can pick up the intent and the level of emotion behind what is being said, which can help you respond more effectively.

> *I'm always fascinated by people at meetings. Half the time, no one is listening to each other, they're all in there making sure they're saying their piece, defending their corner. At a recent meeting, a section head was arguing vigorously for an additional staff member and, after about half an hour, the MD agreed to it. But the section head just didn't hear it and continued to argue. Eventually, someone pointed out to him that it had been agreed and could we please move on. It was amazing to watch but it really brought home to me just how much you can miss if you're totally engrossed in your own little agenda.*

The following tips may help you to hone up on your listening skills:

▶ **Clear away distractions** and concentrate on what's being said. If you can't do that, you're wasting your time and antagonising the speaker – a wound that could hurt you in the future. No one likes to be ignored when they're talking.

▶ **Listen to both the content and the intent** of what is being said. Is the speaker giving away hints of future developments or shifts in policy? What is she really saying? How is she feeling about what she is saying? Being able to read what's behind a message may give you invaluable insights into developments and opportunities for the future.

▶ **Make sure you're picking up the message correctly.** Ask for clarification to make sure you're clear about what's being said. This means not just reiterating what you're been told but paraphrasing the implications as well.

▶ **Listen to the essential facts** and try not to get distracted by the side issues. There's no point in latching on to minor details and ignoring the main points.

▶ **Allow the person to say what they want to say.** Interrupting or talking too much will do you no favours. If the person is waffling, you can interrupt to say things like, 'As I understand it, what you're saying is…' or, 'So, your point is…'. This stops the waffling but lets the speaker know that you've been listening.

▶ **Listen positively.** Avoid being judgemental or letting your prejudices prevent you from hearing what is actually being said.

NON VERBAL COMMUNICATION

Body language plays a crucial part in any conversation. Studies show that over half of all information we receive and understand comes from body language – we speak with our mouths but we converse with our whole bodies.

The way we stand, sit, gesticulate, move around, our tone of voice and our facial movements all give information about how we are feeling. Opening and closing conversations, turn-taking and interruptions are all negotiated (at least partly) through body language.

Research has shown that if there is a discrepancy between what an individual is actually saying, and the impression their body language is giving, most observers give the body language greater significance. Think about what a yawn says when you're talking to someone – far more than any words could. Awareness of what your own body is communicating in the work place will assist you to get your message across (and to interpret what your boss is really saying).

> *I've never been one to show my emotions at work and I've always thought that I kept them well hidden. But one day a colleague said to me "You're angry with me, aren't you?". I was flabbergasted – I couldn't understand how she knew. She said it was because I couldn't look her in the eye and my face was very taut. I'd never realised before how much your body language gives away.*

The main things to be conscious of are:

▶ **Facial expression.** The face is the most expressive part of a person. The shape of the mouth and the angle of the eyebrows are significant expressions of moods and feelings – think about the difference between a smile and a frown. We use facial expression to convey what we're thinking, and feeling, often in close conjunction with our speech. You may not feel much like smiling but try to do so at least once in a while. No one likes talking to a streak of misery for any length of time.

▶ **Eyes.** Your eyes are the most revealing and accurate of all communication signals. Three aspects of the eyes communicate – eye contact, eye movement and pupil size. Eye contact is vital to effective communication. Research estimates that, to build a good rapport when you're communicating, your eyes should meet the other person 60 to 70% of the time. (Don't be too self-conscious and deliberate when you're looking at someone, though.) Lack of eye contact leaves the other person feeling that you are not interested, or worse, you are ignoring them. If you spend your time looking at the floor or the ceiling, it gives the distinct impression that you've got something to hide.

There is thought to be a direct link between pupil size and interest: the greater the interest, the bigger the pupil. The size of the pupil affects the whole expression of the face, making it more accessible and friendly. Observing the pupil size can tell you how satisfied your manager, colleague or customer is.

▶ **Body position.** The position of your body can communicate important signals about whether you're feeling friendly or hostile. Sitting with your arms at your sides will make you seem approachable and receptive. A person in control of a situation, will tend to stand or sit in an upright position. This indicates a person who knows her job, enjoys the work and has no hidden motives in her communication. A person who wants to dominate others or make a determined, insistent statement will tend to have a forward leaning stance while the leaning back slope indicates a person in a defensive or reticent frame of mind.

▶ **Head nodding and shaking.** These gestures have a rather special role to play in conversation. They act as reinforcers, rewarding and encouraging the speaker, and they also play an important role in regulating speech. Nodding and shaking your head at the appropriate moments will convey the impression that you are listening. Tilting your head to one side will make you look interested. Be a little wary of this, however: women (being more sympathetic) tend to nod to show they've understood, whilst men will nod their heads to indicate they've agreed with something. Be careful not to be misconstrued.

▶ **The handshake** plays an important role in the world of work, giving an immediate indication about you when you first meet someone. It is more common in some sectors than in others and it can create a dilemma for women. Men who use the handshake with male colleagues or clients are sometimes at a loss about what to do when they meet a woman. The best policy is, if in doubt, offer your hand. A firm, confident handshake can give off a powerful message about you.

> ❝ I always have a dilemma about whether to shake
> hands when I first meet clients or not. I just can't
> fathom the rules at all. I didn't come from a hand –
> shaking background but, when I came to work in
> London, I was confronted by it. But not consistently –
> sometimes I would be offered a hand, other times I
> wouldn't. I have actually been at presentations where
> the organiser has shaken hands with my male colleague
> but not with me. It may seem like a small thing but I do
> feel that first impressions really count and
> I'm in the dark really as to how it all works. ❞

It is vital that your body language matches what you say. Think of how credible your grumpy supermarket attendant is when she says, 'Have a nice day.' We've all heard the expression, 'It's not what she said, it's the way that she said it.' Don't give a mixed message.

BARRIERS TO COMMUNICATION

There are a number of common barriers to communication and most of us have been at the receiving end of these. By being aware of the following potential barriers, you can become a more effective communicator at work and prevent misunderstandings and mistakes.

Preoccupation: If your head is full of your own thoughts, feelings or worries, you block out what other people are saying to you. Similarly, if you are preoccupied with something else, you will send a garbled message. Mixed messages are the classic result of preoccupation problems.

Emotion: This will always get in the way of clear communications. For example, if you try to talk to a person with whom you are angry, the communication will come across more strongly than the message warrants. If you are feeling vulnerable, you will pick up the slightest criticism as a major put-down. When you're speaking, watch for certain words or phrases which are emotionally charged.

Inarticulateness: Messages get distorted when senders have inadequate speaking or writing skills or when a person does not make the effort to speak clearly. A person who is inarticulate may often be ignored even though she may have something valuable to offer. It is sometimes difficult to distinguish between the best-put case and the best case.

> I used to be so nervous when I was doing presentations that I'd rush through my speech to get it over with. I lost half the audience and the other half would ask me questions because they hadn't understood. That just made me more nervous and more inarticulate. I've had to teach myself to speak slowly and presentations don't phase me half as much as they used to.

Physical circumstances: Noise, constant interruptions, uncomfortable air conditioning or bad lighting are all common barriers to communication. Try to cut down on distractions. If you have ever tried to talk to someone who is constantly interrupted by telephone calls, you know exactly how this feels.

Status: Differences in status between people who are trying to communicate can be a massive problem in some workplaces. People in power can have a major effect on how we communicate. If you're overly concerned with making a favourable impression on the boss, you may be economical with the truth about the sales figures. If you feel threatened or defensive, you probably won't be able to say much at all, let alone take anything in.

Stereotypes: People who think in stereotypes sometimes prevent communication altogether by assuming in advance either that they cannot understand the other person or that they know what the other person will say and do. As common victims of stereotyping, women need to be careful not to do this to others.

HEARD IT THROUGH THE GRAPEVINE?

It's important to constantly keep your ear to the ground, even during slow or no-news periods. When you're out of touch, you lose both information and influence. If you're not visible you don't exist, politically speaking. Worse, you set yourself up to be surprised when something important happens. Keeping your finger on the pulse, however, is very different from being a gossip.

> *There's nothing I love more than a night out with my friends to catch up on all the gossip. But, I've learned from bitter experience not to engage with the gossip at work. I'll listen to it, see if it's relevant to me and my work but I won't chat with colleagues about it.*

Gossip at work ranges from being enormous fun to being downright pernicious. Generally, the more senior you become the less seemly it is to be seen listening to – or passing on – gossip. However, although most professionals would agree that about 90% of the information you glean through the grapevine isn't worth batting an eyelid at, the other 10% or so may be crucial. There are certain things that it pays to listen out for. Here are some examples:

▶ **A black hole of silence.** If there's anything more significant than news it's a sudden silence. It could mean people aren't free to discuss whatever's going on. It may not be a major development but if, for example, a key player is about to depart, possibly involuntarily, you ought to know.

▶ **Major changes.** The grapevine is the early-warning system for any coming upheaval, such as an organisation restructuring or an order to cut your budget in half. If you don't get the word unofficially you easily could make a wrong move.

▶ **Senior management changes.** When top management players change, the entire culture of the organisation changes. Massive defections threaten the organisation and dire predictions will be circulating. Listen long enough to separate the probable from wishful thinking.

▶ **Customer/client defection.** The first hint that a customer or client is about to walk will come from the grapevine. If you are active in your network, you may get confirmation before anyone in your company has heard definitively. No one ever has more advance notice than they need, so use the time to brace yourself and your colleagues for the possible let-down.

▶ **Serious, high-level discontent.** National governments aren't the only places that have bloody coups. Companies undergoing market upheaval or heightened competition have them too. The first victim will be the person who is dumb enough to ignore the sabre rattling.

▶ **Enemy build-up.** If your boss's interdepartmental relationships are slipping, her enemies are forming allies or her power is being seriously undermined, you will get your first hint from the grapevine. You could be hurt unless you've been doing some independent power building yourself.

Of course there are also a few grapevine topics you can usually happily ignore:

▶ Who's having a Ugandan relationship with whom. Sexual peccadilloes are more interesting than they are important. Ignore titillating tales unless they involve a senior manager who is too actively promoting a subordinate's career. Steer clear until one or both parties self-destruct.

▶ Generalised complaints. If it's reported that Mary has said she'll leave if her job isn't upgraded, ignore it. She's trying pressure politics. If she were serious she'd be job-hunting and you'd probably notice her regular absence for interviews.

▶ Generalised paranoia. While it's depressing to hear that your competitors had a record breaking year, it's silly to think they did it just to make you miserable or put your organisation out of business. Lots of this gets passed around, especially when management has no clear directive on dealing with the real problems. It's easy to believe there is a conspiracy afoot when in reality it's a function of incompetence. If you can be positive and communicate that at a time of unrest and upheaval, it will mark you out for the future.

MAKING PRESENTATIONS

> *Whether I'm testifying before a House of Commons Select Committee about social security legislation or speaking to parent-teacher groups about abused children I have to continually work at finding the most effective way to address each audience.*

Making presentations can be very intimidating. However, once you've done your first, it will never be so hard ever again. Be under no illusion, though: brilliant presenters never stint on preparation, no matter how experienced they become. Preparation is the key: a good presenter will spend roughly ten times as long planning and preparing what she is going to say as she will actually saying it.

The classic organising approach to any good presentation has three simple components. Stick to these and you won't go far wrong:

Tell them what you are going to tell them
Tell them
Tell them what you told them

There are an infinite number of presenting styles and the trick is to find the right technique for you. If you go through the following stages of preparation thoroughly, then you set the scene to give your very best performance.

▶ **The content:** First, determine the actual content of your presentation. Identify the subject; work out the agenda – two to four items which will be covered – and break these items down into more detail; determine the body of the presentation; work on the detail of the presentation and then work out your summary (this to be key points only, no new information).

▶ **Your audience:** A crucial part of your preparation is thinking carefully about your audience and the impact your remarks will have. Consider who will be listening; whether there will be one main decision-maker present; also think about the layout of the room and whether you want an informal or formal effect. Collect information on your audience from various sources.

> *I make five or six phone calls to people who are going to be in the audience. I ask them, what's your experience in the organisation, what's your most important concern right now, and so forth. That way you get half a dozen instant allies. If you need some*

*support they'll probably be brave enough to
raise their hands.*

▶ **Visual aids:** Research shows that people remember only
about 20% of information conveyed by sound alone;
a video scores only 40% memorability; whereas they
remember 70% of information conveyed by visual aids.
These not only help the audience remember but also add
emphasis and clarity, providing another area of focus and
attention and making your presentation more enjoyable.
They also save time. Remember the old adage about a picture being worth a thousand words.

▶ **Movement, gesture and voice:** Never forget that the dom-
inant visual is yourself. Only bad presenters hide behind
the razzmatazz of audio-visual gimmicks. When presenting, you have control over every aspect of how your message is put over. You can walk, talk, create images, vary
the pace, gauge reactions and emphasise points. Above
all, use visual material not as a shield, but as a prop to help
you give a sparkling and effective performance. Work on
variety in volume, pitch, pace, gestures and accent. Be
conscious of the need for eye contact.

*I would always advise people not to rehearse in the
sense of becoming word perfect. By all means have
a run through but don't rehearse. You don't
want to get stale.*

▶ **Opening and closing:** If you know that you have a powerful opening and closing strategy, it will calm your nerves
considerably. To open, acknowledge the start of the meeting and welcome and introduce those present (if appropriate) before going on to deliver your dazzling first sentence.
When closing, summarise any key conclusions and agree-
ments reached during proceedings and acknowledge particular contributions.

▶ **The critical review:** Subject yourself to a full critical review. Make sure that the content, sequence and timing of your presentation fit. Have you researched your audience and tailored the presentation to their needs? Have you got all the relevant supporting material and visual aids? Do you have a clear, dynamic opening and closing for your presentation? Have you added interest to monotonous or potentially boring sections of your presentation?

When you wake up on the day of the presentation, take special care over your grooming and do whatever makes you feel assured and able to deliver your best. Allow plenty of time, both to pamper yourself a little, to build your confidence, and to get to the venue in good time.

Once you've arrived, take a good look at the room from the audience's point of view. It may look fine from the podium, but from where the viewers sit there may be serious distractions that you can easily rectify.

When it gets to your turn, take a deep breath. Look at specific people in the audience to command their attention. Look for a few seconds. Then begin, making sure that you speak to the audience and not to your visual aids. If in any doubt, take it very slowly. Women in particular tend to gabble when they're nervous. Avoid handing out information during the actual presentation itself but tell people what they will receive to take away.

Remember, you've worked hard, you're properly prepared, you're well briefed and you deserve to succeed. The presentation will soon be over and you'll be able to bask in the compliments you'll receive. Good luck – you won't need it!

MAKING THE MOST OF VISUAL AIDS

Exercise caution in the way that you use visuals – remember that they are aids not distractions. The following guidelines will serve you well, no matter what visual aid system you are using for your presentation.

▶ **Introduce your subject fully** before you bring any visual aid into play.

▶ **Make visuals bold, big and brilliant.** Fill the space on the screen or chart. Make your main points stand out and use lots of colour to emphasise them. Print words large and use key words only.

▶ **Make visuals really visual.** Don't rely on numbers and words. Use charts, graphs, pictures and colour. The biggest mistake that people make is to cram visuals with too much information. The ideal number of words or pictures is six – the absolute maximum is fifteen per page.

▶ **Use visuals sparingly** so that when they appear they really make an impression. Keep them only for main points and use your voice to convey information that is ancillary to your argument. Refine your images to show only the most important points. Anything else is a distraction.

▶ **Provide a constant format for each page.** This avoids confusion and gives a professional image. For example, you could put a title on each page or put your logo in the corner.

▶ **Practise with the equipment** until you have mastered it. Poor control of the equipment will really let you down.

▶ **Practise your timing.** You will be surprised at how little you can fit into your allotted time. Choose your words and visuals carefully so that you will not be rushed on the day.

Each visual technique has different strengths and weaknesses and it is worth experimenting until you find the technique that best suits you.

Slides are appropriate for a formal presentation. They are particularly useful when you have some standard material that you present on a regular basis. The level of light in the room is important when using slides but try to avoid the mistake of showing slides in complete darkness as this isolates you from your audience. Place your screen to one side, if you can, so that you are centre stage. Remember, you are the most important visual aid.

Flipcharts are much more informal and interactive than most other visual aids. Avoid the common mistake of standing in front of, instead of to the side of, the flipchart. You can use your marker pen to emphasise points by highlighting, circling, underlining or crossing out words. The beauty of using flipcharts is that you can create an impact by writing as you go along. If you are going to do this, put the words on the sheets beforehand in light pencil. Your audience won't see it and it'll save you the stress of worrying about positioning the words on the chart. Don't fumble with the page turns. Dog ear the corners so that you can seize them easily. Leave every other page blank to make sure that the marker doesn't shine through.

Overhead projectors (OHPs) can be used to create either a formal or an informal effect. To get the maximum benefit, put your overheads in frames and make sure they are properly aligned with the screen. Acetates which slide all over the place during a presentation look very unprofessional. Use plenty of colour acetates and coloured markers. If it's appropriate, reveal the image in stages, focusing on what you want your audience to consider. Use a pointer and when you wish to emphasise a point, leave it positioned on the key word and move away. As with slides, do not use an OHP in total darkness since it cuts your audience off from you. Dim the lights gently. Tiny hand movements become enormous by the time they reach the screen, so follow the sequence: on with the visual, on with the OHP, deal with the topic, off with the OHP, off with the visual. One of the benefits of using OHPs is that copies of acetates can easily be made and left with your audience to remind them of the key points of your presentation.

USING THE PHONE

A vast amount of work is done by telephone. Many personnel and human resource experts think that far more attention should be given to telephone training than is currently the norm.

Contact by telephone is very often the first exposure that an external person will have with an organisation. We have all had experience of organisations who have hopeless switchboards and unhelpful receptionists. They are a complete turn off.

It is amazing that employers are not more concerned with ensuring consistently high standards in answering the phone and in making calls. A good telephone manner will often give you a very real advantage in the workplace. Everyone likes to have their calls answered in a brisk, efficient, friendly and enthusiastic manner. The British are notoriously bad at sounding keen to do business on the phone.

When answering the phone: pick up promptly (any longer than four rings is unprofessional); give your name clearly (and your department or function if appropriate); offer to take messages; follow up and check that the promised action has been taken; make notes of the conversation.

When making a call: be clear in advance about what you need to achieve as a result of the telephone call; have the relevant file to hand; ask whether the other person has the time to take this call or if you should call back at a more convenient time; think about the timing of the call for maximum productivity; only hold for a minute, call back if the person is engaged for any longer; make notes of the conversation.

Never: eat, drink or smoke on the phone (absolutely awful if you're on the other end); be negative or evasive; hold two conversations at once; interrupt the caller or use jargon; transfer people around the organisation rather than deal with the query; sound reluctant to take a message or forget to pass messages on.

Intelligent use of the phone will help you enormously in your time management. If you respond immediately to a letter or memo by phone, you will not generally be expected to also write a reply.

Also, do take the time to learn about the different functions on your phone. You'd be surprised at how few people bother to do this: many modern office phones can retain several numbers in their memories which could save you loads of time in looking up and dialling.

> *One of my clients really makes me laugh. In fact, it's a running joke in the industry. They spent over a quarter of a million on their reception area and they have an untrained and fairly gormless seventeen-year-old at reception dealing with the switchboard. It wouldn't cost them tuppence to train her up properly and to institute some procedures. As it is, she garbles the name of the firm, loses the calls, gossips to the other girls in the hearing of people holding. It gives the most terrible impression.*

If you are out of the office a lot and are offered the use of a mobile phone, take it. It can be an invaluable weapon in your armoury of time-management techniques. Mobile phones are best used for fixing meetings and appointments while you're hanging around waiting for a train or for a meeting to start. They are not, however, so good for incoming calls. In fact, it's best to keep them turned off between calls so that they don't interrupt anything important.

If you are only offered a mobile phone for status reasons and you find that its only use is to call people to say you're on your way, then decline: it's an unnecessary toy and you will be liable to pay tax on it in your annual personal tax return.

WRITING EFFECTIVE MEMOS AND REPORTS

It's never too late to develop the skills of writing effective and concise memos and reports. Good writers are made, not born; writing is a process to be practised and mastered. Once mastered, it is an ability that you can use to wield considerable power within your organisation.

In essence a good memo or report will:

Define the problem
Outline a plan
Explore alternatives
Determine a solution

If your piece covers all of the above then you can be confident that it will serve you well. There are two simple rules for good writing: know what you want to say and say it as clearly as you can. Clear writing is the result of attention and care. It is not difficult to learn to write well but it does take time. When writing to colleagues, take yourself through the following process:

▶ **Analyse why you are writing.** Even before you start a first draft, pinpoint what you expect of your reader. Write a note to yourself in answer to this question: What do I want my reader to do (or know) when she finishes reading what

I've written? As you work, periodically consult your purpose statement.

▶ **Anticipate your readers' reactions.** Communications for work almost always have two or more readers. Although you may decide to address your memo to only one person, you should consider as potential readers everyone who has an interest in your topic. Your purpose statement will help you decide who to include on the distribution list.

▶ **Organise your ideas.** Effective operators grow up as writers when they leave behind the crippling notion that they should try to get it right the first time. This widely held belief does not lead to effective business documents; it leads to writer's block. A liberated corporate writer is the one who begins by producing a quick, rough and probably rather long draft starting with the first idea that comes to mind. You must be willing to forgo the temptation to edit the thoughts you are generating. Don't interrupt the process by fussing over word choices, fixing punctuation or rewriting sentences. That sloppy, chaotic rough draft can then be organised and shaped. Move blocks of text around and periodically print out your document to get a sense of the emerging piece.

Keep paraphrasing your own statements until they say exactly what you want them to say. No need to tinker with every word or refine all the small details: it is still too early in the process.

▶ **The final touches.** When you sense that the organisation and structure are right, you're ready to polish your work. Read out loud to yourself and listen to the flow of language. Does anything sound 'off'? Depending on your purpose, the situation you are writing about and the prevailing organisational style, you may wish to use a more formal, impersonal tone. Pick up your cues from the writing that crosses your desk every day. You do not, however, have to pepper your memos with expressions like 'as per', 'proactive' or 'utilise'. Most readers would rather read 'When we last spoke' than 'Pursuant to our previous conversation'.

In addition to avoiding pretentious wording, you should also forgo an unduly cosy, colloquial sound. Avoid clichés, slang, unnecessary jargon and excessive punctuation. (For example, '!!!' is never appropriate.)

Pay attention to format; give your readers visual clues. In longer documents, use white space as well as headings and subheadings that reflect the paragraph's content. Let your reader know at a glance what you've covered and how it's organised.

A good writer's guide can help with the final edit. You may find it useful to compile a checklist of your personal pitfalls to help you clean up the final draft. A memo rife with grammatical and proofreading gaffs can leave an indelibly negative impression on superiors.

If you are writing a major report, it can really help to stand back from it before putting on the final touches. Better still, get a supportive colleague or friend to read through the report and make editing suggestions.

> *I have to write reports a lot in work. On major reports, I used to frequently "burn out" by the time I came to final editing and I just couldn't read it any more. When I hit that stage, I'd call a friend of mine and invite her over for supper. While she read through the report, I'd have a long soak in the bath, cook a nice meal and feel refreshed and ready for her feedback. It really has been so useful for me. I now know all my own writing quirks and watch out for them. Practice really can change your writing style. I don't need my friend to edit for me any more but I do still take a long soak in a bath and emerge ready for that final assault.*

THE DOS AND DON'TS OF CORPORATE WRITING

Writing clearly and concisely for work is something we all have to learn. We are all familiar with gobbledegook in the office – and why it should be avoided. Always remember your office protocol; every company has its own code of behaviour for internal communications. Certain common sense rules hold true no matter where you work:

▶ Do be courteous, factual, specific – and brief. Being businesslike is about saying what you have to say, saying it once and saying it concisely.

> *I have a rule for myself when I'm writing in work. I always write things in draft form first, putting everything down on paper. My rule is to then reduce the draft by 50%. It has really taught me discipline and I am known for my clear and crisp style – many of my colleagues come to me when they're struggling with an unwieldy text.*

▶ Don't put anything in writing that you are unwilling to say publicly. Likewise, don't write anything that you wouldn't want published with your name on it. When your memo leaves your hands it leaves your control. Many an aspiring high-flier has been undone by a fax or the original left on a photocopy machine.

▶ Don't expect something written in confidence to remain a secret. Marking a document 'personal and confidential' may draw the kind of attention you want to avoid.

▶ If you commit negative feelings or thoughts to paper, don't send the memo out right away. You may feel very differently twenty-four hours later. If you think better of your diatribe and decide to dispose of it, keep in mind that the wastepaper basket can be an open book. Use a shredder – either mechanical or improvised.

▶ Don't include nasty characterisations of colleagues or their efforts: avoid words likc 'mcdiocre', 'abominable' or 'naive'.

▶ Don't exaggerate. Avoid inflammatory phrases like 'grossly unreliable', 'very late' and 'major crisis'.

▶ Don't write to someone above your boss without getting your boss's OK first. Going over her head could be mis-construed as going behind her back.

▶ Do put your good ideas in writing and address them to your boss. Let her decide whether to pass them on.

▶ Think carefully about who should be copied a sensitive memo or letter. Many people play political games by 'cc-ing' certain individuals. Remember, copying a client's subordinates on a letter is very bad manners: it implies that she doesn't communicate with her staff.

> *The last thing a manager wants is copious copies of memos passing over her desk every day. It doesn't impress. It makes her wonder how you've got the time to waste on memo writing. Your maxim should be quality not quantity so that, when you do send a memo, it has an effect.*

8 Working Relationships

▶ ▶ ▶ ▶ ▶ DEVELOPING A REWARDING STYLE • SAYING
THANKS • YOUR RELATIONSHIP WITH YOUR
BOSS • THE INDECISIVE MANAGER • THE
DICTATOR MANAGER • THE CONTROL FREAK •
THE DEMOTIVATING BOSS AND THE
UNSCRUPULOUS MANAGER • FRIENDS AT
WORK • OFFICE ROMANCES

One of the distinguishing characteristics of a really effective operator is her ability to forge good working relationships with the people around her. This may be at a variety of levels and with a diverse range of staff but the smart working woman will attend to the quality and quantity of her relationships both within and outside her department and her organisation.

Having a constructive and positive outlook towards others is absolutely key to this. There are some tips here for learning the tricks of energising both yourself and the people around you to have great ideas and to achieve better and brighter things. The importance of your relationships with the team around you can never be underestimated.

Your relationship with your boss plays a key role in your career and we explore the importance of this relationship. We also suggest some strategies for dealing with various types of rotten boss. There are few things as terrible as being lumbered with a stinker of a boss, when you are isolated and vulnerable and desperate for ideas for coping on a day-to-day basis.

Finally, some attention is paid to the more personal side of relationships at work. Many of us are not at all clear where to draw the line between friendliness and friendship in our working relationships. Even more extreme – many of us don't know what to do if we've fallen in love with the company secretary!

DEVELOPING A REWARDING STYLE

Women in particular like to see themselves as nurturing and rewarding. We have all been conditioned for motherhood. This approach can cause conflict with our organisational culture and, to adapt and progress, we can (consciously or unconsciously) adopt an approach that is different to our 'outside' personality.

Think about your own behaviour. Ask yourself the very blunt question: 'To what extent do people voluntarily seek me out; to what extent do they take the initiative in contacting me, communicating with me, sharing ideas and viewpoints with me, and including me in their personal and social activities?"

> *I'd always seen myself as the supportive person on the team. But recently, when one of my colleagues came back after giving a bad presentation, she talked to one of the guys about it. I was gutted, actually. When I confronted her about it, she said she felt that I would belittle her and make her feel guilty. I was shocked. It really forced me to look at how I've changed.*

Study the lists of behaviour characteristics on page 176. How many of these rewarding or punishing interpersonal ploys do you use when working with others? Your answers will give you an indication of whether your work style is primarily that of punisher or rewarder; whether you engender positive working relationships or not. If you have four or more 'punisher' points, you need to change your attitude and approach to people in work.

REWARDER OR PUNISHER?

DO YOU   *or*   DO YOU

DO YOU	DO YOU
Delay automatic reactions; not fly off the handle easily	Lose your temper frequently or easily
Agree with others wherever possible	Disagree routinely
Give your word sparingly but keep it/ keep confidences	Break confidences and fail to keep important promises
Share information and opinions honestly and openly	Tell lies; evade honest answers; refuse to level with others
Stay on the conversational topic until others have been heard	Divert conversation capriciously; breaking others' train of thought
Praise and compliment others sincerely	Flatter others insincerely
Joke constructively and in good humour	Joke at inappropriate times
Treat others as equal as much as possible	Embarrass or belittle others
Question others openly and honestly, asking non-loaded questions	Ask accusing questions
State your needs and desires honestly	Play 'games' with people; manipulating or competing in subtle ways
Talk positively and constructively	Over-use 'should' language; pushing others with words
Express genuine interest in other people	Make aggressive demands of others
Listen attentively, hearing the other person out	Restate others' ideas for them
Give others a chance to express views or share information	Brag; show off; talk only about yourself
Confront others constructively on difficult issues	Make others feel guilty
Negotiate; help others succeed	Solicit approval from others excessively
Share yourself with others, smiling, greeting others	Display frustration frequently
Express respect for values and opinions of others	Overuse 'why' questions

Effective people understand the difference between rewarding behaviour and punishing behaviour. Over the long term a rewarding style of dealing with others makes work a pleasant, enjoyable, achievement-orientated process. It will also help you keep your own and your colleagues' stress levels at a minimum.

YOUR RELATIONSHIP WITH YOUR BOSS

The boss-subordinate relationship is the key relationship in every job: count yourself one of the lucky ones if you have a good boss.

Part teacher and part leader, a truly great boss liberates the best within every one of us. Nothing motivates, inspires or pushes a woman on to ever greater accomplishments more than working for such a rare individual. And motivation is *everything* at work. Ask anyone who is truly motivated in her job and she will tell you: you can achieve ten times as much in a day when you're properly motivated, as you can when you are demotivated and your morale is low.

The trick is both to enjoy yourself and to learn. Watch how your boss deals with you and with the others in the team. One day you will (hopefully) be in her shoes and, if you are not clear about how to go about motivating others, be assured that this is a skill rather than a talent. If you observe carefully, you will learn that the harder your boss works at building a motivated team around her, the more she feels the benefit herself. If you are fortunate enough to work for someone like this at the beginning of your career you will pick up skills that will stand you in excellent stead for the rest of your working life.

The flip side to being a good boss is being a good subordinate. This amounts to more than loyalty and getting your assignments done on time: it means giving meaningful feedback and helping create a framework within which you can be effectively managed.

Unfortunately, most women at some stage in their career will encounter the truly impossible boss. Some bosses seem to resemble characters from a soap opera but it's no joke to real-life women who spend their working lives with these personalities.

> *My boss would approve my budget and tell me to go ahead on a project. Whenever I did that he would say, "I didn't give you the go-ahead on that." This is typical of him. When I approach him early in the day with a problem, he snaps my head off. And to top it all, he's sleeping with my assistant.*

If you find yourself with a bad boss, the worst thing you can do is just sit there and stew. Working under an impossible boss can make you ill or exacerbate existing illnesses. It can also have a major impact on your career, usually for the worse.

> *I was carrying him home in my head, driving myself crazy. Finally, when my family told me they didn't want to hear any more about it, I decided it was time to take action*

Start by trying to understand your own perceptions. Is there a pattern? Have you always felt unappreciated or abused by your boss? Are you overreacting to this particular boss's tone or style, or perceiving criticism as rejection? Are you someone who finds minor criticism devastating? Are you developing a negative behaviour pattern towards your boss?

If you suspect any of this is happening, you can change. Even if almost everyone finds the boss difficult to deal with, you still have some choices. It's unlikely you can change your boss, but you can change your own attitude to the situation. Ultimately, the key to managing a relationship with a bad boss is to have a game plan. First you must take responsibility for your decision of whether or not to stay in the job. Taking responsibility for the choice to stay on puts you in control of the situation.

You may decide it's worth dealing with a difficult boss if you're getting good training or some other important career pay off. Or you may conclude that staying is too costly, both professionally and personally, and the best course is to make a quick exit. Carefully consider the trade-offs you're making. If anxiety about your boss is dominating your life, if you're being made to feel inadequate at work, ask yourself, 'Why am I doing it?'

If you decide that staying fits your agenda, it helps if you tell yourself it's time-limited. If you're there because you're ambitious, see it as a rite of passage. If you were hired as an assistant manager and you want to become a manager, put in your time.

Having taken control of the choice, you will then need to set about changing your attitude. Your boss is not your life. Detach yourself from the situation and realize that you are not going to change your boss. It is a waste of energy for you to try. Focus exclusively on how to get the job done. Working with a boss like this can teach you that by changing your own attitude, you can make an impossible boss tolerable – at least for the time you need to learn the skills to move on. You will also learn what not to do as a manager.

Make sure you take all your holidays, plan things for your weekends and tell yourself *it will end*.

If you position yourself as business-like, calm and detached despite an impossible boss, you'll ultimately be seen as a good manager, able to handle the toughest assignments with poise, able to manage and motivate a wide range of personalities. In the long run you may have your bad boss to thank for teaching you one of the toughest lessons of business: the ability to flourish despite adversity.

It's up to you to keep your eyes open, take control and manage the situation to your advantage. Think of your efforts to make the bad boss tolerable as problem solving. If you understand the dynamics of the situation it can help you distance yourself, at least intellectually. Don't take it personally. Think in terms of your boss's counter-productive style and how it leads to work being done poorly, not just how it damages you.

The following are the most common types of destructive manager (your own particular bad boss may combine the characteristics of two or more of these types):

> **the indecisive manager**
> **the dictator**
> **the control freak**
> **the demotivator.**
> **the unscrupulous manager.**

However awful the characteristics of each of these might be, there may be an approach that can help you manage the day-to-day strain and allow you to continue to progress in your career.

Finally: if you feel utterly trapped, at the point of no return, that's a danger signal. You have to realize that ultimately you have options. If the combination of your unique set of vulnerabilities and strengths and your boss's behaviour is undermining your own sense of self-worth, it's time to move on.

THE INDECISIVE MANAGER

This person may waffle, waver and wobble, but you must be steadfast. This boss is frustratingly indecisive, ineffective and insecure.

> *You can't spend your whole life hoping that she falls under a bus. You must make your boss effective. If need be, help her make decisions – and make her feel that the decisions are hers.*

She (or he) is often so unsure of her standing with her own line managers that she won't give any clear directives. She may be a nice individual who hasn't yet accepted that the role of the boss is to say yes or no. She may report to a bad boss herself, someone who demands she behave as a yes-woman. The organizational culture may require that she spend so much time buttering up top managers and keeping her bottom covered that there's no energy left for the job at hand.

For whatever reason, the hallmarks of the indecisive manager are that she is too nice, too accommodating. She avoids issues and she may have hidden complaints and criticisms that will not come to the surface unless you take action. If you're working for an indecisive manager you need to make her feel comfortable and help her make decisions and set limits.

HOW TO DEAL WITH THE INDECISIVE MANAGER:

▶ Do not confront the indecisive manager. Appeal to her obliquely; make statements that will help to draw her out such as 'We seem to have a problem' or 'I'm not clear about the issues.'

▶ Take the initiative: articulate the options and let the boss help you make a choice. For example, if you have a deadline for a project and you need to find out if it can be extended you could say, 'It's occurred to me that we have two project deadlines right now, do you still want me to continue to work on Project A? Or should I move on to Project B?'

▶ Under no circumstances allow yourself to be so stymied by your boss's indecisiveness that it keeps you from getting your own work done. Say, 'I need the go-ahead from you. The reasons this will go over well for our department are X, Y and Z.' Help her resolve her insecurity about her own superiors.

▶ Change your own attitude; instead of saying to yourself, 'She won't give me the authority,' say, 'If I can work out a way she can feel comfortable with this, then I will get the authority to do it.'

▶ If she never gives you critical feedback on your performance, even when you suspect she feels you're not performing up to par, you may worry that your movement within the organization will be limited. You need to literally *ask* for constructive criticism. Meet with her privately and say, 'I have a feeling something isn't right here. Things aren't working. I need you to give me realistic feedback.' This should clear the air and allow you to have a better working relationship.

▶ As a last resort, if nothing makes the boss move, you may have to work around her. Sometimes it's better to ask forgiveness than permission. Managers up the line may admire you privately if you get something done despite her resistance and without seeming disloyal or stealing her thunder.

▶ Look for the silver lining. Find the redeeming characteristics hidden beneath the difficult exterior, the skills and talents you can learn from. For example, the indecisive manager may be supportive, good at relationships. Find the strength that is the shadow of the weakness.

THE DICTATOR

The dictator breathes fire and brimstone but you must never show you're scared. The annals of business are filled with examples of domineering, demanding, bullying tyrants who wouldn't let go of power.

> ❛ He called me into his office and barked out a series of orders relating to a project that was totally inappropriate for my department. I told him I'd think

> *about it, went back to my office and wrote a lengthy memo explaining why his suggestion didn't work in the context of our history and goals. I never heard from him again about the project.* **"**

Dictators are often company or project leaders. They tend to have a short fuse, be very impetuous and make decisions quickly. Untempered by the need to be diplomatic, dictators run rough-shod over underlings.

> **"** *He was a maniac. The partnership was losing money, he was under enormous pressure and he took it out on us. He had people working seven days a week, made unreasonable demands, and he enjoyed humiliating people publicly with vicious personal attacks.* **"**

It must be admitted that sometimes the dictator style works. In certain industries, at certain times, the dictator is the person who can get the job done. He (or occasionally she) is decisive and gets results. A dictator wouldn't be there long if he wasn't effective. If you can keep this perspective, you can learn to live even with the worst of dictators.

HOW TO DEAL WITH THE DICTATOR:

▶ Reassure him at all times, in subtle or not so subtle ways that he is the boss. The dictator wants to be looked up to as God. But don't fall into the trap of being subservient. You will find more favour with the dictator if you think and evaluate for yourself.

▶ Never show you're frightened.

▶ Never get into a power struggle with him in front of anyone else.

▶ If he is critical of you in public, don't adopt his style. Never shame him in front of others, even if he's done it to you. The best approach is to ignore the remarks. If you ignore by choice, it's not cowardice, it's assertiveness. Your aim is to stick to your own agenda and act as a dignified human being, not to humiliate the boss or to feel humiliated yourself. Later, you can meet with the boss privately and say, 'I need to know more. I want to understand the criticism you have so I can learn from it.'

▶ Don't indulge in saying to yourself, 'I can't live with this, life isn't fair.' It's counterproductive. Substitute this thought: 'He doesn't know a better way of behaving. That's his style. I have to learn how to handle these difficult types to progress in my career.'

▶ Your ability to ride above it all may very well impress your senior management. Remember, everybody will know that this person is a dictator. Most people probably feel very sympathetic towards you. If you can realise that, it might not upset you as much.

▶ When he rants and raves and makes personal attacks, look for the problem, the mutual goal. Focus on what needs to be done. Defuse the anger by asking questions: What is the problem here? What needs to be done right now?

▶ When a dictator loses control, it's because he's feeling insecure. Sometimes you can change the situation by using body language. If you're sitting, stand up. Clear your throat. Look directly at him and say, 'What's the problem here?'

▶ If he embarks on a harangue and seems out of control, find an honourable method of retreat. Suggest a break. Reschedule the meeting. Take a phone call, change the scenery, count to ten, tap your foot. Some people keep their cool by imagining the ranting dictator seated on the loo or dressed in a nappy.

If you recognise that the dictator's behaviour is not personal, the experience really toughens you up. If your constitution allows you to hang in there, and you're extremely ambitious, you could use it as a stepping-stone. However, dictators tend to make others feel inadequate. If you're particularly vulnerable in this respect, look for work elsewhere – unless you love the job. It can ruin your personal life to work for someone like this.

THE CONTROL FREAK

The control freak tends to be skill-orientated, a specialist rather than a generalist. She (or he) is the hands-on manager taken to the extreme – oversupervising, hoarding information, refusing to delegate, resenting independent thought or action. In her need to set the agenda day by day, she may irritate by monitoring morning arrivals, lunch hours and evening departures, giving overexplicit directions and slapping down anyone who steps outside their specific job function. This management style erodes motivation and innovative thinking and encourages people to be overly compliant and fearful of risk-taking.

On the positive side, the control freaks are the glue of many organisations. The control freak usually is very conscientious, takes responsibilities seriously, is dedicated, ethical and hard-working. If you have no time for control freaks, think again next time your plane is circling to land: you'll be depending on the air traffic staff having a boss who demands impeccable attention to detail.

On the negative side, the control freak can sometimes be a career road-block.

> 6 He was the only person in the department when I
> arrived. He said, "All ideas go through me." He
> called the director every morning, then gave me
> assignments for the day, on a piecemeal basis. He set it

up so I had no autonomy over anything. He knew the plan weeks in advance but didn't tell me until the morning of each demonstration. I couldn't work that way. I left when my contract ran out without bothering to renegotiate it. **,**

HOW TO DEAL WITH THE CONTROL FREAK:

▶ Managers like this allow you no independence. Sometimes the only solution is to do it their way. Change your outlook. Remember that the control freak may ensure quality work and that you can learn from this.

▶ Tell yourself, 'I'll do whatever she wants to be done.' Organisations tend to self-select a certain kind of person to work for them. Overmanaging characterises a lot of organisations. Some people like to be given explicit instructions. If you don't, there may be a mismatch not only with your boss but with the place you work as well.

▶ Give the control freak a chance to see you dot all the i's and cross all the t's and get everything done. Then she will gradually relax. Bear in mind the control freak is insecure, afraid that no one can do it as well as she can. By co-operating with the boss's need to be in control instead of fighting it, you will calm her down.

▶ Think of the control freak as an overprotective parent. The best way to deal with her is to drown her in information. The more you give, the less she has to worry and the more she'll let go. The worst thing is to fight it. Then the alarms ring. The boss may think, 'This person is not a team player, this person won't take supervision, this person is trying to hide something.'

▶ Reassure the control freak that you are on her side, while at the same time asserting your own work style.

▶ When it comes to decision time, put the advantages of your preferred options in writing. Give her a chance to think about it. Don't confront her or ask to discuss it further. Provide lots of reasons why your preferred option will work best. Going through the difficult (and seemingly unnecessary) exercise of gathering data to prove your point may teach you a valuable skill in getting what you need in a bureaucratic organisation.

THE DE-MOTIVATOR

The demotivator is a common type of manager: an immediate boss who is a nice guy but couldn't motivate you and your colleagues to save her (or his) life. She literally absorbs energy and just being with her makes you feel exhausted. She is not malevolent but nonetheless you have a very real problem.

> *Everyone likes my boss and that seems to be the only important thing to her. A few days ago I got fed up and told her that morale in the department was at an all-time low. I said I was going to look for a new job. Her answer (and I quote) was, "I don't blame you. Go ahead – and put me down as a referee."*

This sort of boss puts a lot of women into something of a quandary: can it be the case that being a 'nice' boss has its pitfalls? Aren't we women always urging more harmony? Don't we all subscribe to the idea that an uncritical, unruffled manner creates a desirable environment? Well, the answer is: not always. As with children who love tougher parents and respond better within a fairly disciplined family, most of us work harder and are better motivated in a work environment where we know the rules and the lines are clear. People are always happier when they know where they stand.

> *I was so bored at work that I started to do my assignments for my diploma of marketing during the time we weren't busy (which was more often than not). Eventually, I felt so guilty about this misuse of office time that I finally asked the boss if he cared. He said I was welcome to use the time as long as I didn't let his boss catch me. Well, I was astonished.*

HOW TO DEAL WITH THE DE-MOTIVATOR:

▶ Try and work out exactly what is demotivating about your boss. Could it be the case that she's a hands-off manager because she has no orders to give or assignments to make, so she simply leaves you alone?

▶ Determine whether your boss is being straightforward with you. If her hands are tied because of the prevailing company culture, then it may be that she will be having the same problem with *her* line manager – maybe she's as frustrated as you are.

▶ Accept that you really can't do much to change the situation or expect your boss to become a better manager.

▶ Ask for feedback. Lack of feedback is one of the greatest demotivating forces in any situation. Giving feedback – criticizing and praising – is a most important tool in the workplace. It's through feedback that we nudge our colleagues, subordinates and bosses in the right direction, set and modify their expectations and coax them along towards improved performance. Hard as it may be, we must criticize, and we must praise – and so must your boss. Always bear in mind that the feedback business works both ways: if you don't receive feedback from your boss you should ask for comments when a task is completed.

▶ Become a self starter. This is tough, as motivating yourself is one of the hardest disciplines to master. Most people like the comfort of decisions being made for them. It is very difficult to get yourself going every morning – particularly when you're feeling demotivated and low. However, unless you are prepared to seize the initiative yourself, you run the risk of withering away at your desk for want of attention.

▶ Consider yourself as being on a plateau (see Chapter 2) and adopt appropriate coping strategies.

▶ Force your boss to listen to you. Ask for a weekly meeting (it may take only ten minutes) during which you can tell her what's on your mind. Take notes at the meeting so that you will be able to remember what was discussed and what actions need to be taken; write a note of the meeting afterwards for the benefit of you both. Impress upon your boss that she doesn't have to agree to every request you make but that she should be prepared to listen. If your boss cancels meetings once you've set them, it may be that she is not interested in allowing you to succeed. Regrettably, it may be the time to implement an alternative plan.

> *Except for the weekly team memo, our boss hardly ever speaks to us. He spends his time attending meetings. We have no idea what he, as a manager, is doing and he seems to care very little about what we, as a department, are doing.*

THE UNSCRUPULOUS MANAGER

The unscrupulous manager is truly dangerous and you'd best get well out of range.

> *My new boss purposely deflated our void figures in a presentation to the management team. We went*

*over the figures together on the Monday, and she said
that they were higher than she'd like them to be. They
then appeared reduced by 20% on the Tuesday, so it
was pretty obvious she'd done it deliberately. People
from her previous company had warned us she was
sleazy – a liar – before she joined this department,
but I didn't believe she could be as bad as they said.* **,**

Unscrupulous managers are spoilers whose tactics include
undercutting subordinates, stealing ideas and taking credit for
them, sniping at colleagues and sowing seeds of doubt about
their competitors. If unscrupulous managers are incompetent,
they're so good at lying, manipulating, working the office
grapevine and playing people off against one another that they
maintain power.

They are the seducers, flattering their superiors while mis-
treating their subordinates. Unscrupulous managers have
been known to coerce assistants into collaborating in elaborate deceptions covering up extramarital affairs, extra-legal or
unethical business arrangements, manipulation of sales figures, expense accounts or personnel information.

These are the toughest of all the bad bosses to deal
with. They have all kinds of excuses, all types of rational-
isations. They'll try to turn things around and say it's your
problem, that you did the wrong thing, that you didn't
understand.

HOW TO DEAL WITH THE UNSCRUPULOUS MANAGER:

▶ When confronting your boss, use polite, respectful but
firm language. Start with the facts. Review the situation
and your experience of it. Try to do it in an open-ended
way by saying, 'This is the experience I had, these are the
facts as I understood them, this is the position I felt I was

in.' You're giving the boss a chance to respond. If the boss is honest, she (or he) will admit there was a mistake or a misperception. This will clear the air, and it won't happen again. But if it does happen repeatedly and you find the boss denying any mistake, saying it was all your problem, then you must face the fact that you're dealing with somebody who has no ethics, no morals, no values.

▶ Don't make the mistake of thinking you can rescue a boss like this. Do not delude yourself that the boss just doesn't understand, or just has some problems or is not hearing, and you have to straighten her out.

▶ Be prepared to do some soul-searching. Be sure of your own character, ethics and integrity, and decide for yourself where you will draw the line defining what you will and won't permit your boss to demand of you. Then you have to be scrupulous about protecting your own integrity.

▶ The biggest mistake if you're working for an unscrupulous manager is to retaliate in kind. The worst thing is to tell people behind the boss's back that she's unscrupulous. Any boss expects loyalty, and although it's difficult to remain loyal to an unscrupulous manager, don't start going over her head or talking about her in the corridors. Ultimately it will reflect poorly on you.

▶ Never get in the gutter with people like this. This type of boss is capable of using very nasty tactics. You will lose your own sense of self and that's where she wants you. You never win a gutter fight, because your opponent is always more unscrupulous, unethical and ruthless than someone who is not that way habitually.

▶ Analyse the facts. At all times stick to the issues, document your actions. Prove your own value in a visible manner, through your performance.

▶ Privately, one to one, you have to confront these people with their manipulations, their lies, their unethical behaviour, their integrity lapses that trouble you. Make it clear that you won't participate and won't stand for it. This will take some courage.

Ultimately, working for an unscrupulous manager can damage your career and reputation. When you find on a consistent basis that you're dealing with a manipulator and a liar, someone who lacks integrity and would have no qualms about getting you involved in questionable situations, the warning signals must start flashing in your brain. If you're in this situation, you must be prepared to move on. Be aware that by staying you may put yourself in an unethical, immoral and perhaps even illegal position.

FRIENDS AT WORK

Work is often central to forming new friendships, exposing us to a large number of people, including men, with whom we can form ties. Factors that can have a negative effect on friendships, such as getting divorced or having a baby, are more easily overcome when strong work bonds are established.

> *The people I like best are the ones who have jobs that are similar to mine. My whole life is work – I work all day and I'm business entertaining most evenings – other people in the same game understand what you're going through, what your job is all about, why you're not free to socialize at the drop of a hat and where you can get another good job when the time comes.*

Women often meet their closest friends through work and maintain those friendships long after both parties have moved on to different organisations. This is hardly surprising since we spend so much of our time at work. If work now exerts a powerful influence on friendships, the new styles of friendships are also influencing the world of work. The management style of the twenty-to-forty-year-old generation tends to be less authoritarian and more team-orientated than that of the previous generation of managers. The drawback is that people may not be as good at being forthright and direct when things aren't going well. The benefit is that they do tend to be more participatory.

One side effect of work is that women don't have as much time to devote to their friends and that shortage of time actually may spur greater intimacy between them. When women friends do get together they get straight to the real issues: there often just isn't enough time for small talk and conversations tend to have great meaning. So friendships between colleagues at work are increasingly common and women have found that these in-office friendships are most easily formed early on in careers.

There can, however, be drawbacks to being friends with people at work. As we move up through the ranks, we're understandably more comfortable looking outside our own organisations to professional groups, to counterparts in other companies or to people in entirely different fields for close friendships.

> **‘** I wouldn't want to be quoted on this, because it might hurt some people's feelings, but while I'm certainly friendly with some of my consultants, I don't really consider them friends. At this stage in my career, there's too much potential for professional jealousy and for divided loyalties to become too close with anyone through work. I like having friends with whom I can discuss professional issues and problems but I feel safer if I find those friends away from my work and my company. **’**

There is a wealth of difference between friendship and friendliness.

Friendships at work, between colleagues, between clients and suppliers and between managers and subordinates, carry a certain amount of risk. Ideally, a no-favouritism rule is understood and accepted. The danger comes when the colleague or supplier friend is tempted to abuse the relationship. If you find yourself facing friends who expect special treatment, apply the following guidelines:

▶ Clarify the difference between friendliness and friendship. Friendship involves special feelings towards a select few. Friendliness implies a warm, sympathetic attitude that may be shown to all. You can offer friendliness widely. But if you are a person in authority, you will have to avoid the appearance of even the slightest favouritism.

▶ When resolving a feud, involve a third party in the discussion. Avoid one-on-ones when you're an arbitrator. Or if it is desirable to meet individually, give each person equal time and tell the antagonists you expect to meet them later in a three-way session.

▶ Put your cards on the table. You might say to a consultant about to enter a competitive tendering situation: 'We both realise that our friendship creates a complication. I want to make our talk helpful and satisfying to both of us.' If appropriate, explain decisions that are suspect. 'I have given this contract to XYZ because of their special experience with employment legislation.'

▶ Be prepared for the ultimate test. You may face your friend in a situation that pits you against other loyalties – to your organisation, to your own conscience. Feelings may be put to the most painful test. For example, in a contract tendering interview where your friend makes no secret of her expectation to get a favourable decision that in your opinion is not deserved. Subtle ploys include, 'You know I'm the best person for that job' when you know no such thing. She is laying it on and you have to respond without being defensive.

▶ Explain the reasons for your decision. If you lose the friend as a result, one consolation is that the motives for the relationship may not have been genuine anyway.

If your friend holds the same rank as you within the company, you may find that you are occasionally caught between loyalty to your employer and personal feelings for your colleague. Consider your dilemma. In your organisation's interests should you discourage the personal goals? Or in sympathy with the colleague, should you give the best advice you can to satisfy her needs? There is no stock solution to resolve this scenario: even-handed judgement is your wisest strategy. The best thing to do is:

▶ Encourage your colleague to talk. She may be confused and asking for advice. The more she thinks out loud, the more she will clarify feelings and ideas, which makes for better decisions.

▶ Help her to think out the alternatives. You can raise questions about her goals and provide a clear assessment of her prospects in the company. Propose that she explore the prospects and practicality of her goals. Help her sketch out a game plan that could make the present more rewarding.

▶ The last thing you want is to make the decision for her, or in any way influence her decision one way or the other. You can still be a good friend by enabling her to take constructive steps in evaluating her own choices.

> *I learned how to manage people through making mistakes. It's easier for people to tell you what they want to do than for you to tell them what you want*

them to do. But I'm not here to entertain everyone. I no longer mix business with pleasure. I don't go for regular drinks and I don't have family pictures on my desk. For me, that's the best way to avoid potential conflicts with friends when tough decisions have to be made. **9**

OFFICE ROMANCES

6 *We used to go out regularly in a gang after work for drinks. One night – Valentine's night – we just fell into one another's arms after eight of us had stumbled out of an Italian restaurant. People were so pissed that nobody seemed to notice. The next day I told everyone that I was in love and who with but it must have seemed very implausible since nobody believed me until we got engaged.* **9**

It is very common to become romantically involved with someone with whom you work. One estimate (1993) is that as many as two-thirds of all workers have had affairs or are having affairs with their colleagues. This will range from the indiscretion at the office party through to the whole marriage-and-kids scenario.

If you think about it, this statistic is hardly surprising. Many of us are in love with our work, especially in the first few years of our career, and find it all-consuming. We are naturally attracted to people who share the same interests and motivations as ourselves. There is a frisson of shared endeavour and informed understanding. The more intense the job and the organisational culture, the more intense is our need for an ally who will understand, protect, advise and nurture us at work – and at home.

In addition, most of us work long hours and we don't get to meet people in many other contexts. The classic old-style boss-secretary relationship grew as a result of a prolonged intimacy between two people for several hours every day. It is difficult to think of a way of getting to know another person better.

If – for whatever reason – you need to keep it quiet, there is an added dimension. There is no doubt that passion thrives on proximity and secrecy and these affairs are often very exciting.

Every relationship is different and everyone makes their own choices but there are a few golden rules to stick to if no one (especially you) is to be unnecessarily hurt:

▶ Avoid him if he has a reputation for being the office Romeo. He will use you and drop you like he did all the others. And people will be waiting for it to happen.

▶ Avoid him if he is married (no matter how much his wife doesn't understand him).

▶ If it is to be a secret make sure it really is a secret. There aren't many things more pathetic than a secret romance that absolutely everyone knows about.

▶ Avoid him if he's Jack-the-Lad, circulating photocopies of his bum or winning the down-in-one contest in the pub. Very strong chance he will discuss your sexual performance with his mates.

▶ Don't allow him to seduce you on the company premises – even if it is a mutual sexual fantasy. The risks of getting caught are just too high.

▶ Don't use your relationship to secure or confer favours. If either of you is a person in authority, you will have to avoid the appearance of even the slightest favouritism.

If you stick to these, then your office affair is less likely to explode in your face, ruining both your personal life and your career. Of course, you ignore any one of these at your peril but it is sometimes difficult to see things very clearly in these situations. Certainly, if you do make a mistake, you'll be in good company.

> ❝ We both worked for a medium-sized company and he was fairly senior – on the board – whilst I was relatively junior. We kept it secret for a whole year (until he was head-hunted into another firm) in case he was compromised but it was touch and go. People always thought I was remarkably well informed about the dealings of the company and he got a reputation for being in touch with the grass roots. It was hilarious. Between us we knew everything. The whole was greater than the sum of the parts. ❞

9 Resolving Conflict

▶ ▶ ▶ ▶ ▶ STICKY SITUATIONS • RECEIVING FEEDBACK •
GIVING FEEDBACK • SEXISM AND SEX
DISCRIMINATION • SEXUAL HARASSMENT AT
WORK

One of the most difficult things to learn when dealing with a conflict at work is that *it's not whether you're right or wrong that counts, it's how you resolve the issue.* If you focus exclusively on the strengths or weaknesses of the case in hand you may stand to lose more than just an argument.

Women, much more than men, tend to hold on to the notion that everything must be fair. Unfortunately there isn't very much at work which is fair, and in any case, in work-related disputes, fairness isn't really the point. Resolving the problem and working effectively together is the aim. Without some careful diplomacy, stubbornly holding your ground can put you on a dodgy footing for ever more.

It is very hard, but the golden rule is not to let personal feelings enter into work conflicts. A true professional views each conflict and its resolution as a trade-off between professional interests. The higher up you go, the more important it is that you learn to operate like this.

It is a disaster to say anything when tempers are raised. That is a sure-fire way of obscuring objectivity. Once you say something you can't un-say it – which is always worth remembering, particularly when you and your adversary hold different ranks within the organisation. De-escalating a conflict with your boss not only defuses the personal confrontation but casts you in a very constructive role.

When you stop to consider the possible consequences, there are very few office arguments that are worth battling out to the bitter end. Don't always expect a satisfactory resolution on the same lines as you would want in a personal relationship. In most working relationships, it is the ability to compromise (together with a huge measure of forgiveness and not bearing grudges) which is crucial to success. The good news is that, by and large, women behave better than men in their personal relations and it gives us a massive advantage in the workplace.

STICKY SITUATIONS

When emotions run high in the office, it's easy to speak first, think later. Your reply to a colleague's touchy question or observation can either set tempers flaring or turn a potential rift into a problem-solving opportunity. Dealing effectively with difficult situations at work will demand all your interpersonal skills.

As we said at the start of the chapter, it's resolving conflict, not the rights and wrongs, that is important in the workplace. Adopting this as your basic approach will not only lead to a more harmonious working environment, it will also mark you out as someone with finely tuned people skills – skills necessary to move to management level.

There are a myriad of difficult interpersonal situations you will encounter in work and each will demand its own response. There are, however, a few golden rules that will apply no matter what the situation:

▶ **Don't let your personal feelings dictate.** This can be very difficult to do but it's always a disaster to say anything when tempers are raised. Never forget – once you've said something, you can't take it back.

> *I know I probably shouldn't say this but, in my experience, women tend to take problems in work too personally. They are more likely to bring home feelings of anger at how they (or a colleague) have been treated than concern about the sales figures. But, if you put all your energy into being indignant about petty office politics, you won't have the drive to forge a career. We have got to learn to expect unfairness in the workplace – even if that upsets our sensitivities.*

▶ **Think before you talk.** Knee-jerk reactions in emotionally charged situations are a recipe for disaster. Force yourself to really hear what is being said before you give your response. This can make the difference between diffusing and escalating a problem.

▶ **Exercise self-control.** This does not mean that you suppress or deny your feelings or that you sit there and stew. Although it may not sound very appealing, adopting this approach can put you in control of difficult situations. The key to controlling your emotions is to be aware of them and use them constructively.

▶ **Avoid overemotional exchanges** whenever possible. Keeping calm in the midst of an emotional situation will always serve you well and will mark you out as management potential. Find a technique that helps you to stay calm – count to ten, tap your foot, tell yourself, 'This will all be over in a few minutes.'

> *When things start getting out of hand at work, I say "supercalafragalisticxballadocious" to myself and it really helps me. It makes me distance myself from the instant reactions going on around me and gives me that split second to compose myself.*

▶ **Put yourself in the other person's shoes** and think about how you would like to be treated if you were in the same situation, or how you might be feeling. This can much easier said than done – we are, after all, human. But, if you can learn to do it, you can gradually begin to turn difficult situations into productive ones.

▶ **Keep things in perspective.** When you're in the middle of a difficult situation, it's easy for it to become all-consuming and the most important thing in your life. But it probably isn't. Try to keep a sense of humour about it all and ask yourself, 'How important will this seem when I'm eighty?'

▶ **Don't hold grudges.** Even if you have been treated badly by a colleague or boss, you need to be able to learn from the experience and put it behind you. Settling scores never did anyone's career any good – it just diverts your energy into revenge rather than growth. Try and use the maxim 'forgive but don't forget' – evaluate what you've learned from the situation and how you could deal with it more effectively in the future.

Your assertiveness skills (see Chapter 1) will really help you in resolving difficult situations in work. Always keep in mind the aim of sorting the problem and moving on. Here are a few examples of effective responses in some sticky work situations:

▶ **When a colleague says:** 'I have to make a presentation at next week's senior management team and I just cannot be there. Will you give it for me?' **You might want to say:** 'When was the last time you did anything to help me? If your report weren't so key to our department I'd tell you where to stick it.' **But you'll get more mileage from:** 'I'm really swamped, but I don't want our department to lose out. If you'll help me prepare my own report next week, I'll be able to cover for you this time. But be sure to get me all your background research by tomorrow.'

► **When your head of department says:** 'Your sales for this quarter are way down. Have you lot been skiving?' **You might want to say:** 'Given that there's only me and two other full-time people at the moment, you've got a nerve expecting an increase in productivity.' **But you'll get more mileage from:** 'I've also been worried about our sales slump. How would it be if we took on a trainee rep to take some of the routine pressure off the three of us so that we can make more key calls. We are a good team and I know we could get sales back up in no time.'

► **When your trainee assistant says:** 'Why haven't I had a pay increase? I'm going to start looking for another job' **You might want to say:** 'Excuse me, but your attitude is appalling. Don't you know we've just come out of recession? And there's a lot of things wrong with your work. At the rate you're going, you'll not only not get a pay increase, I'll be glad to help you clean out your desk.' **But you'll get more mileage from:** 'I understand how you feel. But there are a few performance issues that we need to discuss before I can recommend you for a salary review.'

RECEIVING FEEDBACK

Dealing with criticism constructively is one of the most difficult and uncomfortable things we face – at work or outside it. Yet the capacity to use criticism productively, as a motivational force is a key attribute shared by effective leaders and entrepreneurs. Ignoring challenging feedback will stunt your ability to change and grow. As the saying goes, 'Good judgement comes from experience; experience comes from poor judgement.'

How you deal with critical comment determines how you feel about your superiors, peers and subordinates and how they feel about you. It may even determine how far you rise.

An American study suggests that one of the primary reasons that certain women have become derailed from the success track is that they have denied the validity of critical feedback. Rather than learn from negative comment, they ignored it, which in turn prompted those above them to believe that they were unwilling to adapt. Among the higher-echelon women surveyed, more than half said that they had overcome other potential derailment factors by getting and using constructive feedback.

Using criticism to further your growth means lowering your defences. Women who benefit from feedback do not duck the critical comments thrown at them because they don't consider them a personal assault. They therefore feel no need to even the score. Instead, the undefensive, receptive woman will use feedback as a tool with which to better herself. She takes the point of the criticism and uses its sharpness to refine her skills.

So why don't more people seek out critiques of their performance? The two most common reasons are simple: first, criticism hurts; second, many of us have not yet recognised its positive aspect.

For some, the wound inflicted by a negative observation is so painful that they block out all such comments. Unfortunately such efforts to protect their self-esteem also keep them from growing. To be able to benefit from criticism you must be willing to make yourself vulnerable. Once you have accepted yourself and your imperfections, you no longer need to present yourself as infallible. You become more open to critical comments because you know that no matter how accurate they are, you still have some worth.

> ❛ It's amazing how productive it can be to lay yourself open to criticism from your colleagues. Because I say "I really made a hash of that this morning," they feel they can also open up about their failings. We really do

learn from our own and each other's mistakes and it means that we're not afraid to give things a try. I love working in that sort of atmosphere – it's really challenging and I've pushed myself to limits I might not otherwise have done.

Many women find it particularly difficult to display imperfections in the workplace for fear of seeming more incompetent than their male counterparts. But look around you – the men in your organisation are not perfect. Does that mean that you immediately write them off? There is no doubt that there can be greater pressure on career women (particularly if they are pioneers or working in a male environment), but be very wary of translating that into insistence on perfection. This approach can actually limit your learning.

If you believe your self-esteem is under attack, you may revert to a familiar defensive pattern. If the criticism is valid, do not immediately infer that you are in the wrong. Once you are on the defensive, you have lost, because you lose control to resolve the matter pleasantly. It becomes an emotional issue. With this response, you are destined to end up in a conflict, because your interpretive style lacks the flexibility to use information productively. People with a more productive, flexible style realise that criticism is simply a difference of opinion. You can learn a great deal about the other person from her criticism. It tells you what her values are. And you can learn a great deal about yourself.

The most immediate way to increase your receptivity to criticism is to view it as information that can help you grow. Of course, not all criticism is equally valuable. To obtain the greatest benefit from it you must learn to appraise criticism so that you can decide whether or not to act on it. Here are several criteria to consider when evaluating the validity of feedback:

▶ **The source.** Is the person qualified to criticise you and your work? Even if she is, that does not mean you have to agree with her. Try and disregard how you feel about the person. Just because you like or respect someone doesn't necessarily mean she is competent to evaluate your job performance.

▶ **The consistency.** Examining the consistency of criticism is important because it helps you determine whether you need to change your behaviour in general or just in the context of one relationship or situation. It could be that you and a particular supervisor have difficulty communicating. If this is the case you can resolve her negative feedback more effectively by discussing the problem with her rather than just by working harder.

▶ **Your energy investment.** Making the changes that criticism may demand takes work. And sometimes it may seem that the change will require you to expend more energy than it is worth. You therefore need to do a cost analysis, assessing as accurately as possible how hard you will have to work to improve the situation. Going the extra mile between excellent and perfect may not be possible – or even desirable.

▶ **The emotional context.** It is important to be sensitive to the emotional climate when you are being criticised. If your boss is angry or hurt from having been recently reprimanded herself, chances are that the criticism you are receiving is overzealous. The best strategy under those circumstances is to stay calm and respond when appropriate. If, on the other hand, the mood of your critic is calm and solemn, take her more seriously. If someone is extremely emotional it is best to let them go ahead and express it. You have to keep cool, stay quiet and get to the real problem.

My boss gives me a lot of criticism and, quite frankly, much of the time it's not valid. I learned, however, that he doesn't mind if I disagree. One time I

> *made the mistake of not telling him directly that I
> disagreed with his criticism of how I handled a major
> media-buying decision. But he knew I disagreed because
> I didn't change the ad schedule. He was furious because
> he felt that by not telling him directly I robbed him of
> the opportunity to change my thinking. Now I usually
> ask for a few days to assess it and then respond to
> him face to face or by memo. Sometimes both.* **"**

Learning to make criticism work productively for you is not an overnight process. There is no shortcut to learning how to restructure your thoughts and how to develop new ways of doing things and taking risks. It is willingness to undergo the process that yields results.

GIVING FEEDBACK

> **"** *I find all this very difficult. I'm pretty reserved
> anyway. What if I criticised something my colleague
> had done and I turned out to be wrong? I'd have caused
> a big argument and some hurt feelings. I'd have to
> retract. It's almost as bad when it comes to compliments.
> What if the job isn't as good as it looks? Won't she go
> off laughing at having taken me in?
> I find it's safer to say nothing.* **"**

Even experienced working women sometimes feel uncomfortable when it comes to giving feedback. Part of the problem is that by committing ourselves to a position, we sometimes assume some risk.

It is enormously important to provide people with feedback and, at the same time, it is enormously tough.

> **"** *I absolutely hate giving feedback at work, whether
> it's in a formal performance appraisal or casual
> conversation over coffee. But to get the job done I*

sometimes have to criticise my fellow team members. I need to find a way to make the experience easier for myself whilst being helpful to my colleagues and still getting the results I want.

Remind yourself frequently that your job is not to criticise your colleagues but to critique their work. If you demotivate them then you're not being an effective manager or colleague. Evaluating colleagues' work and offering constructive comments on how they can improve is an effective way of achieving improved performance. Having said this, you should be aware that it will never be easy. The temptation will always be to equivocate, to take the easy way out. Steel yourself to be truthful and consistent – not only because that's the right way, but because in the long run it's also the most fair, and the most effective.

Of course, this is easier said than done. Even the most effective people find themselves guilty of not expressing how they feel about something a colleague has done, or perhaps not at the appropriate time. It isn't much good to mutter to yourself a week later, 'I should have told him that was no way to handle that situation.' If this happens to you, you must grasp the nettle: reach for the telephone, and tell the person: 'I should have told you right there but as I've thought about it, it's become even clearer that there was something wrong with what you did.'

Some of us have the same problem with compliments. If this is you, you should keep a sign over your desk that says, '*Say something nice!*' As you talk on the telephone or read memos and reports, this sign might prompt you to express what you already feel but would otherwise have kept to yourself.

It is of crucial importance to give praise wherever possible. The ratio of praise to negative comment should be four to one. Unfortunately many people give out comments in the opposite ratio.

> *One of my colleagues had just finished a major report. It was an excellent piece of work but unfortunately when she showed it to me the first thing I noticed was an error which I then immediately pointed out. When I went on to study the rest of the report I could have kicked myself. Later I told her she had done a very good job, but my first reaction ruined the impact of my compliments. She's been upset and angry with me ever since.*

What you say to people right after they do something well is much more important than any plaudits later. People respond to praise, and if you don't use it, you're trying to do your job with outdated equipment. Remember, if people give you their work for comment they are probably anxiously awaiting your reaction. Be very sensitive to the impact your opening comments will have.

> *Feedback will only work for you if you fully explain the context in which you make your comment. Bear in mind that if someone has worked on something for a long time, the chances are that they will have a pretty heavy emotional investment in it. Above all, give criticism gracefully and in private – public ridicule will always backfire and should be avoided at all costs. Also avoid telling people to come into your office or close your office door only when you plan to give negative criticism. Once that becomes recognised as your style everyone will know what's going to happen and you might as well have announced it over the PA system.*

The following guidelines should help you to give more effective feedback so that the situation does not become threatening and unpleasant.

▶ **Be clear about what you want to say in advance.** Practise beforehand if necessary, maybe with someone else if you are really anxious. It can be useful to write down what you want to say.

▶ **Start with the positive.** It can really help the receiver to hear first what you like about them or what they have done well. If the positive is registered first, any negative is more likely to be listened to, and acted upon.

▶ **Be specific.** Avoid general comments such as 'You were brilliant' or 'You were dreadful' – they do not give enough detail to be useful to the receiver. Pinpoint what you thought the person did that was 'brilliant' or 'dreadful'. For example: 'I really liked the way you looked after Tracy when she was upset yesterday' or, 'It makes me angry when you yell across the room at me when I'm talking to someone else'.

▶ **Focus on the behaviour** rather than the person. It is really important to describe what it is that the person does that you like or dislike. 'I think you talked too much at the meeting' is far more effective than 'You're a big mouth.'

▶ **Stick to behaviour that can be changed.** It's not helpful to give a person feedback on something over which they have no choice. 'I don't like your face/height/the fact that you are female etc' is not at all helpful, whereas, 'It would help if you smiled more or looked at me when you spoke to me' is, as it gives the person something to work on.

▶ **Offer alternatives.** If you do offer negative feedback, don't simply criticise but suggest what the person could have done differently. Turn the negative into a positive: 'The fact that you remained seated when Ann came in seemed unwelcoming. I think if you had walked over and greeted her, it would have helped to put her at her ease.'

▶ **Own the feedback.** It's so easy to say, 'You are ...', suggesting that you are offering a universally agreed opinion about the person when in fact all you are doing is giving your own view. It's important to take responsibility for your feedback. Begin your feedback with, 'I' or, 'In my opinion'.

▶ **Give the feedback as soon as you can after the event.** The only exception would be if you are so angry that you would be unlikely to give constructive feedback. What you say to people right after they do something is much more important than any plaudits later.

If you do feel the need to give negative criticism, then it may be easier for your colleague to consider what you have to say if you put it in writing. That way you can ensure that it is delivered in the proper context. Your colleague can then read your critique in private rather than try to assess it and respond while facing you, which can put her in a defensive position. Yelling at people, public criticism, gossip and personal feuds are self-indulgent. Set clear rules and stick to them.

SEXISM AND SEX DISCRIMINATION

      If you want to see what entrenched sexism really looks like, you should take a look at some Japanese companies. Women in Japanese society have always had inferior status. Far from being viewed as serious career candidates, women at work there are segregated, expendable and employed at half-pay to help men move ahead in their lifetime careers. For any eager young professional woman, coping with sex discrimination in pay, performance and promotion is tough enough in British companies, never mind taking on Japanese blatant sexism, when the women nationals in that country are scarcely able to make a dent in their own situation.

We are still the victims of discrimination on grounds of our sex in the workplace. Since this is now illegal (and unacceptable to enlightened employers), a lot of it is more covert than it used to be, but it is still going on and there are very few working women who don't have harrowing stories to tell about their own experiences.

If you are a victim of a serious case of unfair discrimination you must seek help and support from other women in your organisation, from your trade union or personnel department or from statutory bodies (such as the Equal Opportunities Commission). You will also need to be conversant with the law. There are a number of good books that will assist you in combating obstacles.

More common than overt discrimination, however, is the type of unthinking male response that many of us put up with on a day-to-day basis. Sexist behaviour is more prevalent in the private sector than anywhere else, mainly because there are fewer female role models. Neither men nor women are convinced that women should be taken seriously. However, don't delude yourself that there isn't any sexism within the voluntary or the public sectors: it just tends to operate in a more insidious form.

So, how do women cope with day-to-day insulting behaviour? The answer is: with enormous difficulty, but those who want change must make it happen. You will need all of your assertiveness skills and the support of your female colleagues. When you are confronted with demeaning behaviour, you need to fight back – without alienating anyone. Have courage: once you've responded assertively once, you will find it easier to do it again.

This is tough stuff but it is important that you take a stand. Protect yourself as far as possible by keeping the atmosphere as light as you can and outwardly retaining your sense of humour. Some men are merely ignorant and need help in

Here are some common workplace scenarios and some suggested responses.

WORK OUT WHICH WOULD BE BEST FOR YOU:

You are in a meeting with some external people and you're not introduced:

▶ Assume the role of leader: 'Now that you all know each other, we can proceed. I'm Ruth Smith.'

▶ If you suspect this might happen, ask the offending manager, before the meeting, how he wants to structure it and say you prefer to introduce yourself.

▶ Extend your hand and introduce yourself.

Your work has been credited to someone else in public:

▶ Say, 'We're all working so closely together that we are forgetting what's already been discussed. I began work on that idea last month.'

▶ Say, 'I'm sure that James could have come up with the plan himself, but actually it was my idea.'

▶ Say, 'Actually, you should be addressing me. I wrote the original proposal.'

You are confronted with a nude pin-up in a shared office:

▶ Say, 'I didn't know you collected Botticelli.'

▶ Say, 'Please take that back to the little boys room where it belongs.'

▶ Calmly, in full view of everyone, remove it yourself and place it in the bin.

When your colleagues express surprise that your work is good:

▶ Thank them for noticing.

▶ Say, 'I appreciate your praise: Jane hires only the best lawyers.'

▶ Say, 'Thank you. Now I suggest that we let the firm/client/competition know just how good it is.'

The coffee arrives in a meeting and the convenor says, 'Jean, you obviously should be mother' (you are the only woman in the room):

▶ Sit stock still, brazen out the embarrassed silence and wait for one of the boys to pour.

▶ Say, 'I think that Mike has a much better mothering technique than me.'

▶ Say, 'But it must be Father's Day sometimes.'

You are told a sexist and demeaning story:

▶ Say, 'Why did you tell that to me?'

▶ Say, 'I haven't heard a pathetic joke like that since I was in the playground.'

▶ Without saying why, excuse yourself for a brief, but noticeable, period of time.

coming up to acceptable standards of behaviour. There is no point in making an enemy until you've ascertained whether you are dealing with ignorance or real sexism.

> *Being both Irish and a woman, I get fairly regular comments and innuendo about my intellectual capabilities. Over the years, I've developed a strategy of using humour to disarm whilst still getting the message across. It gives me more control over the situation and I'm also much less likely to suffer the 'uptight feminist' label. I know it's far from ideal but at least those situations don't totally erode my confidence any more.*

SEXUAL HARASSMENT

Sexual harassment is just about the most serious and harrowing form of conflict in the workplace and is very difficult to deal with constructively.

A broad definition of sexual harassment would include repeated and unwanted verbal or sexual advances, sexually explicit derogatory statements or sexually discriminating remarks made by someone which are offensive to the worker involved. Anything of this type will cause the woman to feel threatened, humiliated, patronised or harassed, and will interfere with her work performance, undermine her job security and create a threatening or intimidating work environment.

Sexual harassment can take many forms, including leering, embarrassing remarks or jokes, unwelcome comments about dress or appearance, deliberate abuse, ridicule, the offensive use of pin-ups or pornographic pictures, repeated or unwanted physical contact, demands for sexual favours, or physical assaults. The key factors are that it is unwanted and persistent.

One thing must be made clear here: women are not at fault. Provocative dressing and/or behaviour, or oversensitivity to sexual jokes are not the causes of sexual harassment. Office romances that have gone sour are not the source of complaints of sexual harassment. Men harass women not through high spirits, flirtatiousness, excessive hormonal activity or sexual desire but in order to bully and humiliate us. The harasser wants a victim, not a playmate, and a woman modest in dress, make-up and comportment is just as likely – maybe even more likely – to be harassed.

Even in the 1990s, harassment is quite widespread. In general (although not always) the old prey on the young and the powerful on the less powerful. A female subordinate under thirty-four being harassed by a male over thirty-five is the most common scenario. There are a large proportion of victims in the eighteen-to-twenty-four age bracket and we owe it to our young colleagues to look out for them if we work with a known offender.

A relatively few individuals may be responsible for a hefty percentage of harassment cases. Chronic harassers – men who bully one woman after another – share a common goal: intimidation. These men must be watched. If someone is capable of harassing a colleague, they're also likely to take advantage of people in other ways and it is known that workplaces with high rates of sexual harassment also have high rates of racial harassment, discrimination and other forms of unfair treatment.

Harassment also becomes more common when women enter predominantly male workplaces or breach the formerly all-male domain of upper management. The higher up we climb, the worse the harassment can get, since men feel threatened and use this behaviour to deter our advancement.

It is essential that working women recognise the difference between social interaction at work, which involves social relationships *mutually* entered into, and sexual harassment, which is the *imposition* of unwelcome attention or action on one person, often by a person in a superior position.

Sexual harassment can take many forms, and differences in attitudes of workers can mean that what is perceived as sexual harassment by one person may not be seen as such by another.

Different kinds of workplaces can also produce different experiences of sexual harassment. For example, often when sexual harassment is talked about it is in the context of the office, where there is a clear-cut division of status between female secretarial staff and male management. There are, however, many other instances of sexual harassment. For instance, teachers and other workers dealing with young people can face sexual harassment from them.

The common link is that the action is unwanted by the woman. Sexual harassment is a display of power over the recipient and is designed to undermine, isolate and degrade that person as a worker. Sexual harassment also undermines any attempt to achieve equality for women workers within a workplace.

Dealing with harassment as an individual woman takes real guts. The best thing to do is to let the perpetrator know – loud and clear – that if the behaviour doesn't stop, you will turn him in. Bullies can only operate if they are allowed to bully.

> Trying to ignore the problem is the most common response. A disapproving look or turning away in disgust seems a bit inadequate but most women were conditioned to never make a scene so it is entirely understandable. However, in almost every case, a firm "no" will work better than ignoring the problem.

It is very easy to advise women to be assertive but very tough to actually do it. This is because most victims are in fairly powerless situations, where they are already isolated and alone. After all, he wouldn't be harassing you if he didn't think he could get away with it. The most common scenario is that nobody will believe you or take you seriously when you tell them and this further undermines your confidence. If you are able to document harassment – in dated written notes or on cassette (or even videotape) – it will help you, even if you don't intend to report it. If the situation escalates later and you're forced to take action, you will need evidence of the problem. One woman was able to win a case by leaving her dictaphone on in the office during an incident. Even if you never report the incident, gaining some control over the situation through documentation will help to preserve your self-esteem.

> *When you're being bullied, it makes you feel inadequate. It tells you things you're not very proud of, like accepting what's happening to you even though you know it's wrong. But it's a trap. Because you have to earn a living, you don't tell. And because you don't tell, it just gets worse and worse.*

Confronting an individual and making it clear that you will not put up with this behaviour and, if necessary, will seek redress is almost always the best course. Take up the issue as soon as possible. If you feel too intimidated to do so on the spot, tackle it the next day. Don't wait too long. If you allow yourself to become a victim without saying anything, the situation can escalate. And, for your own self-esteem, you need to know that you have tried to change the situation. A threat of redress is usually enough to stop the harassment in its tracks. Filing a complaint is a gruelling process, to be avoided if at all possible (although if you do have to lodge a complaint do not despair, the law is on your side and there are a number of organisations that will support you).

Obviously, it is better to enlist the support of your organisation well before you need to get into any confrontational encounters. Sexual harassment is a subject many companies feel uncomfortable with and tend to ignore. A recent survey showed that the vast majority (88%) of companies had no formal policy on harassment at work. Even worse, more than half of them said the harasser never faces dismissal and it is the victim who is most likely to be relocated to another job.

Despite legislative changes, the issue of sexual harassment remains largely neglected. You may well have to take the lead in getting your organisation to face up to the issue. You could contact the National Harassment Network for support or work with your personnel manager to institute policies and procedures for dealing with sexual harassment in your organisation.

This is one area of conflict at work which is very difficult to deal with positively. The General Institute of Personnel Managers published a report in September 1992 which said that harassment at work – racial, sexual, and other types – is on the increase. This increase will not be stemmed unless all of us who are affected take a stand. If you are being victimised by a man, ask for support and assistance as soon as you can. If you are approached for support from a colleague then be prepared to help as much as you are able – you never know when you may need the favour returned. There is always safety in numbers.

10 Harnessing your Stress

▶ ▶ ▶ ▶ ▶ SYMPTOMS OF STRESS • YOUR SUSCEPTIBILITY
TO STRESS • HOW TO TELL YOUR OWN COPING
STYLE • USEFUL GUIDELINES IN THE CONTROL OF
COMMON TENSIONS • HOW TO COPE WITH
CHRONIC NEGATIVE STRESS • BURNOUT • STRESS
MANAGEMENT IN ORGANISATIONS

Everyone suffers from stress.

The most quoted example of a stressful lifestyle is that of the high powered executive business man with endless meetings to attend and planes to catch. The fact is that this caricature (if he still exists) is likely to be a lot less stressed and a great deal better supported than the working woman needing to prove herself in a junior position in a male dominated office.

The bad news is that stress is to be found in every sphere of our lives and that we women generally get more than our share since our lives are (by and large) more complicated than those of our male counterparts.

The good news is that we are better equipped and are more inclined than men to find ways to deal with stress. Women are much more open to learning ways that will help them to be effective and efficient – particularly at work.

Stress, in itself, is neutral. It is how we react to it that makes it a positive or negative force in our lives. In fact, too little stress can be as bad for you as too much, leaving you feeling lethargic and depressed. You need stress to help you write that report on time; to force you to review your presentation again and again until it's perfect; to ensure that your estimates for next year's budget are right. This sort of stress is considered to be positive. When the situation motivates us to think clearly, act decisively and feel challenged – it leads to change in our lives and encourages us to achieve.

When a situation induces chronic anxiety or hostility, however, when we feel threatened rather than challenged, when we become obsessed – that is negative stress. If negative stress is not quickly diffused, it brings a long list of troubles. Creative stress management requires preventing short-term stress from becoming chronic and long-term.

How we respond to a potentially stressful situation (known as a *stressor*) is influenced by two factors: our general approach to life and how many stressors reign down on us at once. What is important to remember is that learning to manage the stress in your life can lower your susceptibility to its debilitating effects. Research overwhelmingly shows that we can learn to change our approach and thus convert negative stressors into positive ones.

There is an optimum level of stress compatible with health, both mental and physical. The art is to live a full life with a minimum of wear and tear, to live more intelligently. Resourceful working women will turn potentially damaging stress into high achieving energy. This chapter deals with stress as it affects you at work and how to channel that stress into tangible achievement.

SYMPTOMS OF STRESS

Stress produces a whole array of both physical and psychological symptoms. In the workplace, however, the emphasis tends to be on physical manifestations.

For generations, men have had physical ailments which are a direct result of stress in work and no one thought any the less of them. Dying of a heart attack proved how hard you worked. Short of dying, the valiant breadwinner in the grey suit could have ulcers. Today it is trendy to have back pain. Whatever ailed them, men did not complain about feelings or psychological problems, just physical pain.

Unfortunately, career women have picked up the cue. Today we report the same kind of problems as men do. Just like men, women find it more appropriate to report such physical symptoms of hard work rather than emotional problems, because showing psychological weakness is the kiss of death in this competitive world. Physical consequences, on the other hand, are perfectly respectable and cannot be dismissed as 'moodiness' or 'all in the mind'.

Of course, not every physical ailment is a sign of work-related stress but you should be acutely aware that your aches and pains may be your body's way of signalling 'Enough!' to the stress that is causing the problem. Although stress-induced adrenaline can be very positive, when there is no let-up, when the adrenaline doesn't stop flowing, the stress overwhelms the body's ability to handle it, resulting in anything from a migraine to a heart attack.

It has long been understood that patients with physical symptoms who seek help – and often their doctors as well – do not understand that the underlying cause is stress. What happens is that the symptom is treated but as soon as it is brought under control, another pops up. A women with an irregular menstrual cycle may, once it has cleared up, become overwhelmed by excessive cramping during her otherwise normal period. This is a typical stress symptom.

Classic symptoms of negative stress are hives, stomach upsets, hyperventilation, muscle spasms, chronic fatigue, irritable bowel syndrome or even outbreaks of cold sores. One of the most obvious indicators of stress is muscle tension – painful spasms often follow as the initial tenderness is ignored. The exact symptoms depend on each individual's particular physical vulnerability.

Researchers are beginning to paint a clearer picture of the relationship between physical symptoms and stress. Studies have been undertaken on the effect of stresses on the immune system, particularly of the effect on menstrual cycles. Constant stress can weaken the immune system, leaving you open to illness.

> *I have now identified my "weak spot" as my stomach. After years of tests, pills and frustrating hours with the doctor, two months with my homoeopath helped to identify my stomach problems as my body's way of saying "Stop". But the wonderful thing is that I can now control it through diet. As soon as the symptoms appear I know I am overdoing it and I know I can control the immediate physical side effects. That sense of control does more to relieve the stress than anything I know.*

Although revealing your emotions can be a hindrance in the workplace, you ignore the emotional symptoms of stress at your peril.

There is an increasing body of evidence about the link between mind and body in both our susceptibility to and ability to recover from illnesses. Emotions are the vital mind-body connection. As our emotions fluctuate, chemical reactions that can either improve or damage our immune system are released. Positive emotions bolster up our immune system, negative ones deplete it.

The most common stress-induced emotions are anxiety, loneliness, worry and hostility. Go-getters are not inevitably at risk of stress overload as long as they're well balanced. It's the hostility that stress can bring which is a major problem. Hostility is not the same as anger. It's a mixture of cynicism, self-involvement, mistrust and anger. A hostile person believes that everyone is out to get her. Bosses let you down, friends lie, boyfriends cheat.

> *About two years ago, I was caught in the classic vicious circle of drinking and smoking too much, not eating or sleeping enough because I was so stressed out, which only made the whole thing worse. But the most frightening thing (and what convinced me to finally go and see a counsellor) was when I began to mistrust my friends and people at work. I was convinced that they were all out to get me and I was totally sceptical of their (genuine) attempts to help me out. It was like I was a different person.*

Ask yourself the following:

Do you always feel pressed for time?
Do you hurry when you eat?
At the end of the day, do you feel stretched to your limits?
When you're angry, do you sulk and keep things bottled up inside?
Do you always like to have the last word in an argument?

If your answer is yes to most of these questions, your stress levels are getting out of control, making you hostile. Such negative feelings create a downward spiral that leads to habitual depression and mistrust. Try to avoid cynicism. It's unhealthy, not sophisticated. The world is not out to get you and if you practise tolerance and keep things in proportion, you will realise this. You can, with stress-management techniques, learn to eschew your hostility.

Stress researchers estimate that interpersonal conflicts probably account for more than 50% of stressors for women compared to only 20% for men. Women managers say that they worry about firing people, about the personal lives of the clerks and secretaries, and about changing office workloads when it might adversely affect personal lives. They are also concerned about how others perceive them. These are obviously positive and useful concerns, but they are not always appropriate. Most men would not have these as paramount considerations.

> ❝ The working woman's so called "fear of success" is probably better defined as a fear of failing in other areas of life, especially failing to live up to traditional expectations of our role as daughter or girlfriend or mother. Concern with interpersonal relationships is generally very positive, but without balance it can lead to indecision and stress. ❞

Worry is a particular problem for women. Studies have shown that two to three times as many women as men are chronic worriers. Worry can take the form of some faulty thought patterns that come into play during times of stress:

Selective envy (the grass is always greener)
Catastrophic extrapolation (I suppose this is only the tip of the iceberg)
Polarised blaming (it's all my fault – or hers)
Projection (assuming others think and feel as you do)

Merely recognising these patterns can inspire more suitable reactions. We can reduce tension simply by acknowledging that interpersonal concerns can cause stress and by allowing ourselves to be caring in the appropriate setting.

Women are attracted to work environments where they can set up socialisation patterns that they find comfortable. Many are drawn to self employment for this reason: women start over a third of all new businesses in the UK. In her own business a woman can set policies. She has control over her work environment and its socialisation pattern.

SUSCEPTIBILITY TO STRESS

Stress does not affect us all in the same way. Our personality, lifestyle, history all affect what we find stressful and what level of stress we can handle. At different times of our lives, we will be able to absorb different levels of stress. Some of us thrive on deadlines whereas they induce panic in the rest of us. Writing reports is a joy for some, for others they bring on a migraine.

Certain types of jobs, however, are more susceptible to producing negative stress than others. A workaholic lifestyle does not necessarily predispose a woman to a life of stress. The level of control you have over your job, rather than the level of the job itself, appears to be the key.

A survey of 10,000 British civil servants found that the most stressed-out were not the high fliers but the lowest in the pecking order – the most overworked and least in control of their working lives.

Research findings from Sweden indicate that jobs with high demand but low control cause women more stress than they do men. This would confirm data from America showing that the type of woman with the highest risk of heart disease is a clerical worker with an insensitive boss, three children and a blue-collar husband. Since other studies also show that most men are still not doing much housework, such women are under tremendous time pressure in performing their dual roles with little support from others; putting them squarely in the category of someone under high demand with low control.

❝ I've recently been promoted to management and I can honestly say that I experience nothing like the stress I felt in my first job in a typing pool. Apart from the relentless tedium of the work, I was totally at the mercy of other people. On bad days, I could have two or

*three managers screaming at me because of their
deadlines. It was me who was put under pressure
because they were late getting the
work done. I had absolutely no say.* **❜**

As well as being more in control of their work, executive
women are also better financially supported. This greatly
relieves many pressures and allows them the time and space
to set priorities, recognise what can and cannot be changed,
acknowledge their own needs and determine the price they
are happy to pay. Also, more affluent women are able to celebrate successes along the way – treat themselves to that mas-
sage or buy the scarf they have been admiring.

Developing your resilience can really help. Resilience is
recognising our ability to successfully influence events in our
lives. If we have a sense of control and self-worth, we can work
for the most beneficial outcome. Chapter 1 on developing a
sense of control will assist you in building your resilience.

Resilience also teaches individuals to read physical signs
of stress and then to develop strategies to overcome them. A
typical resilient strategy would be when an individual faces a
stressful situation over which she has no control; she should
bolster her self confidence by meeting a separate challenge.·

❛ *My boss used to systematically undermine me. It
was the worst job I ever had – I used to dread going
to work. I felt so out of control of my life. Then I decided
to give up smoking – it was a tall order as I'd been quite
a heavy smoker for fifteen years and I'd tried to give up
on numerous occasions – and I was very stressed. But this
time I was determined to succeed, just to show that I
was in control of something in my life. Well it was four
days of abject pain followed by a perpetual feeling of
sheer triumph. This was much helped by the fact that my
boss smoked forty a day and was forever trying
unsuccessfully to kick the habit. That was five years ago*

HOW SUSCEPTIBLE TO STRESS ARE YOU?

I sometimes climb stairs rather than take the lift   TRUE/FALSE

I generally get things done on time   TRUE/FALSE

I can usually find time for myself   TRUE/FALSE

I enjoy receiving compliments   TRUE/FALSE

On average, I get seven to eight hours
sleep a night   TRUE/FALSE

I know what's important to me   TRUE/FALSE

I do regular exercise   TRUE/FALSE

When I'm annoyed, I will say so   TRUE/FALSE

I'm prepared to give my opinion   TRUE/FALSE

I generally know why I'm doing what I'm doing   TRUE/FALSE

My body weight is right for my size   TRUE/FALSE

I really try to see my plans through   TRUE/FALSE

I can start conversations with people
I don't know   TRUE/FALSE

I take responsibility for my decisions   TRUE/FALSE

I eat regular meals   TRUE/FALSE

I find it easy to say 'thanks' to someone
who's been helpful   TRUE/FALSE

I am not afraid to make mistakes   TRUE/FALSE

I can ask for help when I need it   TRUE/FALSE

I find it easier to confront difficulties than
to avoid them   TRUE/FALSE

I can have a laugh with my friends   TRUE/FALSE

and I'm still not smoking. The day I took control was the day I started to cope with that bastard. 🙶

Women in non-traditional jobs are also more susceptible to stress. With no or few female work colleagues and, more importantly, few female role models, women in traditionally male working environments can feel particularly vulnerable and isolated.

Try the exercise on page 227 to see whether your approach to life means you are overly susceptible to stress. Count up the number of 'false' responses you have. If you score more than fifteen, you are highly susceptible to stress and it may take little to push you to chronic stress levels. You really need to look at your approach to life and try to change your lifestyle and perceptions so that they leave you more resilient and better able to cope with stress.

If you score between eight and fifteen, you are relatively stress susceptible and could do with changing some of the 'false' responses to 'true' ones. With not too much adjustment, you could change your life to a low stress susceptible one.

If you've scored less than eight, you are quite stress resilient. This does not mean to say that you will never experience negative stress but your approach to life probably means that you will experience it less and not as severely as those who scored higher.

IDENTIFYING YOUR OWN
COPING STYLE

Most of us fall into one of two basic stress categories: confronters or avoiders.

When *confronters* are under stress they want to know everything they can about the situation. They question everything and worry about everything. *Avoiders* tend to push things away, dealing with things by not dealing with them.

Which style works the best? That depends on the circumstances. Coping through avoidance seems to work better in short term crisis situations. It allows you to keep emotional control over a situation you have no control over. Individuals who handle stress this way also have an advantage in dealing with everyday hassles; whereas confronters tend to get anxious in situations they can't control or they don't understand.

Keeping your feelings bottled up, however, has its limitations. Experts agree that confronters seem to handle stress better over the long haul: their more active coping style helps them face, and eventually resolve, major life problems.

On the other hand, when avoiders are confronted with a situation they can't ignore, such as the death of someone close, or a redundancy, they often have trouble reaching out for help or finding a way to deal with it. Avoiders are also less likely to notice the physical warning signs of stress and may not attend to them until they become bigger problems such as high blood pressure, skin problems and ulcers. They may not notice that they are feeling tense until it gets out of hand.

Most people occasionally worry and sometimes we all push things away but the majority of us stick to one coping style most of the time. To effectively cope with stress you need to identify your own personal stress style. You can then tailor a relaxation programme to meet your needs. The exercise on pages 230–231 will help you identify whether you are a confronter or an avoider. Imagine that you are in the situations described and then tick all of the statements that apply to you.

If you have more avoider points you tend to a more emotionally-focused coping style. If you have more confronter points you tend to use more of a problem-focused style. Knowing your coping style will help you to select suitable tactics for managing your stress levels.

If you are an avoider, you are fairly level-headed. You also, however, have a tendency to avoid dealing with things

You have just finished giving an important presentation to a potential client company. Although you were well prepared you can't tell how it was received. The managing director is supposed to let you know in the morning whether you will get the contract – this could seal your promotion. You would:

a) Go out to dinner with a friend and get blotto
b) Go through your notes again to see if you missed anything
c) Take a longer than usual run in the park
d) Ask a colleague how he or she thought it went
e) Go back to your hotel room and take a nap
f) Try to analyse the expressions the board members had while you spoke
g) Leaf through a journal you don't usually read
h) Plan what to say if they tell you they are not interested

It is rumoured that due to a large scale drop in orders several people in your department will be laid off. Your manager has given the senior team an evaluation of your work for the last year. The decision about redundancies has been made and will be announced in several days. What would you do?

a) Continue your work as if nothing special were happening
b) Try to figure out if you have fulfilled your present job responsibilities
c) Go to the pictures and take your mind off things
d) Ask colleagues if they know what your bosses' evaluation of you said
e) Push out of your mind all thoughts of being made redundant

you find unpleasant. Your ability to block out the external world can be used to your advantage when you feel tense, since avoiders probably make good mediators. A good avoiding technique is to close your eyes and slowly count back-

f) Think about which colleagues the supervisor might feel have done the worst job

g) Tell your partner you don't want to discuss your chances of being let go

h) Try to remember any arguments or disagreements you might have had with your boss that might have lowered her opinion of you

You are on an plane going to a conference in Manchester. A half hour before landing the plane unexpectedly goes into a deep dive and then suddenly levels off. After a couple of minutes the pilot announces that nothing is wrong, although the rest of the ride may be rough. You are not convinced that all is well. How would you react?

a) Calmly finish your novel

b) Call for the flight attendant and ask what the problem was

c) Make small talk with the passenger beside you

d) Carefully read the information provided about safety features in the plane and look for the emergency exits

e) Settle down and read a magazine or write a letter

f) Talk to the passenger beside you about what might be wrong

g) Order a drink or take a tranquilliser

h) Listen carefully to the engines for unusual noises and watch the crew to see if their behaviour is out of the ordinary

Give yourself an avoider point for each time you answered a) c) e) or g) and a confronter point for each time you answered b) d) f) or h).

wards from ten, concentrating on letting the tension lift out of your body as the numbers decrease. Reading, doing crossword puzzles, watching television, going to the movies or going on a long run are also helpful.

Because you don't pay such close attention to the physical manifestations of stress, a method such as biofeedback which measures your body's responses and signals a rise in heart rate or blood pressure can teach you to recognise when you are tense. In catastrophic situations such as a death in the family, avoiders should seek out a support group or counsellor (see Chapter 4) who could help them face the crisis.

If you are a confronter, you tend to a natural worrier and somewhat highly strung. While your proactive approach to stress is effective over the long-run, you may get upset in situations you can't control.

To keep day to day stress in check, you should set aside a half hour worry period at the same time and place every day. If you start to worry at other times write down your concerns then put them aside and go back to whatever you were doing. You should consult your notebook during your assigned half hour, examine how rational your fears are and see if you can come up with any solutions.

If you have a mixed style you are adaptable. You probably don't get overly concerned by small stresses but face big problems when it is necessary. If you are feeling tense any of the above methods may help. How can you tell if you have chosen the right relaxer for you? The simple answer is that you should look forward to the activity, enjoy it while you do it and feel better afterwards. If this is not the case, then you have chosen the wrong technique.

CONTROLLING COMMON TENSIONS

If you can incorporate all or some of the following suggestions into your own lifestyle, you will find that tension may be pre-empted and stresses more easily managed. Don't try and tackle them all at once, pick one or two that you feel would really benefit you. When you've incorporated them into your life, you can build up your resilience by tackling some other ones.

▶ **Talk over your worries.** Everyone needs to do this at different times in their life. Choose a friend, relative or professional helper you can trust. This may relieve your strain and help you to see what you can do about your problem (see Chapter 4 for hints on support systems).

▶ **Treat yourself.** Escape from the problem – even if only for a while. Lose yourself in a change of scene or interest. There is no merit in 'sticking it out' and suffering. Escaping for a short while will help you to be clear-headed when you come back to the problem. Have a bath, go for a swim, treat yourself in whatever way you like.

> *When things start getting out of hand for me, I treat myself to an aromatherapy massage. Not only does it really relax me but it makes me feel so good about myself that I feel much better able to cope.*

▶ **Learn to accept what you cannot change.** To ignore this leads to unhappiness, cynicism and bitterness.

▶ **Deal with one thing at a time.** Select the most urgent task first and get on with it. Forget the rest for the time being. This will help you to achieve something and the other tasks will seem easier when you get round to them. Tension and worry make even an ordinary day seem unbearable. This need not be a permanent state.

▶ **Agree with somebody.** Life should not be a constant battleground; avoid entrenched interpersonal conflicts.

▶ **Manage your time better** (Chapter 6) and delegate. Use a system that works for you, not against you; take one thing at a time and beware of overdoing workaholic behaviour; create time buffers to deal with unexpected emergencies.

▶ **Plan ahead.** By saying No now you may prevent too much pressure building up in the future.

▶ **Try not to be a perfectionist** in everything. If you expect too much of yourself all the time you can create a constant state of worry and anxiety. Decide which things you do well and put your major effort into these first.

▶ **Plan your recreation time.** Allow some time for a hobby or recreation. Unplanned time often becomes wasted time. Make variety part of the planning. This will result in you returning to your work or to your problem with a fresher outlook.

▶ **Exercise is a brilliant de-stressor.** It reduces the level of adrenaline released by pressure or anger, produces 'good mood' agents (endorphins) in the brain and leads to a sense of well-being and relaxation (some individuals even become addicted to exercise).

▶ **Learn methods of relaxation.** You are aiming to be in control of your body and learning how to counteract tension and anxiety. This will result in you unlocking tension in every part of your body and even preventing tension in the future. Experts recommend massages, sex, hot baths or deep relaxation, though perhaps not all at once!

▶ **Avoid addictive substances.** Too much nicotine, alcohol, coffee or tranquillisers will only make the situation worse.

▶ **Get enough sleep.** Rest to recharge your batteries. Sleep not only breaks the cycle but it can also strengthen the immune system. Sleeping pills are unnecessary if your lifestyle can be changed. Know when you are tired and do something about it; it is difficult to go to sleep when feeling either anxious or angry. If you need help to get to sleep, try using passiflora which you can buy at any health food shop.

▶ **If you become sick, give in and go to bed.** Do not try to carry on as if you are well.

COPING WITH CHRONIC
NEGATIVE STRESS

We should all be on guard against negative stress overload at work. Warning signals of this may include the following:

▶ emotional exhaustion with tiredness, irritability or outbursts of irrational anger, proneness to accidents, depression and excessive caffeine and alcohol consumption

▶ low productivity accompanied by feelings of low achievement, high absenteeism and a high sickness rate

▶ depersonalisation – treating individuals as if they are objects.

Physical symptoms of stress are becoming so common that some individuals are tuned into the underlying cause at the first hint of an ailment, be it an allergic reaction or a tense shoulder. Instead of simply reaching for an antihistamine or calling a masseuse (although both of these will help with the immediate problem), the smarter response is to analyse the stressor and then to do something about it. If you can't get rid of the problem, then at least you can learn how to change your response to it. This might change your health or even save your life. Above all, you need to avoid burnout.

Although many of the stresses in life can be put to good use – and lead to solutions – it doesn't always happen that way, even with all the right physiological gambits in play. Sometimes stress is a way of hanging on. To determine whether stress at work has become chronic, look for signs of the four Ds:

Dependency needs increase
Decision-making is difficult
Depression dominates the emotions
Disorganisation – even panic – sets in.

BURNOUT

Burnout develops when an individual works too hard for too long in a high-pressure environment and ignores or fails to recognise the warning signs. The burnout victim is exhausted on all levels – physical, emotional and attitudinal. Burnout knows no age or status limits: it can affect the idealistic trainee, the struggling junior executive or the managing director.

Situations which lead to burnout are often characterised by the fact that they:

▶ Are repetitive or prolonged
▶ Engender enormous burdens
▶ Promise great success but make attaining it difficult
▶ Expose the person to risk of attack for doing their job, without providing a way for them to fight back
▶ Arouse deep emotions – sorrow, fear, despair, helplessness, pity, rage. To survive, the person tries to harden their 'outer shell' to contain feelings
▶ Arouse a painful, inescapable sense of inadequacy and often of guilt
▶ Leave the person feeling that no one knows, let alone cares, what price they are paying, what punishment they are absorbing

People at risk of burnout tend to feel indispensable, have high levels of energy but don't know when to stop, have high expectations of themselves and others but are poor delegators. They live with their foot constantly on the accelerator; they

All of these symptoms are normal unless they do not subside in time. If they don't subside, priorities must be shifted, work delegated, management techniques changed and faulty thought patterns identified. A therapist can often help, and it is to women's credit that they are far more inclined than men to seek professional help when they need it.

know where the brake is, but choose not to use it. These over conscientious perfectionists with 'hurry sickness' are the most vulnerable to burnout. They are used to being in control and are the least likely to ask for help when things are beginning to go wrong.

People suffering from burnout usually have the following characteristics:

► Chronic fatigue
► Anger at those making demands
► Self-criticism for putting up with the demands
► Cynicism, negativity and irritability
► A sense of being besieged

The victim is struggling to keep going and urgently needs help. She is reluctant to go to work. Chronic insomnia and agitation have resulted in clinical depression and the risk of suicide. Road accidents and relationship breakdown are common concomitants. Alcohol or drug abuse may become established.

If burnout is recognised and treated early, almost all women will make a complete recovery. However, if it is left to gather momentum, a psychiatric referral may become necessary and there is a risk that burnout can become permanent. More sleep and exercise, a daily relaxation technique and reduction of alcohol and caffeine intake all help to prevent professional burnout. For a more balanced life, working women should aim for creative calm in their day-to-day lives.

Perhaps women's most important tool in rising to the challenge of negative stress is communication. Women undergoing stress in work organisations rely on social support systems as a way to offload the stress. It is particularly effective against acute short-term frustrations and stressors. It's another asset that many women have that men do not.

Women can also benefit from their tendency to be open with others. They can relate an irritating incident to their secretary or partner. They are also likely to solicit and benefit from non-verbal comforts such as hugs.

If you are under acute stress, the **HALT** programme can really help you to deal with the pressure in the short term. Although getting to the root of any stress is the best way to dissipate it, sometimes, emergency measures are needed. If you can do the following, it will really help you through that short-term panic:

H – avoid getting HUNGRY
A – avoid getting ANGRY
L – avoid getting LONELY
T – avoid getting TIRED

11 Managing your Health

▶ ▶ ▶ ▶ ▶ MANAGING YOUR DIET • CONTROLLING WHAT YOU EAT AT WORK • BOOZE, FAGS AND DRUGS • EXERCISE • MENSTRUATION • WORK-RELATED BACK PROBLEMS • HAZARDS OF WORKING WITH VDUs

There is no use having the most wonderful career path mapped out, or the most brilliant prospect of reaching the top, if you do not look after your health in order to be able meet that potential.

Managing your health is about understanding your body sufficiently well to be able to utilise your energy cycles, increase your stamina, beat that fatigue and enjoy yourself.

In Chapter 4 we discussed support systems – all invest-ments in our health and well-being. This chapter retains a holistic theme with some guidance on nutrition, exercise and the issues of menstruation and hormonal cycles. It also deals with some of the more conventional health hazards that women experience in the workplace.

We have taken a positive rather than a punitive approach to health. We are all human. There is little point in adopting a strict, rigid approach to health which may make you physi-cally fit but leave you feeling miserable. Without too much effort, we can all change our diet to give us more stamina to meet the challenges of our lives and still enjoy it. Controlling the use of drugs – caffeine and alcohol in particular – can be much more effective than total abstention. Exercise should be fun and leave you feeling energised, not punished.

Wise working women quite quickly become sensitive to the needs of their bodies as they understand that without their health and stamina they are lost. You will be amazed how, with a little application, this approach will become a way of life.

MANAGING YOUR DIET

Athletes often consume large amounts of carbohydrates a few days before a race to give them that extra push at the end.

Your own finish line may be the completion of an important report to be given at a top-level presentation, or that crucial promotion exam. Whatever it is, a carbohydrate-rich diet can help you keep up your energy through ten- and twelve-hour days as you build up to your big event.

Many women balk at high carbohydrate diets, since conventional dieting wisdom has ingrained in us all the need to cut back on bread and potatoes. Dietitians now generally agree that this approach is wrong and that the healthiest diet is built around complex carbohydrates. Complementing complex carbohydrates with rice and beans, fruit and vegetables and small amounts of low fat dairy foods, lean red meat, fish and poultry will add up to stamina-building nutrition.

Instead of carbohydrates, it is fat that should be identified as the main 'baddie' in a working woman's diet. Having said that, fat is the carrier of flavour and aroma so nobody wants to go without it completely. Fat also imparts texture to food (think of the difference between nearly fat-free sorbet and fat-rich premium ice cream). The secret is to cut down on the *amount* of fat in your diet by reducing your craving for more fat-laden food.

Traditionally, nutritionists have suggested what *not* to eat in a rather punitive way. Our approach is more positive since it emphasises what women *can* eat: it seems obvious that the best way to convince people to make healthier food a staple diet is to give them the opportunity to *enjoy* their food. The approach follows some simple principles:

▶ **Concentrate on what you *should* eat rather than on what you should not.** If lunch is a chicken leg with crusty wholewheat bread and a fresh green salad, thoughts of greasy pizza may not be on your mind. If you buy a really decent juicy orange for dessert, you may not crave ice cream. This will need some application in the early stages but if you are prepared to persevere then you will find that you will re-educate your palate in time.

▶ **It is better to eat less, more often.** Grazing is good for you. Nutritionists now suggest eating five times a day for better health. These five may only be servings of fruit and vegetables. Choose between vitamin A-rich selections such as cabbage, carrots, spinach, sweet potatoes; vitamin-C rich choices such as grapefruit, melon or berries; high-fibre choices such as dried apricots or figs; a serving of cabbage or the cabbage family vegetables. If you eat five servings a day from these four categories you may be less likely to overindulge in foods that are not as good for you.

▶ **Eat more fruits and vegetables *not* less ham and cheese.** Research shows that people who regularly consume fruits and vegetables tend to have lower rates of several kinds of cancer. If you wish to cook them, stir-fry your vegetables wherever possible in a hot non-stick pan with only a tablespoon or less of olive oil. Remember also that steaming is better than boiling vegetables.

▶ If you are vegetarian (and even if you're not) be sure you **get enough iron and protein**. Becoming anaemic or even border-line anaemic saps your energy and makes you susceptible to illness.

▶ **Watch your salad dressing.** You usually cannot simply remove the fat, but you can use a balsamic vinegar (expensive but so different from ordinary vinegar that it's worth it) and less oil. A standard oil and vinegar dressing is three parts oil to one part vinegar, but a one to one mixture of olive oil and balsamic vinegar is acceptable.

► **Explore cooking with lighter foods**, substituting certain non-fat ingredients to give foods a smoother texture. For instance, cooked and puréed garlic can be used as a basis for pesto and you need only add a little oil. You can add gelatine to some soups and sauces to thicken them, instead of using fat, or if you do not like to use animal products at all, agar-agar made from seaweed and available from health food shops will do the trick. Try using corn-starch and arrowroot rather than butter to thicken sauces. Whole eggs are often used to bind ingredients together in recipes, but egg whites will work just as well.

► **Find the best health food shop in your area** and have a browse. If you haven't been to one for a few years, you will be pleasantly surprised at how much fun they are these days. The better ones will have someone on hand to advise on nutritional matters. Take it slowly and non-punitively. They also have some lovely (and good for you) sweets – carob tastes nearly as good as chocolate.

► **Take a vitamin and mineral supplement** if you must but don't make a religion of it. Better to eat a diet which provides everything you need rather than rely on supplements.

► **Keep a careful eye on the amount of salt you consume.** Never add salt to your food before tasting it. The average daily consumption of salt in this country is nearly twice the safe limit set by the 1990 WHO report. Watch for hidden salt in crisps, peanuts, ketchup, pickles and so on.

► **Variety is the spice of life.** The Japanese believe that a balanced diet will contain at least thirty different items every day. It is acknowledged that they have very good dietary habits. Incorporate as many different things as you can into your meals to ensure a good spread of vitamins and minerals.

▶ **Drink plenty of water.** Very few of us drink enough water. The female body (in particular) needs a lot of water to keep it running smoothly. Smart women drink around five to eight glasses of water a day – on top of the other liquids that we all ordinarily consume.

If you feel able to adopt only one of the suggestions outlined above then that has to be to eat more fruit and vegetables. This one simple expedient will revolutionise your energy levels.

After you have reduced the fat in your diet for a while you may not even miss it. Positive nutrition is all about re-educating your taste buds. People who switch from whole milk to skimmed, for instance, often find whole milk too creamy and thick when they taste it again later.

> *I used to devour salt with everything and I thought I would never be able to do without it when my doctor told me to cut it out of my diet. It was hell for the first three months – I kept getting cravings. But it can be done and it is worth it. Now, I can't imagine how I could have eaten things with so much salt in them.*

Many diets overlook the glaring question of taste. If you do not like fruits, vegetables and other healthy foods you will not eat them. Taste is the main reason that people choose the foods they do. Take heart if you really do not like healthy foods but would like to. Taste is acquired.

Small children often need to taste new foods ten or even twenty times before they like them. It may be that the same phenomenon exists with adults. This is partially because we are used to certain tastes but also because we are biologically programmed to like certain tastes and dislike others. Everyone – even newborn babies – likes the taste of sugar. Babies likewise reject sour and bitter tastes but with time and experience grow accustomed to them. As an adult, you can acquire some tastes and change your preferences.

CONTROLLING WHAT YOU EAT AT WORK

It can be quite tough to reform your diet at work but, with a few minor adjustments, you can dramatically change your eating routine.

Many of us rely too heavily on endless cups of coffee to sustain us throughout the day. This is hardly surprising in light of recent evidence which showed that caffeine was better even than steroids in increasing the immediate performance of runners. Unfortunately caffeine is pretty addictive, its effects are rather short-lived and it wreaks havoc with people's (especially women's) bodies.

Coffee can cause insomnia, anxiety, restlessness, nervousness, irritability, agitation, depression, palpitations and headaches. These symptoms can be produced in some people by the equivalent of two cups of coffee a day. Tea, Coca-Cola and Diet Coke also contain caffeine and you may wish to consider switching to decaffeinated versions of these drinks. Most of us are familiar with the 'coffee low' effect, felt mainly in the late afternoon when even the caffeine is no longer kick-starting our bodies, our mouths are dry and we feel tired and irritable.

Nobody is suggesting that you quit drinking coffee completely. We are all human, after all and it is useless to expect us to be paragons of virtue. However, if you can cut down the number of cups you drink (three a day is a reasonable number) and schedule those for before 3.00 in the afternoon, then you will feel the benefit very quickly. Not only are you likely to sleep better but you will find that you are less likely to be irritable. Also, you will really feel the energising effects of that cup of coffee when you do have one. It puts *you* in charge and there is an enormous amount of satisfaction to be derived from the controlled use of stimulants. Women who have successfully cut their coffee intake have done it by substituting herbal tea (which gives a lift without the buzz) and by viewing each coffee break as an occasion.

The following suggestions may help you develop a more healthy eating routine at work:

EATING IN THE WORK CANTEEN

It can be difficult to find healthy food choices in works canteens. You could try asking your catering manager or employer or union to consult with the local community dietitian about how healthy your canteen food is and about offering healthier choices if possible. If necessary, you may have to bring fruit (fresh and dried) and chopped vegetables in with you if you are to maintain your stamina. Healthy canteen food could include:

▶ Pizza made on wholemeal bread

▶ Sardines or baked beans on toast

▶ Whole-grain breakfast cereals which are not sugar- or honey-coated served with skimmed or semi-skimmed milk

▶ Plain popcorn sprinkled with paprika or parmesan cheese

▶ Roast chickpeas or sweetcorn

▶ Breadsticks, wholegrain crackers, crispbreads with low-fat toppings.

PACKED LUNCHES AND SNACKS

Trying to think of interesting and tasty packed lunches day in day out can be difficult especially if you are looking for healthier choices. You could try some of the following ideas:

▶ Pasta or rice salad. For example pasta shells, pepper, cucumber chunks, cold chopped chicken, tuna or kidney beans

▶ Soup, baked beans, or tinned pasta in a wide-necked thermos flask

▶ Raw vegetables such as sticks of carrots or celery, sweetcorn and salad vegetables or mixed chopped vegetables

▶ Fresh fruit such as apples, oranges, pears, or peaches or mixed chopped fruit

▶ Currant buns without icing, scones or teabread

▶ Plain low-fat yoghurt or fromage frais with fresh fruit or fruit canned in natural juice

▶ Sandwiches with thick cut bread, rolls, crispbreads. Chappatis with filling such as lean meat, chicken, egg, mashed banana, cottage cheese, half-fat hard cheese, tuna, sardines, chopped raw vegetables, bean and nut spreads.

BOOZE, FAGS AND OTHER DRUGS

Lots of us drink too much. One in six women in the eighteen-to-twenty-four age group drink more than the recommended healthy limit (fourteen units per week). Estimates suggest that 200,000 British women are drinking at a level that is definitely harmful (more than thirty five units per week). There is

TAKEAWAYS AND EATING OUT

Takeaways are often a convenient way of having a meal at work but many are also high in fat. If you eat them only occasionally then there is no problem but if you eat take aways regularly for your lunch then try to choose from the following ideas:

▶ Baked potato without butter and with low-fat fillings such as cottage cheese, baked beans, ratatouille, chicken and mushroom, tuna or chili con carne

▶ Soup and roll

▶ Wholemeal buns with burgers. Mayonnaise could be the fattiest part of the burger so use salads instead

▶ Beanburger in a wholemeal bun. Sandwiches with low-fat fillings. Shish kebab in pitta bread with salad

▶ Large helping of plain noodles or rice with stir-fried vegetables. Tandoori chicken or chicken tikka with chappatis or rice.

also a trend towards women drinking more the further they go up the organisational ladder. Ask yourself if you display any of these warning signs:

▶ Getting angry when other people discuss your drinking

▶ Making drink a top priority in your life

▶ Having an accident or injury because of drinking

▶ Needing to have alcohol at hand

▶ Getting into trouble over drinking – problems at work or a drink-driving offence

▶ Feeling sick, shaky or sweaty in the morning or in the middle of the night

BUSINESS LUNCHES:

The British Heart Association guidelines suggest that
women should aim to consume only 30% or less of our total
calories in fat and, of course, many restaurant dishes have a
higher proportion than this. Prudent eaters get around this
by holding down the fat content of breakfast and dinner,
for it is the total amount of fat in our diet that counts, not
what is in any one meal.

There are, however, some things that can be done to
reduce your fat intake and maintain your stamina in the
afternoon:

▶ When you are ordering in a restaurant, ask for the
sauce on the side so you can control the amount. After a
while a teaspoon or two will be enough, more will seem
excessive, oily or fatty

▶ Whenever possible order pasta. A pasta dish with a
carbonara sauce is comprised mostly of complex
carbohydrates

▶ Go easy on the wine at lunchtime. Drink a glass of water
after every glass

▶ The effect of even the most traditional heavy cuisine
can be offset by ordering fruit for dessert. Once you get
back to work, a peppermint tea in the afternoon will
help your digestive system to cope.

▶ People seeming worried about your drinking

Unfortunately, many of us feel a bit defeated in trying to tackle
our drinking habit on a rational basis, since much of the
literature available seems to be rather alarmist and doesn't
match up with the reality we see around us.

> ‘ It's all very well them saying keep to within fourteen units a week but quite honestly it's quite common for me and my friends to go out and consume fourteen units a day on occasions and I wouldn't say that I had a drink problem. Mind you, it isn't every day. ’

Unlike changing your diet, which can be tackled positively, it is difficult to find a non-punitive way of advising working women on their drinking habits. A list of 'don'ts' is a real turn-off. However, even though most of us are under a lot of social (and other) pressure, there are guidelines we can adopt if we think we may be drinking a little too much:

▶ Lay off the spirits. Stick to beer and wine (and wherever possible add water to your wine). If you must drink spirits then dilute them as much as you can with mixers and ice.

▶ Drink lots and lots of water – both while you are actually drinking alcohol and at all other times. Water is your body's best friend in metabolising poisons.

▶ Don't drink every day. Some women make it a rule not to drink on Monday, Tuesday and Wednesday of each week. Others give up completely for one week in four. Most of us have less formal mechanisms for giving our bodies a break. Whatever you choose the principle is the same.

▶ Stick to white wine rather than red wine if you can. Red wine contains tannin and countless other nasties which mess about with women's bodies.

▶ Don't drink at lunchtime if you can avoid it (very *passé* in any case these days) and certainly don't do it every day.

▶ Don't get discouraged. The liver is a massively regenerating organ. If you've had a binge then knock it off completely for a little while and you will soon feel the benefit.

Of course, if you are displaying most or all of the danger signs outlined at the beginning of this section then you probably have a real problem and should seek assistance from your GP, Alcohol Concern or Alcoholics Anonymous immediately. The sooner you face it, the easier it will be to deal with it.

As with drinking, none of us need to be told not to smoke. If you are a heavy smoker, then giving up is the single best thing that you can do for your health: It is also the single hardest thing you can do and don't allow anyone who has never smoked preach at you about your habit.

Many of us took up smoking in the wake of the women's movement when smoking and drinking were symbols of our emancipation. Unfortunately when the boys began to give up smoking in large numbers, a lot of us carried on puffing away, unwittingly providing role models for our younger sisters and daughters.

If you do smoke then obviously the best thing that you can do is plan to give up now. There are any number of books, nicotine gum/substitutes and self-help aids on the market which will assist a little. However, this task can never be underestimated.

Don't expect it to be easy and don't expect to be able to do it on your own. Get as much help and support from anyone you can – family, friends, your therapist, your GP – and talk to women you work with who have given up successfully. Be prepared for failure and don't allow it to knock you back completely. Remember, you can do anything if you want to.

> 6 *It can be done. I was twenty nine when I gave up –*
> *cold turkey – smoking forty a day for fourteen*
> *years. Somehow I didn't want to be a smoker for more*
> *years than I hadn't been a smoker and it was getting*
> *close. I had tried to give up on numerous occasions*
> *before but had always failed. This time I was*
> *determined and I had to take up swimming at the same*

time to do it. It was sheer hell for the first week but it got easier after that. Having said that, it was three years before I stopped wanting cigarettes and five years before the idea became completely repellent. So it's a long haul. But it was the best thing I ever did. I still derive enormous pride and satisfaction from it.

If you don't want to stop smoking or if you're not strong enough right now to tackle this area of your life then you probably won't need to be told to:

▶ Leave a long stub

▶ Smoke the mildest brand you can

▶ Put off the first cigarette of the day for as long as possible

▶ Cut down on the opportunities to smoke

Be very wary about smoking excessively at work – especially in front of the higher-ups or opinion-formers. The last thing you want is a reputation as 'Fag-ash Lil'.

The good news is that the damage is reversible. Within three years after quitting, an ex-smoker's lung capacity and risk of heart attack is about the same as it is for someone who has never smoked.

As with cigarettes, women seem to be more vulnerable to drugs, both prescription and black market, than men. Why this should be is not entirely clear but may be to do with some of the themes mentioned elsewhere in this book such as conflicting roles and adverse societal pressure.

Again, you will not need to be told that drug abuse of any kind is likely to do you in. Yes, you can come across women who have been addicted to heroin for eight years, or who have been taking tranquillisers for twelve years, still managing to hold down successful careers and juggle their home and family. However, be under no illusion: most drug addicts don't have steady jobs, let alone manage to grow in their careers. Women who can continue to function whilst abusing drugs are in the minority, they are unhappy and a massive amount of their energy goes into their habit. Energy that could be expended on other things – including sorting out their lives.

The short message is: successful people do not abuse their bodies by taking dangerous drugs. If you feel that you could be in danger from drug abuse or drug addiction, then get help now, not later. You run your life, your habit must not be allowed to do so.

EXERCISE FOR ENERGY

The phenomenal growth in the fitness trend in the 1980s was largely due to more and more women taking up sport as a way of coping with increasingly stressful lifestyles.

It is clear that the most effective way of increasing your stamina, raising your energy levels and improving your looks and health is to take regular aerobic exercise. Perhaps the best way to do this is to join a local sports or fitness centre. Although local authority provision is patchy and private sector health clubs are very expensive, if you shop around you should be able to find somewhere to suit you. If you can, get a professional to advise you on an appropriate exercise pro-gramme. If not, you won't go wrong with a bit of brisk walking or a schedule of swimming, provided you start gently and ease yourself into your new regime. The extraordinary thing about exercise is that you will feel the effects in only a few days. It is hard work but immensely rewarding.

The added advantage of joining a health club or sports centre is the social dimension. For years, men have net-worked around sporting activities. We have all heard the sto-ries of the megadeal being done on the eighteenth tee. Women too can use the exercise environment to broaden and consolidate their network.

 One of the best career decisions I've made in recent times was to join a gym near work. I was totally out of

shape and I've obviously benefited in that respect but it's had a much deeper impact than that. My ability to withstand the pressures in work has been heightened, I've got bundles of energy and I've met a great bunch of women. But more than any of that, it taught me to keep my career in perspective. I joined when I was in the throes of a classic stress syndrome. I was eating, living, sleeping work and my work was suffering. Now, I know that work is just one part of my life.

We are all familiar with the reasons why we should exercise regularly: the physical and psychological effects have been well documented. Some of the time, however, the whole idea of exercise can be offputting because of the punitive way in which it can be depicted. To the busy working woman with a hectic social and domestic life, the idea of traipsing off to leap around in a leotard can be anathema. However, much as we may not want to hear it, the busier and more stressed you are at work, the more you need to exercise. And exercise does not have to equate with shedding buckets of sweat.

If you're not an innate exerciser, try to view exercise as time out rather than a chore. Pick an activity that suits you and your personality. Some people love team sports whereas solitary pursuits are more appropriate for others. You may find the hectic aerobic-type exercises invigorating or the sheer idea of it may strike you with terror. Calmer exercises can be just as beneficial. If you're the type of person who joins a health club, can't keep to the schedule and drops out after a few visits, aim for activities that don't have to be timed. Without too much effort, you can integrate an exercise routine into your busy life.

I've never been a sporty type. But because of nagging guilt, I'd launch myself on a new fitness programme every spring – joining a club or whatever. Within six weeks I can guarantee that I'd have lapsed and the guilt would just build and build. Eventually, I decided it was madness and my fitness programme is now walking to work (which takes about twenty-five minutes) and cycling to the supermarket or whatever. The trick is to pick an exercise regime that tailors to your life, not the other way round. **,**

As with many things, your approach to fitness has a lot to do with your attitude. There are always plenty of excuses for not exercising but if you seek out opportunities that dovetail with your day-to-day life, you will be amazed at how you lived without it. If you have children, for example, you can build exercise activities into the time you spend with them. Swimming and walking, in particular, are activities you can share with your children. Playing football or hide and seek is very good exercise for all of you.

Even if you have little time for visiting the gym or the pool and there is no lunchtime aerobics class near you, there are several ways you can incorporate a little exercise into your everyday life:

▶ Instead of taking the bus, walk to work or to the station. If it's too far, then walk the first five stops or get off several stops too early. You can increase the number of bus stops as your fitness increases.

▶ Don't take the lift, use the stairs. Running up stairs is great exercise. Always walk up escalators.

▶ Don't sit when you can stand. Don't stand when you can walk. Don't walk when you can run. Always stretch your physical activity to a level higher than that which is strictly necessary.

▶ Learn exercises that can be done unobtrusively during meetings or whilst you are taking a phone call from a client. Exercises such as pelvic floor lifts, ankle rotations and pulling in your stomach are good examples of worthwhile activities to tone your muscles. No one will be the wiser.

The time and energy invested in sports and fitness are well worth it. Not only do you reap the health benefit but the rewards will filter through to your professional life. The challenge and physical discipline will give you a sense of self-esteem. This is a feeling that more and more women are getting used to.

MENSTRUATION

Menstrual problems, particularly premenstrual tension (PMT), are much-talked-about subjects these days. For many years such problems have been largely ignored by the conventional medical profession, but at last doctors are beginning to take them relatively seriously.

A survey in *She* magazine estimated that as many as 84% of women suffer from some form of PMT (also known as congestive dysmenorrhoea). Unfortunately, PMT may well affect our ability to function effectively and to hold positions of responsibility. One of the big problems for working women is whether to announce the PMT when it arrives.

Obviously, amongst friends and family, some warning is sensible, since symptoms (including irrationality, depression, aggression, lack of concentration, food cravings and insecurity) can lead to very odd behaviour indeed. Women have complained of midnight feasts, absent-minded purchases, forcing their partners to hold torches while they weed the garden, frantic cleaning and polishing fixations, as well as the more usual tears and carving-knife scenarios.

In the workplace the question becomes more difficult. Whilst a 'Warning, PMT!' announcement might explain our bout of obnoxiousness, it is hardly a good advertisement for womankind as employees in general, or for you in particular.

It is very hard for someone who does not suffer from PMT to imagine how peculiar it is.

> ❛ I remember one day I was in the lab chatting with my colleagues, when I felt as if I was undergoing a transformation. I got it into my head that my workmates were actually planning to sack me. Then when I looked over what I had written in my report I decided that it was all rubbish and that I deserved to be sacked. Suddenly I couldn't understand what it was I was supposed to be writing about in the first place. Rotten swine, I thought, how dare they trick me into writing about something incomprehensible in order to get me sacked. I went out at lunchtime and ate three Wagon Wheels. ❜

Stating the cause might convince colleagues that none of this is personal but it is nevertheless perceived as an admission of weakness. It is also special pleading and we know the argument: if women want equality, they cannot expect to have allowances made for them. The *She* survey revealed that while 32% of sufferers take time off work because of PMT, fewer than a third of them feel able to give the real reasons.

The following tips may help you deal with PMT:

▶ Modify your diet: avoid alcohol, caffeine, yeast, animal fat, sugar and cigarettes; eat potatoes or seeds at frequent intervals.

▶ Take nutritional supplements: vitamin B6, magnesium, oil of evening primrose, all seem to alleviate symptoms.

▶ See your homoeopath or herbalist: symptoms of stress and anxiety are relieved by motherwort, oats, passiflora and vervain.

▶ Physical remedies: exercises in the loo at break times can help; other ideas include not crossing your legs (restricts energy flow), massaging your feet, checking if your jaw bones are straight.

▶ Know your cycle: make a note in your diary of when your period is due. This will act as a reminder not to set up important meetings at that time.

▶ Enlist support: try and find at least one work colleague (a woman, most likely) whom you can tell without losing face. Ideally, develop humorous banter about it.

▶ Painkillers: as a last resort. Remember, the more often you use them the less effective they may be when you really need them. On the other hand there's no point in suffering unduly.

The best thing you can do at work is to try and control your PMT and if you have to reveal it, do so to only truly loyal colleagues, whilst hanging on to your sense of humour. Try not to get so obsessed that you cannot keep a sense of proportion.

I become some sort of paranoid demon for two days every month. I never really used to know what was happening or why until after the event. Now, I keep a note in my diary and check it out every time I start feeling odd. My colleague knows the code in the diary and her "Oh no, it's Mrs Bates, time to lock away the knives" does more to diffuse the situation than any amount of painkillers.

Unfortunately, PMT symptoms may get worse as you approach the menopause which is worth bearing in mind if you are a sufferer. The message is: do not put off finding help because you can just about bear it now, as it may get worse as you get older. Be systematic about seeking assistance and make people take you seriously.

WORK-RELATED BACK PROBLEMS

Back pain is responsible for the loss of over sixty million working days every year and that, statistically speaking, is as if a city the size of Coventry simply had to stay home with a bad back every single day. It loses industry £3 billion a year. Office workers who spend anything from twenty-five to forty hours a week sitting down, are especially at risk – more so than manual labourer and workers.

If this is a problem in your workplace then you should seek the co-operation of your management to take some action. You can treat as well as prevent back pain with osteopathy and chiropracty plus physiotherapy. You may well avoid work-related back trouble totally by looking at the ergonomics – correct sitting and working postures including a few DIY posture rules and a decent chair/worktop at the proper height for you.

> ❛ It is notoriously difficult to sort out industrial disputes involving back problems, whether I'm representing employees hoping to claim back pain compensation for pain or injury caused by their work, or employers disputing a claim they feel is unfair. This is because 80% of chronic cases do not even show up on X-rays. There is no doubt that prevention is better than cure. ❜

Tips for avoiding back pain:

▶ Chairs must be adjustable for height so that your keyboard is elbow height.

▶ Seats must support you without pressurising the back of your knees and be wide enough to allow hip movement. Tilt has to be adjustable (a slight forward angle is helpful but too far and this is tiring to sit on). Back rests have to be adjustable. Arm rests can be a boon but again, they need to be adjustable.

▶ Do not sit with ankles or legs crossed.

▶ Do not overreach to open a draw or answer the phone (keep them close to you).

▶ Keep your feet flat on the floor, put a phone directory or a briefcase underneath them if it helps.

▶ Use a sloped surface for reading to avoid neck strain against the weight of your skull.

▶ Place your computer screen directly in front of you. Placing it to one side of your desk will lead to upper back strain.

If you find that you are suffering from the occasional twinge, the Back Pain Association recommends the following useful exercises for office backs, office necks and office shoulders:

1. Shrug your shoulders up to your ears then push them back down again to relax them. Repeat three times.

2. Tighten tummy muscles as you breath out. Count to five and release slowly. Promotes good posture.

3. To stretch and release tension in your spine: stand tall, feet slightly apart. Place both hands in the small of your back. Keeping knees straight push hips forward and shoulders back.

If any of the above feel uncomfortable then you must stop at once and if the problem proves to be more than the occasional twinge, seek professional help and guidance immediately.

Preventive back-care treatments for employees subsidised either wholly or partly by your employer can save a lot of money. Local osteopaths and chiropractors will probably be very receptive to organising preventive and treatment clinics on-site.

WORKING WITH VDUs AND
OTHER OFFICE HAZARDS

VDU safety is an important and contentious issue. The National Radiological Protection Board continues to proclaim that, 'VDUs are not a proven health hazard', but clinical evidence to the contrary is mounting. VDU-related health problems include obvious things like backache, headache, eye-strain and repetitive strain injury (RSI). In addition to these, VDUs have also been linked with higher miscarriage rates, birth deformities, skin and eye problems. You should always be cautious and take adequate protective precautions when working with these machines.

There are a number of things that you can do to minimise your exposure to potential hazards caused by working with VDUs:

▶ Don't use your screen for more than four hours a day if possible.

▶ Adjust for brightness and contrast every time you switch on.

▶ Take a break every hour.

▶ Don't wear rubber soled shoes or trainers; they will increase static.

▶ Have regular eye tests

▶ Install an anti-static earth screen (available from most computer suppliers)

▶ Fit an earthed, anti-static mat to put under your VDU, keyboard and computer.

▶ Keep an ioniser on your desk.

Repetitive strain injury is a general term for a large group of muscular skeletal problems of the upper limbs (neck, shoulder, arm, elbow, wrist, fingers) and includes things like tennis elbow and tendinitis. The trigger is overuse of soft tissues like muscles and tendons as a result of repetitive movements and is prevalent amongst journalists, VDU users and programmers.

Apart from pain, symptoms include weakness in the affected parts, tingling, swelling and numbness. Preventive measures include regular rests from keyboard work and a careful look at your work practices, seating, desk layout and general ergonomic design, otherwise these symptoms will probably recur.

Your eyes are at risk from fluorescent lights and a dry atmosphere with low humidity as well as from VDUs. The best sort of lighting is daylight. Failing that, up-lighters reflecting soft light off the ceilings, or the new flicker-free fluorescent casings and tubes for the ubiquitous office strip light are best. The flicker-free principle is that the flicker to and fro is too fast for the human eye to register so that the result is fewer work headaches for those who are sensitive to this. The tubes and fitting cost twice as much as ordinary ones but are 30% cheaper to run and pay for themselves within a couple of years. Both Philips and Thorn do these high-frequency ballasts and tubes.

Try keeping a glass of water (or better still, a vase of flowers) on your desk to help with the humidity. If you have an office humidifier, don't let it go above 40–50% and avoid bugs being circulated around the building by insisting that it is cleaned out every two to three months. If it one of those portable units, this ought to be done every day. One in thirty-three offices workers is thought to suffer from humidifier fever thanks to dirty units.

12 Dressing for Success

▶ ▶ ▶ ▶ ▶ BUILDING A PROFESSIONAL WARDROBE •
GUIDELINES FOR THE BASIC WORKING
WARDROBE • SHOPPING FOR THE BASICS •
ORGANISING YOUR WARDROBE • GROOMING •
SKIN CARE FOR BUSY WOMEN • MAKE-UP FOR
THE WORKPLACE • HAIRCARE

Dressing for work is one of the things that men have got absolutely sussed: traditional men's working fashion is a great example of well balanced-dressing.

Because of their societal limitations and their more rational approach to clothes, men seem to work on a smaller wardrobe scale than women, based on logic and necessity. They collect clothes with a long-term view. They maintain a small wardrobe, which encourages a consistent individual style more naturally than an extensive wardrobe of unrelated categories.

This chapter borrows this approach by introducing the concept of the basic working wardrobe for women.

With a basic wardrobe the key has to be versatility. You need maximum options from a minimum amount of clothes. Think about how you would pack a suitcase in order to cover every possible eventuality. Limited space forces forward planning and precise organisation which means you prune the selection down to versatile and favourite separates.

How you look *is* important to your career. Don't ever think it isn't. Your inner self is armoured and complemented by your outer presentation. Your image at work begins with the visual impression that you make.

It isn't for nothing that the neglect of the outer self is listed as one of the classic symptoms of depression. To be well turned out is both a mark of healthy self-respect and a sign of respect to those with whom you interact.

There are, however, many approaches to being well turned out. It could mean a tailored outfit and little make up, more casual clothes teamed with a pristine haircut: the important thing is that you have considered your impact. It is not the specific components that count but the whole, or more specifically, the attitude you display towards yourself and others.

Even for the most seriously minded career woman, attention to personal appearance is neither frivolous nor vacuous. The notion that women dress and apply make-up simply to attract the sexual attention of men is both false and insulting. Be under no illusion that this theory is generally propounded by men who choose to assume that if a woman wears attractive clothing it is to signal sexual availability. This assumption should be treated with the contempt it deserves.

What follows is guidance on creating an image through your clothes and your grooming that will reinforce your career aspirations.

BUILDING A PROFESSIONAL WARDROBE

It is quite difficult to begin to build a work wardrobe from when we start our first jobs. Most of us have grown out of the 'clothes obsession' stage and are now interested in finding practical, easy-upkeep solutions to our image problems.

Many of us begin with a sort of left-over-from-college wardrobe: a lot of tatty casual clothes together with the odd thing like a good silk shirt that's a bit too large or a leather skirt in a funny colour that doesn't go with anything – in short, a mishmash. We aren't yet sure quite what our style is and when we have just started work we cannot afford to blow our entire salary on clothes.

However, it is worth giving it your serious attention, even in the early days. You are better off having two or three outfits that look smart than attempting to wear something different every day of the week. Nobody expects someone in their first job to have an abundance of different clothes. Remember, in almost every working sector, the big players (of either sex) seldom look sloppy and a neat-well-groomed look need not cost very much.

Begin slowly and take your time to develop your own individual style. Use your common sense. It is pointless to invest in clothes which you can't afford the time or the cash to maintain. Don't buy clothes that need ironing if you don't have the time and avoid clothes that need regular drycleaning if your budget doesn't stretch that far.

The idea that you need plenty of money to look distinctive is outdated. At last the fashion industry is beginning to realise that many of us treat our clothing budget as a long-term investment rather than disposable income. There are advantages in a small budget. It forces you to be disciplined, to think hard about how much you really want every article you buy.

> *When I first started work, one of the older girls in the office gave me some brilliant advice. She said if you can buy only one thing, buy the best black skirt you can possibly afford: short or long, full or tight, but black. This was great advice. It took me ages to find the right one but when I did it went with everything and I always felt confident whenever I wore it. I still wear that skirt eight years later, it was the best investment I ever made.*

A large wardrobe may be more of a hindrance than a help: the wider the choice, the harder it is to establish a consistent style. Wearing different clothes every day is not necessarily a sign of being well dressed. Also, time is more important than a large budget. Find time to look after your clothes, however inexpensive they may be. If you treat them properly it will reflect in how you look – and they will last longer.

Even though most of us cannot afford them, it is worth keeping an eye on the annual designer collections, since the high street shops will reflect these styles within weeks (or if you're really keen you may find that you can buy the real thing at knock down prices in your local designer studio sale). Perhaps because of the last recession, fashion houses are beginning to feature the kind of clothes that career women have all along been saying they want: classic styles that don't go out of fashion at the end of each season. In particular, Donna Karan and Calvin Klein are worth watching.

Working women need friendly, accessible clothes that don't look too wildly different from the clothes we are already wearing. That is to say, women's wear that behaves more like men's wear. This does not mean women wearing severe male-look-alike suits. What it does mean is that jackets and skirts and dresses of last season do not look *passé*. Instead of a fashion revolution every few seasons, we are aiming for a civilised evolution.

GENERAL GUIDE-LINES
FOR THE BASIC WARDROBE

> *When I feel comfortable, I feel confident. That's important because in my job you need to look authoritative.*

When considering the clothes you will need for work, strive for an updated but classic style. As Coco Chanel said, fashion fades but style remains. Classic does not mean boring, old fashioned or unattractive. Today's classics are elegant and very becoming.

For the more fashion-orientated businesses or in the creative sectors you have a wider range of choice and can be more 'fashionable'. For more conservative sectors aim for contemporary, elegant classics. Keep the following in mind when collecting your basic wardrobe:

▶ **Buy clothes to last**. The clothes you loved last year should stand you in good stead for this year; small touches should enable you to update an outfit.

▶ **Be prepared to cut your losses**. If something doesn't suit you, don't wear it. You will look and feel uncomfortable. Forgive yourself if you make mistakes and try to learn from them. Either give that shirt to charity, or if it is a decent label, sell it through your local nearly-new outlet. One woman's poison is another woman's meat.

▶ **Aim to have at least one stunning work outfit**: something that you know will always work for you and make you feel great. This will stand you in good stead for any challenging days when you need that little bit of extra confidence.

▶ **Respect your clothes**. Every item of clothing, from the foundations to the finishing touches, should be chosen with care. If not, you are wasting money on clothes which won't fit, co-ordinate or suit you. All your clothes, shoes and accessories should be cleaned and maintained on a regular basis.

> ❝ I schedule an evening every three months when I stay in and attend to my clothes. You know, sew back on hooks and eyes and hanging loops, fix falling hemlines – that sort of thing. I decide what I need to send to the drycleaners. I also polish all of my shoes really properly. Apart from that I do no clothes maintenance at all except to chuck all my dirty things into my automatic at the end of each week. I never buy

clothes that need ironing unless they're dryclean anyway. I carry around one of those pocket shoeshine things and occasionally buff my shoes up on the tube – but that's all I do.

▶ **Dress according to who you are**. You do not necessarily need to spend lots of money on the latest fashions. The key is to choose clothes that reflect your personality, suit your face and body shape and are appropriate for you.

▶ **Pay attention to detail**. Women who have a polished groomed look with appropriate make-up and hairstyle tend to earn more and are promoted faster. Don't sell yourself or a great outfit short by not bothering with the final touches.

▶ **Review your look**. Make sure that you have access to a full-length mirror – not a cheval one, which may distort your body shape – in which you can view yourself top to toe, front and back, each morning.

▶ **Always consider your comfort first**. Remember that every outfit you wear may have to last from 7.00 a.m. through to anything up to midnight. Avoid tight clothes and uncomfortable shoes.

▶ **Be yourself**. There is always scope to have an individual style, no matter how conservative the sector in which you work. Slightly zany jewellery, a colourful scarf or some sensational shoes will make an ordinary outfit into something with real personality. None of us wants to subscribe to the clones industry.

SHOPPING FOR THE BASICS

Just like our male equivalents, powerful women tend to be well over forty, so the slinky models of the fashion designer's fantasy world are hardly suitable role models. Although women who are established in their careers obviously can afford to

AN EXAMPLE OF A BASIC WARDROBE
FOR WORK

The following selection of clothes would provide you with
an excellent basic wardrobe whether you shop with Armani
or with Marks and Spencer.

1 full length wool-mix coat
1 gaberdine raincoat
1 suit comprising: 1 short skirt
                           1 pair trousers
                           1 loose fitting jacket
1 loose-fitting shirt in washable polyester
1 plain shirt in silk
1 pair trousers
1 longer-length skirt
1 tailored jacket
1 cashmere-mix twinset
1 sweater
2 handbags (different colours)
2 pairs court shoes (different colours)
1 pair penny loafers
2 belts (different colours)
various scarves in different colours

To extend this wardrobe the following season, you could
add, for example:

1 kilted skirt
2 further chemises (different colours)
1 pair culottes

swathe themselves in the elegance of Armani or Jasper
Conran, many prefer more middle-of-the-road labels; sober
imitations of Chanel, instead of the real thing. Many of us dress
as if we have shares in one of the high street chains such as
Alexon or Jaegar – companies which specialise in understated,

conservative office wear. There's nothing wrong with this, as long as you feel comfortable. By sticking with one or two collections, you will at least ensure a consistency of style.

If you're still in your twenties or thirties and not yet in this budget bracket, or if you wish to be a little more adventurous, make sure that you stick to shops and brand names you can trust.

When choosing styles for work, look for an elegant fit (save tight clothes and plunging necklines for after hours, even if you have a stunning figure). Choose classic lengths, with skirts slightly above or just below the knee. Buy good-quality, well-made clothes from reputable places. You are seeking co-ordinated pieces in up-to-date classics. Avoid one-off designs that won't work with anything else in your wardrobe. You also won't do yourself any favours in badly made or ill-fitting clothes, or the latest fads.

When looking for colours, remember you wear the colour, the colour doesn't wear you. Also, you want to be taken seriously. Look for neutrals as your best investment in jackets, coats and suits (solids are the most versatile to co-ordinate) and bear in mind that darker shades convey more authority.

> *I know it sounds very boring but all the successful women I know wear gently tailored suits in soft muted colours such as medium grey, stone, petrol blue, soft navy, blue or violet, medium warm turquoise, soft ivory, warm pinks and peaches.*

If you are buying clothes from a chain, you can 'lift' an outfit by changing the buttons on a suit or jacket – particularly if they're a visible feature. Mass-produced clothes seldom carry good buttons since this adds considerably to the cost of manufacture. Replacing cheap buttons with decent ones will give you a better appearance, lending individuality and refreshing an outfit. A good department store in your area will carry a good range or go to a specialist fabric store.

If the chain-store suit that you've bought is basically good but doesn't look too well finished, it is a good idea to invest a little time and energy in replacing fastenings or letting the hem down and taking it up again properly. This attention to detail will all add to you having a more polished appearance.

> *I buy all my suits from Marks and Spencer but I find that most of the skirts are too "A-line" in cut. What I do is get my local drycleaner to alter the skirt shape and, while he's at it, to redo the hem so that it doesn't look machine-finished. This adds about £15 to £20 to the price of the suit, but it's well worth it as they always hang better and nobody ever thinks they're from a chain store.*

The fabrics you allow into your working wardrobe need very careful selection. Stick to natural fabrics, such as wool, cotton, silk or blended natural fabrics. Bear in mind that 100% pure fabrics will tend to crease, so investigate blended fabrics such as wool and terylene mixes. Seek out fabrics which are easy to care for, with a smooth finish.

Avoid materials that are difficult to maintain, such as linen, embroidered fabrics, fine knits, and so on. Don't buy fabrics that wrinkle easily or that are skimpy, sheer or fussy. Never buy anything that is totally polyester (the only exception to this being easy care polyester blouses).

Skirts: Choose skirts that are slightly too big rather than slightly too small. Not only will they hang better but there is nothing more uncomfortable than 'pulling' out of a waistband.

Fortunately these days, we have a wide range of skirt lengths to choose from. Gone is the time when one length dictated. Be honest with yourself concerning what lengths are possible for you. Consider your height, your proportions and the shape of your legs. The tall woman requires a good-length skirt, as she can look lanky if too much leg shows. Short women know that they look squashed in long and voluminous skirts and need to display some leg otherwise they'll look even shorter. You can enjoy short skirts at any age provided you have decent legs. Don't go overboard with short skirts for work, though: you do want to be taken seriously. You can wear a shorter skirt to work without it being a distraction, provided you team it with opaque tights.

If you know that your legs aren't your best asset, choose longer-length skirts. The most popular hem length for working women is on the knee. Ultimately, however, your figure, profession, weight, and personality will be the deciding factors on the type of skirt you choose.

Blouses and shirts: Seek out classic loose-fitting shirts and blouses in soft colours to complement your suits and jackets. Look for bodies which will further enhance a smooth polished line. If you haven't got rid of your shoulder pads yet, now is the time to retire them. The softer lines are more elegant.

Avoid shirts or blouses with tie bows at the neck. This is a very frumpy look best left behind. Plain silk shirts may have a tendency to look a bit crumpled but this won't be noticeable if you stick to prints. You can't go too far wrong with at least one decent white or ivory shirt in your wardrobe.

Jackets and suits: Probably the biggest chunk of your clothes investment. Choose very carefully with a view to these items lasting you for three or four years. If you only buy one jacket each winter or summer the fact that it costs that bit more won't hurt so much. Don't buy suits unless the component parts work separately, since you may wish to split them on occasions. A good investment is both skirt and trousers to match the same jacket.

Trousers: Amazingly, there are still some organisations – particularly in the private sector – which balk at women wearing trousers to work. If you are in any doubt, ask other women at your workplace and don't wear trousers to an interview with a company that you suspect is very conservative. Trousers for work can look immensely smart provided you have good hips – go for a great cut and you won't go far wrong.

Never wear trousers with high-heeled shoes. Your tummy tends to fall into the front of your trousers giving you a very strange look. Stick to loafers or flat boots.

Coat: Your coat may not be your most exciting clothing investment but the quality, style and condition say a lot about you. Buy the best quality you can afford: a generously cut wool coat looks a lot better than a skimpy cashmere jacket. Treat your coat properly: have it cleaned regularly and rest it between wearing on a proper (not wire) hanger. When you get to the stage of being able to afford more than one coat, invest in a decent mac and don't allow it to become grubby.

Shoes: The expression 'well heeled' is a very evocative one. Do pay particular attention to your shoes. Look for quality leather in neutral tones. You won't go far wrong with classic courts or pumps which are updated in style. Court shoes need not be boring – there are many styles which are fun and fashionable. Your shoes should be the same colour or darker than your skirt or trousers.

Try to avoid part leather and part man-made shoes; check inside and out before you buy them. You also won't get much wear out of fashion colours which make the shoes a statement, white shoes in any style, or trendy styles which detract from your outfit. Grey leather looks dreadful. Your comfort and posture are very important to your total look, so avoid too high a heel.

Handbags: Your handbag should be a good size in proportion to you, preferably in a neutral colour to co-ordinate with your shoes, suits, and coats. Seek out elegant but functional designs.

You won't do yourself any favours with big, chunky masculine styles, fashion colours or bags that are too casual or too fussy in detail. It is better not to carry both a handbag and a briefcase together as it looks awkward. If you need both, try keeping the handbag inside the briefcase.

Tights and stockings: Your hosiery is an essential finishing touch. Choose elegant shades which will blend with your work clothes and shoes. Go for neutral tones in ten to fifteen denier to blend with your skirt and shoes and don't buy cheap nasty tights which will ruin the rest of your carefully put together look. You won't go far wrong if you choose tights which contain lycra or tachel which have a very sheer appearance.

As a rough guide, the shorter the skirt, the darker should be your stockings in the same colour of the shoe or the outfit. Always wear black tights with black skirts. Avoid overly patterned, colourful or sexy styles for work. Bright colours, dramatic designs or lycra that is too shiny will draw too much attention to your legs.

Don't forget to consider buying good-quality opaque tights to go with some of your outfits. They are very slimming and will help you achieve a co-ordinated look. They also last a lot longer than ordinary sheer tights. Look for opaque tights marked 'satin' or 'cotton velvet'.

Needless to add that hosiery should not sag and should be free of ladders. Smart women keep a spare pair in the desk drawer. Finally, you can get away with pop socks under trousers and longer-length skirts (more hygienic as well).

Underwear: Invest in pants and other foundation garments that give you a sleek outline. The best type of pants for work will be high-waisted and cut high in the leg. Bikini knickers tend to be uncomfortable with tights and give you a visible knicker line. Try to avoid this: aim to have all your seams in the same place. You may find that body stockings will give you a smoother line and are more comfortable and practical.

If you buy body suits, ensure that the poppers are covered and won't dig into your skin. Don't go for pretty frilled underwear for work as you will find it difficult to wear it under anything.

Pay particular attention to your bras. An amazing seven out of ten women in the UK wear the wrong size bra. Go to a department store to be properly fitted from time to time – a properly fitting bra should never leave red marks or welts against the skin. Remember also that your bust size will change. Have yourself remeasured if you have had a period of weight loss, pregnancy, severe stress or strenuous exercise.

If you're poor at the moment and can't afford to invest much in underwear at present, you're better off owning only a few articles and washing them through a bit more often, rather than settling for cheap knickers or bras which will give you a lumpy line and will probably disintegrate quickly in any case.

Accessories: Accessories add colour, texture and interest to your outfit and can provide many variations to your look. If they are well chosen you can wear them with most of your wardrobe. You don't need drawers full of scarves, belts and costume jewellery, only a few contemporary styles which help you update your clothes from previous seasons.

The key to using accessories in your business look is neither to overdo or underdo it. The clanging bangles and large hoop earrings can be overkill (depending on your face and hair) whilst the twee pearl choker and gold stud earrings are the opposite. When choosing earrings, make sure that they are not too tight or too heavy as they will quickly become uncomfortable. Jewellery designs should be simple but current. For inspiration visit the department stores or high street boutiques near you and see how they accessorise outfits in their displays.

Belts give a finish to your look. Choose good-quality leather. Avoid chunky or flashy buckles and fashion colours which won't be as useful as neutral tones. If you have a very good waist, you will look great in big wide belts.

Scarves and shawls add character, flair and colour to the most sedate, classic suits and dresses. A large square can work with your suits and dresses or brighten up your coats when worn on top. Choose interesting patterns and colours which will add drama to, but co-ordinate with, your main items. A light or cool wool or viyella are your best investments.

> *I was invited to quite a high-powered businesswomen's lunch last year and I agonised over what to wear for ages. I was expecting all these thrusting dynamic career women to reflect the image of the working gal in the Hollywood films – you know, the youthful six-foot Barbie doll with waist-length hair, a miniskirt, stiletto heels and a dainty little briefcase. What a relief to discover that instead of wall-to wall legs and shoulder-pads, the place heaved with sober navy suits, dog-tooth checks and the kind of dorky sensible court shoes that wouldn't get caught in the grating on the underground. I looked almost trendy.*

ORGANISING YOUR WARDROBE

Answer the following questions honestly:

▶ Have you ever noticed that you are better dressed when you're on holiday?

▶ Do you often open your wardrobe which is full of clothes and say you have nothing to wear?

▶ Do you keep clothes that fitted you when you weighed less in the hope that one day soon you'll be that size again?

▶ Have you got drawers full of unwelcome gifts that weren't you but you feel guilty about giving away?

▶ Do you keep clothes that you know never suited you: those relics you bought on impulse and regretted after one wearing?

If you have answered yes to more than one of these you need a radical reorganisation of your wardrobe.

▶ **Remove anything and everything that doesn't fit you now.** Be honest with yourself. Forget the dream about being the ideal size ten. You are who you are. Accept yourself. A couple of extra pounds may just require a few new styling techniques. Start a pile of clothes which you are eliminating from your wardrobe. Those in good condition and a fairly recent style can be sold. What's left should be given away to friends or charity.

▶ **Eliminate anything you haven't worn for two years.** This will be tough, but if you haven't, chances are you won't again this year. Look over each article carefully. Unless you can come up with three good reasons to keep it, decide whether to give it to charity or put it in the resell pile.

▶ **Pull out the wrong colours.** You want a wardrobe of colours that suit you and work for you. Get to know which ranges of colours make you look your best and co-ordinate with one another. Keep only clothes you wear away from your face – skirts and trousers – that are in the wrong colours. You can at least get the right colours where you need them most – on the top half. For expensive jackets and suits in the wrong colours that you need to get wear out of, use blouses and scarfs in the right colours with them.

▶ **Hang clothes by category.** Invest in decent hangers. Group your blouses together, then skirts, dresses, trousers, etc. Separate your shirts, hanging jackets and skirts as individual items. Even though you may never wear the jacket as a separate item you can always wear suit skirts with a sweater, for example, to double the wear.

▶ **Maximise hanging and storage capacity.** Visit your local department store for ideas for wardrobe systems – poles, baskets, hanging bags, racks, etc. A few well-chosen storage systems can double the capacity of your wardrobe.

▶ **Go through your shoes.** Use the same criteria for fit, style and colour when deciding which shoes, sandals, boots, etc, you keep and which you eliminate.

▶ **Separate clothes into summer and winter.** Keep your summer and winter wardrobes separate, storing your winter clothes away in the spring, and your summer clothes away in the early autumn. The wrong weight clothes add clutter to the wardrobe and benefit by a rest from sunlight and dust for half the year.

GROOMING

Grooming is the key to good looks – a healthy skin, good haircut, cared-for nails will all add a polished finish to whatever else you do. Attention to the details of your business look take away distractions when dealing with people, help you look confident and professional and, unconsciously, signal success.

Nails and hands: Nails should be keep well manicured or buffed. Unless your nails are absolutely stunning and you're prepared to spend the time and energy keeping them highly polished, avoid colours except pale, neutral shades. Use a moisturiser on your hands.

Perfume: Choice of scent is highly individual and the same scent will not smell the same on two different women. Don't overdo it for work. If you put on your perfume in the morning and can still smell it yourself ten minutes later, then you are probably wearing too much. Save the musky romantic scents for the evening. For day, use light floral or citrus fragrances – you don't want to make your colleagues feel sick.

Glasses: There is no doubt that glasses make a professional look intelligent, mature and authoritative. When you have glasses on, people think you're earnest and sincere – and they believe you'll be transformed if you take them off.

There are a number of younger women who wear glasses rather than contacts, predominantly because they feel the need to look more mature. It has even been known for serious careerists with 20/20 vision to add substance to their corporate image with non-prescription glasses. Looking over the top of half-glasses is a well-known ploy for emphasising a point or intimidating someone in negotiations.

> My office clothes are less staid than they should be but I get away with it because I wear glasses to work instead of my contacts: they definitely make me look more serious.

SKIN CARE FOR BUSY WOMEN

A great-looking skin, which glows with vitality and energy, will always give you more confidence in your work. There is nothing to beat a healthy lifestyle to give you healthy skin: you need to drink lots of water, watch your caffeine/booze/fags intake and eat well – plenty of fruit and vegetables (see Chapter 11). Couple this with a good skin care routine and your skin should always look its best.

Choosing the correct skin-care range is a bit daunting if you're not used to it. Make sure you go to a professional who is able to help you make the correct choice. Keep your eye on press reports by beauty editors, rather than on advertisements, to point you in the right direction for a skin-care range. When buying skin care the consultant or beauty therapist should look at your skin when it is free of make-up. Do not be surprised if she touches your face, the texture of your skin is vital to the diagnosis. She should be able to answer all your questions about the effect of each product and why they are necessary.

When choosing a skin-care range, here are some key points to remember:

▶ Never use skin care that is perfumed: perfume sensitises the skin.

▶ Never use a product that feels harsh or stinging on your skin.

▶ Never use a product that contains alcohol.

▶ Be sure you know exactly what you are doing with each item before you leave the beauty clinic or store. Don't be afraid to ask questions.

▶ A good therapist/beauty consultant will record the details of your purchases for future reference.

▶ A good skin-care range will have back-up literature to guide you through the use of the products.

Once you have chosen which skin care range you are going to invest in, you then need to decide which products you will need. The basic items for effective skin care are:

Facial cleanser. This should be suitable for your skin type. Quite often, we have a misguided conception of our own skin type and because it was oily and spotty at fourteen, we assume it has stayed that way. It really is worth the time and money to have a qualified beauty therapist diagnose your skin type. Most likely, you will need a cleansing milk or foaming cleanser. Do not use soap or a cleansing bar as these contain caustic soda which strip the skin's natural oils (caustic soda is used to clean drains!).

Facial toner. This is an essential, if frequently neglected, part of basic skin care. A toner will fully rinse off the remains of your cleanser before you apply your moisturiser. After you've applied your toner, blot your face with tissue to prevent dehydration through evaporation of the product.

Treatment cream/moisturiser. This is essential for daytime use. It should be light and non-greasy. While it treats the skin, it should not be so heavy that it precludes the application of your make up. Ideally, it should combine UVA and UVB filters.

Night treatment product. This is the counterpart to your daytime moisturiser and is richer and stronger to provide more treatment benefits.

Eye cleanser. Search for one that is not heavy. Many are too rich and can lead to puffiness and stretch the delicate eye tissue.

Eye cream. Use it at night to delay the signs of ageing and to soothe and desensitise the eye area. Apply your eye cream in small, patting movements. Do not rub as the eye area is very delicate.

If you are not a regular skin-care user, do not buy all the products at once. Take your time and familiarise yourself with the routine of application. If there is a problem with an item, a skin reaction, for example, good suppliers should provide a solution. Always, however, test the product on your facial skin before buying. If need be, go for a walk with some of the moisturiser on before committing yourself to the product. It is worth investing in a decent product range – quality skin care products will last longer and prove more effective.

Once you've mastered the basics of good skin care, you could progress to investing in exfoliants and masks which are available in most ranges.

> Because I've never been a big make-up person, I had neglected my skin care too. I avoided beauty salons and skin-care departments thinking they weren't for me. Then, about two years ago, I was given a voucher for a beauty salon and went for a facial. Not only was it a wonderfully relaxing experience, it introduced me to skin-care products that suited me and my skin has vastly improved. I still go religiously – once a month – for a facial, mostly because it's time out for me and it's great to be pampered once in a while.

Once you have selected your products, it's important to get into a routine. Instigating a strict morning and evening regime will really pay benefits. In the morning, the regime should be: cleanse, tone, moisturise. In the evening, it should be: eye cleanse, cleanse, tone, eye cream, evening treatment product.

MAKE-UP FOR THE WORKPLACE

Studies show that women who wear make-up are perceived as more capable. They earn more and are promoted faster.

The objective of your make-up for business is to look polished and understated. The key is to select the right shades for your own natural colouring. Also, you need to use today's techniques for applying make-up to ensure you make the most of your own features. You can often tell how old a woman is simply by how she applies her eye shadow and blusher. It's easy to get into a rut, so experiment and learn some new tricks in getting a fresh, up-to-date make-up finish.

▶ Foundation should be one shade lighter than your skin tone as it 'warms' the skin. It is necessary to give a smooth appearance to your face. Set it with a heavy application of translucent powder followed by dusting off. Choose a good foundation and powder that is designed to last all day. It should contain ombosal as an ingredient – this will soak up grease throughout the day.

▶ Use blusher that blends, not screams – either powder or a cream/powder blend, not a cream-only blusher.

▶ Avoid bright or frosted eye-shadow: use only neutral shades for work – navy, brown, grey, olive, peach, soft pink or ivory. Remember that light shades will enlarge your eyes whereas dark shades will contract them. Use a light shade over the eyeball and a dark shade in the outer corner to shape and define. Do not use shadow right up to your brow bone. The less eye make-up you wear the better, and it is vital to apply it in the light in which you will be seen.

▶ Be sure your mascara allows people to see your eyes. Too black or brightly coloured mascara is distracting. Also do not have it on too thickly. Never use waterproof mascara: it causes eye allergies and is difficult to remove at night.

▶ Use a lip liner in a shade darker than your lipstick to give definition. A lip liner matched to your favourite lipstick will stop colour feathering into lines around your mouth and will give a finished look.

▶ Subtle lipstick shades are more professional than bright colours. Avoid wet-look lip gloss in favour of a rich cream base. Don't wear bright red lipstick if you don't have time to keep touching it up. Put on your first application of lipstick with a brush and then blot it with a tissue – this will stain your lips before you add a second coat of your lipstick and is well worth the extra effort as the lipstick will then last very much longer.

▶ Go soft on eyeliner if you use one. The full black outline is too heavy for business and you should only apply eyeliner to the outer eye corner, not around the whole eye. Use a cotton bud to soften the edges.

▶ Finish your eyebrows if they're not perfect. Cleanse off any foundation with a damp cotton wool bud and brush your eyebrows into place.

The basic working woman's make-up bag will contain a powder compact for touching up during the day along with an eyeliner, lip liner and lipstick. You don't need to carry the contents of your dressing table around.

HAIR CARE : ESSENTIAL TO
A GREAT LOOK

Never underestimate the importance of your hair to your overall image. Your hair frames your face and is critical to the impact of your business look. Hair that is not well looked after communicates a lack of discipline in your personal life: people may think that will spill over into your professional work.

Begin by getting your hair into good condition. A healthy diet is essential, as is choosing the correct shampoo and conditioner for your hair. Many shampoos bought from supermarkets or high street chemists are ordinary detergents with colour and fragrance added. These leave a residue on the surface of your hair which will build up to dull your natural shine and weigh your hair down (the 'two-in-one' products are even worse – they really burden your hair). You are far better off using one of the professional shampoos and conditioners available from any reputable high street hairdresser. These need not be that much more expensive – they are much more concentrated and you use about half as much as with a mass-produced brand – and the effect will be so much better.

Alongside attending to getting your hair into good nick, you need to find the right hairdresser for you. Do some research. A salon should be clean and hygienic (particularly with combs and scissors), and the staff should be presentable and friendly. The general environment should feel happy and confident – you are looking for somewhere where the staff are interested in you and not in themselves. It is always a good idea to have a consultation with a stylist in a salon before you commit yourself: any decent hairdresser will be delighted to give you a free consultation and you then have the choice of making an appointment then and there or telling them you'll call later. If you really want to test their skills, go for just a wash and blow dry and observe them in action.

If you're not impressed with the stylist, if she (or he) presents you with problems rather than with solutions (you know you have flyaway hair, you need to know how to deal with it) and doesn't have a positive and constructive outlook, get the hell out of there and find another salon. Never forget that you are buying a service and refuse to be intimidated into accepting anything that isn't right for you. The experience should be enjoyable and you should feel comfortable – if it feels like a trial then go somewhere else.

> If you should see a great haircut in the street, don't be afraid to ask the woman where she got it done. Ask her which salon and which stylist. It's one of the best ways of finding a good hairdresser and it's guaranteed to make her feel like a million dollars.

Choosing the right style also needs some thought. The ideas and experience of your stylist offer a guide but at the end of the day it's your head and you need to feel entirely comfortable with your hairstyle. If you feel you are being talked into something you're not sure about ask lots of questions. If you're still not happy, don't be bamboozled: stick to your plan or leave without having the cut done.

You need to give some thought to what you want before you go to the salon: make a list of things that you need to communicate to your stylist (for example, if you can't blow dry your own hair to save your life, this is crucial information for your stylist before she cuts your hair). It is also a good idea to wear clothes that reflect your personality, that are typical of you and how you want to look. Make sure that you are not to blame for getting the wrong haircut through giving the wrong impression or an inadequate briefing.

A decent haircut will not need a massive amount of maintenance. You will be able to finger it into place and it will look good; of course if you do more than this then it will look even better but the point is that the haircut does the real work for you. If it's a struggle to make it look good then you'll probably only look great one day in fifteen and you can guarantee that it won't be the day of your key presentation.

> I recently had my hair cut very short for the first time. Short and spiky. It is the most successful haircut I ever had. My hairdresser suggested it the very first time that I met him but I was trying to grow it out and he always followed my instructions. Over the months I realised it wasn't working and I went back to the salon and followed his advice. He was right, I look five years younger, but it was my decision and he always respected my wishes.

When you and your hairdresser are choosing your style it is helpful to use visual information – pictures of haircuts you've snipped out of magazines or a style book belonging to the salon. Consider the shape of your face: if you're in any doubt about this, scrape all the hair of your face and draw around the image of your face with a marker pen on the surface of your mirror. Then think about the overall impact of your suggested cut. Whilst it is important to create a sense of balance to your face, you don't want to contradict your own features. Angular faces (square, oblong, triangular) look silly with soft, curly styles and are most exciting when framed with crisp styles, asymmetric and geometric cuts. You don't want a mismatch of images. Having said that, a strong haircut could give a very hard impression: you may prefer to opt for the same definitive haircut but with softer, more broken-up edges.

By contrast, a soft face demands a soft hairstyle. For example, a round face can look unbalanced and awkward with a severe straight fringe. If your face has soft features, frame it with an appropriate style. A heart-shaped face needs something to be happening at jaw level to balance the shape.

Try not to hide behind your hair. If your face can take it, get your hair back for work. Short hair or hair tied back off your face makes you look more open and receptive. Think also about the context: a fussy hairstyle doesn't work with a slick business suit, so make sure your style complements your face shape, your look and who you are.

Give the same amount of attention to your hair colour. If you're thinking of changing the colour of your hair seek good professional advice. Wear very little or no make-up to the salon so that your natural skin tones can be seen properly. If you go for all-over colour you need to be clear that you are making a commitment: you will need to have the roots redone every six to eight weeks (the straighter your hair, the shorter the interval). If you think you won't be this dedicated, opt for highlights or for a colour bath (an all-over colour which will last for about eighteen washes and fade progressively).

Think about whether you are prepared to invest the time and energy to maintain all-over colour, as working women really cannot afford to let their roots show without looking as if they've let themselves go. If you go for all-over colour, don't choose the shade you were at twenty, go a shade lighter. It will look more natural. Highlights or lowlights may be a better option as they disguise grey without the roots effect; colour baths are also a safe option since the white hair will take up the colour about 50% less than the rest of your hair, giving a gradual result.

13 Home and Cash

▶ ▶ ▶ ▶ ▶ BOOSTING YOUR SALARY • MANAGING YOUR
CASH FLOW • FINANCIAL PLANNING FOR
WORKING WOMEN • PENSIONS SCHEMES •
REDUNDANCY • MANAGING YOUR HOME •
INVESTMENT FOR LESS HOUSEWORK • TAKING
WORK HOME

There isn't a working woman who doesn't need to think about how to balance home and work more effectively, whether you have a partner and/or children or not. In order to keep a check on what you should be doing and what someone else could do for you, you require efficient systems, well - thought-out routines and brilliant planning. This includes knowing precisely where your money is going.

Money management is all too often a new area for working women. This has got to change.

For starters, we can't expect pay rises each year. The recession of the early 1990s has set a new tone for how we are going to live. The notion that an individual might do better and better and earn more and more each year even if they remained in the same job with no new skills, was the great dream of the post-war generation. The belief was that, if only the government did its job there would be an irreversible trend upwards and that our children would always be better off than ourselves. This belief cannot now be sustained. The party is well and truly over.

Women now need sane money-management tactics for an external economic climate of no growth or slow growth. Of course this doesn't mean that we can't grow as individuals – we can and we will – it just means that we need to take control over our money and our homes and not let them take control over us.

BOOSTING YOUR SALARY

Work patterns are changing very rapidly. Many of us are salaried but, increasingly, more of us are moving into some form of self-employment or a flexible mode of working. Certainly the days of working for one large corporate or public sector organisation from the cradle to the grave, with the automatic expectation of yearly economic advancement, have ended.

Within this context, your challenge is to remember that just because things have changed, it does not mean that at certain periods in your career you won't be able to ask for more in the way of a remunerative package from your employer. The secret is to know your own worth and not be afraid to hold out for it in negotiation.

Tactics to boost your confidence when negotiating salary are:

▶ Sharpen up your attitude towards your own worth. Investigate what is the norm in your field and industry. *You* must believe that you're worth more money in order to convince others.

▶ Learn to negotiate. (See also Chapter 3.) If this skill is completely alien to you, practise in a safe arena, such as a local car boot sale or an auction.

▶ Remember your assertiveness training (Chapter 1 will point you in the right direction) and use these skills to practise asking for more money. Any feedback you receive will be very valuable.

▶ Rehearse your arguments. Work out a presentation before you make an approach. Stress your strengths and achievements. Don't focus on weaknesses.

▶ Be sure you're giving your employers the right message: take me seriously. It's never too late to turn around their impression of you.

▶ In any salary negotiation, don't threaten to leave unless you can actually follow this through. If you can't, it will only weaken your position. Having said that, if your attempts to gain a rise are continually unsuccessful, why not look for another job?

▶ Don't forget perks. If your boss insists there's no more money, how about a car, travel allowance, health-care scheme or even luncheon vouchers? It all boosts your salary and will increase your negotiating power.

▶ Most important of all: never be ashamed of wanting more money. Remember you *are* worth it.

> *Putting a price on my work is still really difficult for me. I've been working as a freelancer for four years now and I'm bloody good at it. I can negotiate until the cows come home but for one thing – my daily rate. I still find it very difficult to place a monetary value on my work. I know I end up charging less than my male counterparts and I know they have no problem getting it. I suppose I was never brought up to value my skills in a monetary way – I was brought up to be a good wife and mother.*

It is always helpful to show your employer how indispensable you are. Has your role increased profits or boosted market position? Find any way to link your job to cost-effectiveness. If you are a brilliant team leader, it's likely that staff turnover has been low. This, indirectly, could have saved your department a fortune in recruitment and retraining. Become observant: take a look around your organisation and ask yourself, 'Who earns the good money and what do they do to achieve this?' Find out what the system is for earning more. Ask about appraisals. What are they looking for in your job?

Offer to take on a project that needs doing – the new filing system, for example. Approach your boss and say you're prepared to do this at a weekend. Then move in to negotiate extra money by asking, 'Do you think the budget could stand it?' This shows two things: you obviously want to be paid for extra work, yet you are displaying sympathy for your boss's need to keep within a budget.

Generally though, it is still the men who receive the higher pay awards. The past decade was very hot on deregulation, including pay structures. Employers were encouraged to throw out pay scales and replace them with merit awards and performance-related pay. Women have, so far, lost out in this new pay flexibility. A study commissioned by the Equal Opportunities Commission shows that whilst employers use merit pay to bring rates into line with the market, it usually goes to men.

However, the good news is that employers are now firmly wedded to flexible pay structures, and this means there is scope for you to negotiate a merit increase. There has never been a more important time to make sure the gains of working women aren't lost because of the recession.

> **6** I was skint. I knew that equivalent officers in other boroughs were paid more. I compiled a dossier of information on what was standard for my specialism and then I sat on it for three months. Eventually I plucked up courage to approach my boss. Do you know, I think he was relieved. I think he'd been trying to justify giving me an increase and that this was the ammunition he needed. I got an upgrading and an increment. **9**
> And it was backdated.

MANAGING YOUR CASH FLOW

It's amazing how few of us keep track of our personal expenditure. Working women who manage budgets of hundreds of thousands of pounds are frequently overdrawn in their personal accounts. We may have numerate degrees, and even MBAs, but women's relationship with money is often very complex and confused.

> *My husband once pointed out to me that my attitude to money and food was quite bizarre. I'd think nothing of spending eight or nine quid on smoked salmon for a convenient starter and then skimp on the lemon – dividing one between four people, all to save fifteen pence.*

Keeping accounts is easy: all you need is a record of what comes in and what goes out. If you're on a tight salary (and even if you're not), you need to put together the basics of a domestic cash-flow system if you aren't going to come unstuck when a big bill comes in.

Enlist the support of your bank and your bank manager. And shop around until you get a decent service. Weigh up the pros and cons in the same way that you would a potential project at work. For example, interest-paying current accounts seemed like a great idea at the start, but now they're looking less attractive (if you overdraw, the interest charges are pretty steep and now that interest rates have fallen, the rates paid on these accounts have plummeted below 2% net).

Take informed decisions and consider these guidelines for prudent money management:

▶ Aim to have all of your outgoings fall at the same time each month, preferably just after your salary goes into your account, so that you know just how much disposable income you really have.

ANNUAL FINANCES

		Jan.	Feb.	March	April
I N C O M E	Salary				
	Freelance fees				
	Rent from tenants/lodgers				
	Interest on savings				
	Other income				
	TOTAL				
E X P E N D I T U R E	Mortgage/rent				
	Service charges				
	Ground rent				
	Repairs/maintenance				
	Water/sewage rates				
	Council tax				
	Property Insurance				
	Other Insurance				
	Pension plan				
	Gas/electricity				
	Phone				
	Health costs				
	Car insurance/tax				
	Petrol/parking				
	Tube/bus pass				
	Childcare/school costs				
	Hire purchase				
	Credit agreements/cards				
	Food shopping				
	Household items				
	Clothes/shoes				
	Haircuts/cosmetics				
	Entertainment				
	Membership fees				
	Bank interest/charges				
	Other				
	TOTAL				
	MONTHLY + or −				

May	June	July	August	Sept.	Oct.	Nov.	Dec.	TOTAL

▶ The world is now divided into two sorts of people: those who pay off their credit cards at the end of each month and those who run up ever-increasing amounts of debt. If you are one of the latter group, cut up your credit cards now.

▶ Keep only one credit card: that way everything gets charged to the same account and paid by the same account.

▶ Don't get credit from shops. The interest rate is astronomical and the default rates pretty punitive.

▶ Don't leave sums of cash in current accounts. Transfer cash into a savings account as soon as possible.

▶ If you switch to a building society account on grounds of better interest, beware: they are still not as good as the high street banks at routine banking duties. If your needs are simple this won't matter, but if you need more flexibility look to one of the more proactive banking services (First Direct is targeted at working women).

▶ If you find yourself very broke and not clear why, write down *all* of your expenditure in a pocket notebook. You'll soon find out where the money is going.

The starting point to controlling your finances and making them work for you is to work out an annual or monthly assessment. Only when you know how much you are spending on what, can you start to make longer-term financial decisions and plan for the future.

A sample annual financial planner is provided on pages 292–293. Your own income and expenditure will obviously be particular to your circumstances but it is a useful guide. You need to be specific and include all your expenditure and income. Only when you do this will you know what your overheads or basics are and what disposable income you really have. Allow yourself some leverage for unexpected events – car breakdown, a leak in the roof, a friend's wedding.

> I got a great piece of advice which has really helped me through all the inevitable "emergencies". When I'm working on my annual accounts, I divide my income by eleven but my expenditure by twelve to get an average monthly figure. This gives me one month's salary to play with for the unexpected. And if the unexpected doesn't happen, I can treat myself at the end of the year.

If you have never done any annual or monthly costings, do it *now*. How can you plan or know what options are open to you until you have a clear idea of your current financial position? It really is a good idea to keep an eye on it on a monthly basis. Until you track your spending over a few months, you will not be able to make a realistic assessment of what your money can do for you. You may well be amazed at how much you actually spend on some items and reviewing your expenditure over a few months will highlight areas that you need to get in order.

> If you asked me how much I have in my account, I wouldn't have a clue. I'm one of those people who will keep on spending until there's none left. I did try to take myself in hand and I realised that, for someone like me, the only way to have any "rainy day" money was to have it taken directly from my account. Because I never see it, I never miss it.

FINANCIAL PLANNING

Women's lives have changed radically in the last forty years, both socially and financially, but it is still the case that our lives are very much conditioned by the generations of women who left money matters to men.

Even today, in some households, it is the man who always pays the bills and manages the household. In other households where the woman actually pays the bills, the man may still retain control over long-term financial planning in the home.

Thankfully, modern working women are beginning to understand and value personal finances. Nonetheless, the idea that we women aren't quite in control of the more important aspects of our finances is still buried deep in our psyche. We may have seized control of the rest of our lives but most of us still balk at taking charge of our financial destiny.

It is now time to stop pretending that money isn't important to us and that it is in some sense unseemly to appear overly concerned about it.

> *In the drive not to be seen as hard career women, some of us have devalued the importance of money. In trying to give the signal that our career is about dignity and self-respect, we may well have inadvertently given the signal that money is not a motivator. And I think we have even convinced ourselves of that. We can quite happily deal with a situation where a male colleague earns more than we do and not stake our claim to greater financial reward.*

Whether we like it or not, the truth is that money imparts freedom and independence. It is not just a case of being able to buy a new pair of shoes or a holiday without having to ask a man. It's the freedom to make genuine choices about your life and career – to finish a bad relationship, start your own business, invest in training, take a trip around the world.

Many of us will have a broken pattern in our working lives – whether due to children or other causes – and, whilst this represents an obvious opportunity, the danger is that it may place us on the financial margin. Having effective financial plans in place can really help to buffer you from financial dependency.

More than ever before, we need the confidence to take control of our money, to redress the balance of financial power and to start planning beyond our next pay cheque. Thirty years ago it was unheard of for a woman to get a mortgage. Now one in every five home-buyers is female.

The banks and building societies are now fully aware of the fact that we account for well over 40% of the labour force and that about half of all married women go out to work. Their marketing teams are extremely conscious of the fact that the number of working women is still growing, bringing with their salaries the need for financial services.

> **Women could be much better at money than they or the financial industry gives them credit for. A substantial but growing minority manage all the family finances including filling in their husbands' tax forms.**

As with many things in the world, there is some disagreement about whether women need special financial services. Most building societies, for instance, are against the idea, but many financial advisers will tell you that any woman with more than a current account needs financial advice. Tax consultants generally believe women need more attention because of their different circumstances (mainly that their careers and earnings are likely to be disrupted by childbirth).

> **The banks may well be responding more to women's financial needs but they are doing so in a very rigid manner. As far as I can see, they are based on the notion that we will all have partners and children at some stage. I have neither and that seems to be a problem. The last financial adviser I went to actually tried to sell me a policy for dependents because he was sure 'I would have them some day'. I was disgusted. I wish that someone would open a bank for women who don't fit the stereotype.**

If you want to retain control of your finances, it may be that holding a high street bank account is no longer enough. As soon as you feel you have moved beyond this stage, it will be worth your while to invest in some financial advice. Choosing independent financial advice helps you take the first step towards making much more of your hard-earned cash. The next step is finding the right independent financial adviser.

Never buy services from anyone who isn't registered with FIMBRA (Financial Intermediaries, Managers and Brokers Regulatory Association). As the government's watchdog, FIMBRA endeavours to ensure that its members provide the best advice to the public, matching clients' needs with suitable financial services products. Members must prove they are taking all reasonable steps to do this and breaches of the rules are a serious offence. FIMBRA cannot, however, guarantee total impartiality or quality of service and you will need to shop around to find the right service for you.

To get the most out of a financial adviser, you need to spend some time thinking about what it is you want from life; whether you are likely to have interruptions in your career and when they are likely to be. In short, you need to appraise your career and personal goals (see Chapter 1) and brief your financial adviser on exactly what you want. Don't let them sell you off-the-shelf products if they do not serve your needs. The more time you spend preparing, the more likely you are to walk away with financial plans that will suit your particular life and aspirations.

> *Never forget that, at the end of the day, most financial advisers are little more than sales people and you have to be in control of the relationship. Don't let them bamboozle you into buying their pet product. Make sure that you end up with whatever products will help you realise your future dreams.*

PENSIONS

Most people do not take pension planning seriously until they reach their forties. Consequently, the average Briton retires on less than half their final salary. Despite lower living costs in retirement, this is likely to mean a considerable drop in living standards. The situation is more attenuated for women with breaks in their careers to care for their family and longer life expectancy. A twenty-five-year-old woman who takes a five year career break might have to pay as much as 50% more than a twenty-five-year-old man, to obtain the same personal pension in retirement.

There is also the demographic time bomb to consider. By the time today's thirty-year-olds are at retirement age, over half of the British population will be over sixty-five.

It is obvious that planning for an adequate level of pension is crucial. The longer you postpone pension planning, the more it will cost.

> ‘ I can't believe I'm saying this really but it is important to invest in a decent pension. I'd put it off for years because I didn't see the need but as I'm approaching my forties, retirement suddenly became more of a reality. I suppose I had never really thought about myself as an older person. Because I've started so late, I'm really paying through the nose and I wish I'd started when I was in my early twenties. ’

Women are increasingly being targeted as a lucrative market for pension and life investment products. In spite of our growing sophistication in relation to financial planning, there is still a large group who are potentially very vulnerable when it comes to what is probably the most important financial aspect of our lives – planning for retirement.

Nobody really seems to understand pensions. For example, more than a quarter of married woman expect to rely on their husband's pension in retirement. This could be the biggest financial mistake they ever make. Because of the high divorce rate, woman can no longer afford to do that. And it is not just rights to a husband's income after retirement that are at stake. There is also the question of payment if he dies while still employed. With death benefits for final salary schemes running at a lump sum of up to four times salary, plus any widow's death-in-service pension, we are talking substantial sums. By law a wife has no automatic right to her husband's death benefit, so that her claim has to be judged by the pension scheme trustees with other claimants, such as his new partner. A wife may receive only a percentage of benefit, or even nothing at all.

All this underlines the argument that if you have independent means you should be taking out your own personal pension contracts – unless you're in the (increasingly less common) bracket of being in a good employer scheme and likely to stay there for a long time. The benefits from an occupational pension scheme operate in a different way as they are not directly dependent on fund performance. More commonly they are determined by your years of service and your final-year salary. A typical scheme requires you to have forty years' service to obtain the maximum pension, which is two-thirds of your final salary.

General guidelines for pension decisions are:

▶ The younger you start, the cheaper it is and the more choices you have to say, retire early or provide a bigger pension.

▶ Make the most of all your pension opportunities – your state entitlements, personal or company schemes and any frozen pensions you might have.

▶ Decide on what proportion of your salary you want when you retire. Be realistic. You may well have fewer financial commitments (your mortgage, for example) but there are also added costs associated with retirement – health care being the primary one. If your dream is being able to travel, will your pension provide you with the means to do that?

▶ Select a reliable and competent independent financial adviser to assist you in planning your pension and personal finances in general.

▶ Review your pension (and your other financial services) at least once a year.

Given the insecurity in the employment market, paying into personal pension schemes puts women very much more in control, provided we carry on making contributions in the eventuality of going freelance, switching to a flexible contract or starting our own business.

> *My marriage didn't last and I am glad now that I never stopped making contributions. It was traumatic enough without the financial problems – I couldn't imagine what it must be like to be a woman in your fifties and to have to face life without your own financial means.*

There is no doubt that women are at a disadvantage when it comes to retirement. Women's career paths are more likely to be interrupted, not just for children but because it is still tougher for them to get to the top. We can't always get where we want to go with a conventional employer so we are forced to find new ways to work.

Relying solely on the state is a very bad idea, likely to result in real financial hardship in retirement. A woman will need thirty-nine full years' National Insurance contributions to qualify for the maximum on the State Basic Pension (currently about £55 a week for a single person and £90 for a couple). The State Earnings Related Pension Scheme

(SERPS) supplements the State Basic Pension for employed people. For those retiring after the year 2000, National Insurance contributions and lifetime average earnings will determine the level of benefit (currently to a maximum of about £80 per week).

There is a big debate raging about retirement age. In the light of the Barber judgement (which said men were discriminated against because their state retirement age was five years later than for women), most companies have levelled up to sixty-five rather than down to sixty. Women in company pension schemes are likely to have to wait longer to retire. Personal pension plans, on the other hand, allow some benefits to be taken much earlier, normally from the age of fifty.

REDUNDANCY

Probably the greatest financial challenge you can think of is facing sudden (or even expected) redundancy. When your are made redundant, you may be entitled to:

 wages, bonus or commission
 pay for holiday leave you are entitled to but have not taken
 money in lieu of notice if you are being let go immediately
 a redundancy payment.

Your contract, if you have one, will tell you what your employer has agreed to pay if you are made redundant. It will also say what holidays and period of notice you are entitled to. If you have nothing in writing, or did not agree terms with your employer, you will be entitled to the statutory minimum redundancy payment – if you have been working for your employer for at least two years and have worked for at least sixteen hours a week. The actual amount of your statutory entitlement will depend on your length of service, your age at redundancy and your salary. The rules for working out your statutory entitlement are quite complicated and you should take advice about whether or not the amount you are being offered is correct.

Although the shock of redundancy can leave you paralysed, you need to sort out the financial implications as soon as you can. Keep your nerve and take the following action:

▶ **Seek guidance.** Some employers make the services of professional advisers available to their staff at the time redundancies are announced. Don't refuse this help, however angry and hurt you feel. You need all the assistance you can get with sorting out the financial implications of your new situation. If your employer does not offer this type of service, ask in your local library or Citizens Advice Bureau about what help is available locally. Perhaps there is someone in your network who could discuss the financial implications with you?

If none of these apply to you, it may well be worth considering paying for professional financial advice. Time spent on financial planning at the initial stages will really help to reduce the impact of redundancy on your life and save heartache.

▶ **Find out about your entitlements.** Research what redundancy and social security payments you are entitled to. Contact your local social security or Department of Employment office and ask for their information brochures. There is a whole array of entitlements available, including assistance with your mortgage, so make sure your search is comprehensive. Stick with it – even if it is very frustrating and you constantly seem to be hitting your head against a bureaucratic wall. Difficult though it may be, try to avoid feeling that you are accepting handouts. Remember, you have contributed to the welfare system all through your working life and you are only getting back what you are due.

▶ **Use your redundancy payment wisely.** Avoid the temptation to splash out on a new car or an expensive holiday. Try to take a longer-term view. Far better to keep the money to give yourself treats as you hit those low spots.

▶ **Undertake a total financial review.** Develop a coherent strategy for financial planning in your life. You need to take stock and review your finances in the light of your current situation. Remember, you can put a temporary hold on things like pensions, life insurance and savings policies. Don't feel trapped by your current obligations.

> *I put my head in the sand for the first year after I was let go. I continued to live as I had when I worked – in fact, I spent more than I used to. I suppose I just refused to face the fact that I had less expendable income. I ate up all my redundancy money and worked up debts on my credit cards. Of course, it all came to a horrible end. It's taken me three years to sort out some of my debts (I'm working again) but my one bit of advice to anyone who is made redundant would be to grab your finances by the horns and cut your cloth accordingly.*

There is no doubt that you will have less expendable income when you are unemployed and you will not be able to afford everything you did when you were working. But you need not live the life of a hermit. There are a lot of services and facilities that are either free or offered on a concession basis to people who are unemployed. Keep your eyes open for these and write them down in your diary or filing system.

MANAGING YOUR HOME

Managing a home is hard work. Because it is a classic trap for women, housework is a very emotive subject, and almost all of us consider it a burden we could do without.

How do working women find time to work, run a home, have a social life, and still enjoy leisure time for themselves and with their family?

Most ideas for coping with a home are simply common sense and consist primarily of thinking about the way in which you get through each day and considering whether it could be improved.

A lot of it comes down to applying the discipline of time management to our home lives as well as to work. After all, running a home is a lot like running a business. A home has resources to look after, and time to allocate, and routine activities to be covered, leaving room to enjoy your leisure time. There may also be several individual lives, personal goals, preferences and commitments to consider as well as the overall goals of the household (or team).

If you don't live in a single-person household, you may find it useful to keep track of everyone's schedules using a monthly overview or plan which you can put on a notice board. If you use different colours for each person, you can quickly see potential clashes or where special arrangements have to be made. You may also need a weekly plan, to see who is best suited to offer lifts, do the shopping, or who will be late home or eating out. Use this to record principal daily jobs and the initial of who has been allocated to do them. This can quickly solve disputes about who was the last person to wash up. Also on your pin board keep a list of emergency contract and service numbers.

Encourage everybody in the philosophy 'a place for everything, everything in its place' to avoid time wasted in hunting for keys, scissors, sticky tape, phone messages and so on. Some things go astray more often than others. Agree house rules for telephone messages (after all, it could be your head-hunter). Use an expanding file to keep important things together. Each person can have a section for their post, phone messages, reminders of things to do and questions which need to be answered. You could use the other sections for bills to be paid, letters and stationery, special projects, shopping lists and entertainment (including ideas, as well as tickets and brochures). The sections in your file are also ideal for more permanent filing and your headings could include things like receipts, insurance, credit card, bank, tax, garden, birth certificates, passports, guarantees and so forth. Keep a central database of contact numbers and addresses.

Home management is not only about storage and systems. Just as in work, it's a matter of managing your time as well. Plan your time carefully to make the best use of your energy levels. Like work, don't be overambitious in your planning and try to complete tasks once you've begun them. If you clear everything away when finished with, and take things with you as you move from room to room, you won't be faced with having to return to clear up at the end of the day.

> *I have to confess that I do all the organising of my home from my office, usually in my lunch hour. I keep my household accounts there and everything. I just seem to be in a better frame of mind to tackle finding someone to clean the carpets or ringing the gas board or paying the phone bill when I'm sitting at my desk. Most of the people I need to reach work standard office hours too so it would be difficult to get them at other times.*

As with most things, you can cut down on shopping and cooking time and hassle if you institute systems. The key is forward planning.

Discipline yourself and encourage everyone else to make a note on the shopping list (by the larder, by the phone) as soon as they open the last (or penultimate) jar, tube or packet.

Shopping usually divides into the routine and the special. List regular items and keep it with you in case, say, you get time to go shopping at lunch time or get to leave early one evening. Keep a note of things like forthcoming birthdays: you never know what interesting small shops you may find when you are between two external meetings or away at a conference.

If you use anything in bulk (such as bottled water or disposable nappies) investigate whether you can get a local shop to deliver these articles. Find out also what your milkman has to offer: you can get eggs, yoghurts, bread and a whole lot more through him, provided you're diligent about paying.

> *Never go shopping for food when you're hungry – you always buy more than you need. If you're really broke, write a list and be sure you stick to it. I work in the retail trade and I know that supermarkets rely on about 60% of your purchases being impulse buys.*

Above all, schedule yourself time to relax, and be sure to stick to it. Having your own time which isn't taken up with the ironing, household administration or redecorating is as important a part of work and play as your responsibility at work or to your partner or your college course.

Although homes can be as demanding as work, they are essentially places to relax. With a little thought about the time you spend there, you can be sure of getting the most out of them for yourself and the people you live with.

INVESTMENT FOR LESS HOUSEWORK

Your aim is to minimize the effort and free up as much of your time for leisure and social activities. Invest in as much labour-saving equipment as you can afford – view it as a necessary expense of working, on a par with the cost of travelling to work.

▶ An automatic washing machine is a prerequisite – particularly if you have kids. Make sure the machine you choose has a fast spin (1,000 rpm or faster), which cuts down on drying time enormously and is much more important than having lots of elaborate wash programmes.

▶ A useful alternative is to use a launderette with a service wash facility. Get the very best stream iron you can afford.

▶ As soon as you possibly can, avail yourself of a dishwasher. Most kitchens can accommodate a dishwasher somewhere: there are several models that are only eighteen inches (half a unit) wide or there are counter-top dishwashers that will fit on your draining board. This is not a luxury item if you are out at work. Never buy china or saucepans that won't go in the dishwasher, no matter how beautiful the kitchenware is.

▶ Other useful equipment could include food processors, microwaves or electric toasters provided you're going to make full use of them. If they're just going to gather dust in your kitchen, don't give them house room.

TAKING WORK HOME

Taking work home from the office is not necessarily the same thing as getting work done at home. Along with the contracts and reports loaded into the briefcase at the day's end, we often pack the best intentions which can be weightier than any amount of paper.

Certainly the after-hours environment offers a less stressed alternative to the nine-to-five scenario. Who wouldn't rather tackle that report from a comfy chair, with your shoes off and your answering machine on? Many working women maintain that they can accomplish more in two hours of uninterrupted time at home than in an entire day at their desks.

> *Work that needs to be carefully examined – say, legal contracts – I do best in the quiet of my front room.*

If you can't get the necessary peace at work and your home offers a quieter place to get the task done, make sure you view your work from home as part of rather than in addition to your working hours. If, at the start of a project, you know you will need quiet time at home, flag that up with your boss at the start and build it in to the programme. If you have regular 'quiet' work – monthly reports, for example – agree with your boss that you will work the day or morning before the deadline at home. The aim is to be task-orientated about work you take home. Use the quiet afforded by your home to achieve specific tasks, not as a way to put in more hours.

> *I somehow managed to turn my forty-hour week into a sixty-hour week without realising it. I didn't want people at work to think I couldn't handle my job, so I took home work every evening. I commandeered the dining table which really irritated the people I lived with and I seldom went out. Eventually, one of my friends pointed out what was happening and told me that I was becoming obsessive about my work and a bore. Because I couldn't control it, I now never take work home.*

Don't believe for a moment, however, that home is distraction-free. Such seductive diversions as family, friends, the phone and the telly can beckon, undermining our best efforts. Also, for some workaholic women, turning their home into an office extension can make for a miserable personal life.

> 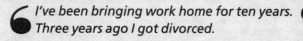 *I've been bringing work home for ten years. Three years ago I got divorced.*

So how to balance the pressures of after-hours productivity with personal time? Bring home realistic goals. Nothing will discourage you faster from even opening your briefcase than knowing there's more in it than you can actually get through.

Give some forethought also to exactly where in your home you can be most productive. For many women the kitchen table doubles as desk. For others, though, being in the thick of the activity can provide incessant distraction. You may find that you spend an hour rereading the same page.

Yet wherever you work, deciding when to get down to business will also affect your efficiency. Some women are most productive in the early-morning hours when they are recharged by some sleep and the house is quiet. If getting up with the sun isn't your time to shine, consider taking out the work after an early-evening aerobics class or on a lazy Sunday afternoon.

If you are taking work home every week, beware. No matter how busy you are, this is a sign that you are becoming a workaholic and your time management skills are ineffective. If you need the quiet of your home for some of your work, negotiate with your boss to work from home for a morning or however long you need. Don't get into the habit of seeing home work as additional to the office – something that you have to do every week. If you do, you are caught in the trap of the workaholic – 'If I don't take this work home, I won't be able to achieve.' You will also eat into your precious free time and be in danger of losing your friends.

14 Babies?

▶▶▶▶▶ YOUR WELL-BEING WHILE PREGNANT AT WORK •
WHAT TO WEAR • NEGOTIATING YOUR
MATERNITY LEAVE • KEEPING YOUR JOB ALIVE
IN YOUR ABSENCE • RETURNING TO WORK •
ALTERNATIVES TO THE NINE-TO-FIVE •
CHILDCARE PROVISION FOR THE UNDER-FIVES •
CHILDCARE PROVISION FOR THE OVER-FIVES •
COPING WITH A SICK CHILD • RETURNING TO
WORK AFTER BRINGING UP YOUR CHILDREN •
HOW MOTHERHOOD AFFECTS YOU

There are any number of excellent books to be found in your local bookshop or library which can tell you everything you need to know about having a healthy and happy pregnancy and birth. Unfortunately, there are fewer sources of advice on how to cope with a pregnancy and then a baby whilst also trying to hold down a job and continue to build your career. Such advice as is available tends to be centred on what is good for the developing baby, rather at the expense of the poor beleaguered mother. This chapter unashamedly puts *your* needs first since we categorically believe that what is good for you and your career will ultimately be good for your baby and family.

The demands on you at this time are pretty harrowing but if you are well prepared you are better able to cope with what's in store. Pregnancy is only the start. Combining a dual career as working woman and mother can be a daunting task. Any woman who successfully copes with a home, a family and a career really *knows* about management.

As a working mother, you will find that you either think about or do what needs to be done, or you think about it and delegate it to someone else. Whichever way, it is generally you who makes decisions and takes responsibility for seeing them through. This may not be fair but it is usually the reality of the situation.

This chapter will help you deal with the pressure of the dual career of mother and working woman. Hopefully, it will also help you to understand and celebrate the extra dimension that this gives you over your fellow managers.

YOUR WELL-BEING WHILE
PREGNANT AT WORK

The most obvious thing to attend to when you're pregnant is your physical and emotional well-being. Working when you're pregnant can be quite difficult, especially if you feel sick and tired in the early months. Or utterly exhausted in the last few weeks.

> It was awful at the beginning. I've never in my life felt so drained, and of course, I didn't look pregnant, I looked just the same – I had absolutely nothing to show for it. I used to get home from work and go straight to bed and Brian thought I was really ill. Nobody at work knew I was pregnant so I couldn't make any special case. Then suddenly, at about three months, I was all right again.

The key to a healthy working pregnancy is to listen to your body. Be very sensitive to your own needs and put these first. It really isn't worth making any noble sacrifices at this stage. To keep yourself going and to care for your growing baby, bear in mind the following points:

▶ **Be sure to eat properly.** Try to have something to eat before you start work in the morning. At least cereal or toast. If you really can't face it, have a snack later on when you feel less sick (bananas are good for queasy stomachs). Include some fresh fruit in what you eat at lunch. If you can't get fruit where you work, take it with you from home.

▶ **Conserve your energy.** Submerge your workaholic tendencies and curb your ambition for a few months. Something has to give. Do not volunteer for any activities over and above the call of duty. Pare your external commitments down to a minimum, particularly in the first three months.

▶ **Plan ahead.** Bear in mind that in the second three months (second trimester) you will have a lot more energy. Accordingly, schedule your more difficult projects for this time.

▶ **Rest whenever possible.** Try to have a quiet sit-down after lunch even if it is only for a short time. Take another breather in the evening, and if daytime resting is out of the question, at least make sure you get a good rest in bed each night.

▶ **Put your feet up whenever you can.** If your legs feel at all tired, throw your vanity out of the window and wear support tights (the new high tech versions are very sheer). Sit down whenever you can – but not with your legs or ankles crossed.

▶ **Cut down on travelling.** If your journey to work during the rush hour gets very difficult for you, talk to your boss about the possibility of working slightly different hours for a while. If you can afford it, get a taxi from the station when you're tired.

▶ **Schedule enough time for antenatal activities.** These don't impinge much at the beginning but by the last trimester you will be going to your doctor or midwife once a week and you may also have antenatal classes to attend, not forgetting such events as the scan(s) and the tour of the delivery ward. All of these will eat into your working day and whilst you are legally entitled to time off from work for them all, be aware that they take up extra time and energy that you may have planned to use to finish off projects before you go on leave.

▶ **Prepare to give up work in good time.** There are countless apocryphal tales of megasuccessful women working up until the hour before they go into labour. Most of them are pretty exaggerated. By about thirty-two weeks, most of us don't have a great deal of energy and find it difficult to muster the stamina to get through the day. You won't do much for your reputation if you're exhausted, and your developing baby needs you to rest so that she can grow. (Most of the baby's weight is put on during the last few weeks – but not unless the mother is well rested. Your long-term aim is for a heavier baby: big babies are more physically stable and sleep through the night better.)

Unfortunately, it isn't only your body you have to consider. Pregnancy has a profound effect on your psychological well-being as well as your physical health. There is an awful lot going on inside you and it takes up a great deal of emotional and mental as well as physical energy. You will find that your hormones have gone completely haywire and that you don't always treat situations rationally.

This is not the time to take on stressful situations. If your normal style is to confront stress at work then try to adopt more of an 'avoider' approach (see Chapter 10), at least for the duration of your pregnancy. You really don't need any hassle: you are quite vulnerable and much less able to cope with it than when you are not pregnant. Now is not the time to prove any points or take on any new challenges – save these for when you've got back to normal on your return.

As you enter the third trimester, do not be surprised if you become somewhat self-absorbed and introspective. Many of us have this experience and it's perfectly natural. Suddenly your priorities are elsewhere and it is as well to give in gracefully to this as it is too powerful to struggle against. Rest assured that you will come out of it again, and in the meantime, concentrate on yourself.

WHAT TO WEAR

Many of us spend years finding the right clothes to cultivate the image we want for our work, and it is a bit of a trial to then have to find appropriate clothes to wear during our pregnancies when we are a different shape.

Chain-store maternity clothes are not particularly inspired, although obviously decent things can be found if you look hard enough. There are some very posh maternity-wear shops but the clothes are expensive and most of us resent having to fork out a lot of cash for things that we may only wear for a few months.

There are also a number of companies (mainly run by women) which offer maternity clothes by mail order. You will find these advertised in pregnancy and parenting magazines and it may be worth you getting a few catalogues to give you some ideas to work on.

> ‘ I found it very difficult to get the clothes right. I thought I was being so clever, in the early days, when I bought two pinafores which I thought I could wear over all my ordinary shirts. Well, they didn't look at all businesslike – sort of blousy and earth-motherish – and very pregnant, even when I was still quite small. Eventually I bought an elasticated pair of trousers and a skirt and wore these with loose tops and my suit jackets. This was much more the image I was trying to create. I only wore the pinafores at the weekend. ’

Tackle the problem of your maternity wear as a special mini-case of a basic wardrobe (see Chapter 12). It is important to be comfortable during this time. Get yourself measured and properly fitted with maternity bras when you're about six months pregnant – or before if you are experiencing any discomfort: you can always get refitted for a larger size later.

At the beginning, sort out those clothes that you will never be able to wear during your pregnancy such as your tighter skirts, blouses and trousers (you may be able to prolong your use of these with a nappy pin and piece of elastic around the button and through the button hole) and either pack these away for the duration or put them out of sight at the end of the rack. This is a good time to have your ordinary suits cleaned, mended, etc. Hopefully you will still have a few things left that you can continue to wear (unwaisted dresses look quite smart with a contrasting jacket).

Check out all your colleagues who have been pregnant before for the loan of maternity dresses and separates. In some offices the same clothes do the rounds on several occasions and no one is any the wiser. See if you can team borrowed clothes with things from your own wardrobe to make new outfits.

Depending on your budget, buy one or two elasticated skirts and/or pairs of trousers in neutral colours, together with a couple of loose fitting tops which can be mixed and matched with your existing jackets and accessories. You may also want to invest in at least one decent maternity suit or dress for more important work situations.

Be realistic. You will need at least five outfits for work. It's daft to buy new clothes in desperation at seven months because you've got nothing to wear, when you could have got better value out of them by buying the same articles at four months.

Wear flat or low-heeled shoes whenever possible. Try not to buy new pairs of shoes during your pregnancy, as your feet will swell a little and it is common to find that shoes are too big for you afterwards.

Pack your maternity wardrobe away carefully after the birth – you never know if you may need it again or if you can lend it to a poor deserving pregnant colleague who is at her wits' end about having nothing to wear!

BREAKING THE NEWS AND NEGOTIATING YOUR MATERNITY LEAVE

Choosing the moment to tell your employer that you are pregnant (particularly if it's your first baby) can be tricky. Most of us wait until we are about fourteen weeks before we say anything, figuring that most miscarriages occur during this period and if the pregnancy doesn't work, there's no point in unnecessarily rocking the boat. Others hang on until after they've had their first scan at eighteen to twenty-one weeks. You need rock-hard stomach muscles to pull this off and if in any doubt, don't try it, since your boss may not ever trust you again if she guesses before you tell her.

In an ideal world, your boss will be a positive manager and supportive when you break the news. If you have this sort of boss, lucky you. Unfortunately, many working women discover that their employer's attitude towards them changes irrevocably once they have informed them of their pregnancy. There is a minimum level of support that your employer has to offer legally but if they are not generally supportive, don't expect them to suddenly become enlightened overnight. It is as well to know your statutory employment rights during your pregnancy before you broach the subject with your boss.

The most difficult part can be negotiating your maternity leave. If your employer is unsympathetic, you will need a fighting spirit, along with a realistic evaluation of your chances, to negotiate anything above the statutory maternity entitlement.

There are effective and ineffective ways to negotiate your maternity package. Here are some hints:

▶ Try to present your arguments clearly and concisely without being unnecessarily confrontational.

▶ Try not to adopt a self-righteous attitude – it will turn everyone off, especially managing directors or chief executives who are resistant to change.

▶ Be brave: no matter how difficult it may seem, it's definitely worth a try. Organisations are changing swiftly these days.

▶ If direct confrontation doesn't work, going around the problem might prove more fruitful.

▶ Team up with other colleagues. Although individuals can and do effect major policy changes in recalcitrant organisations, going it alone is not the only route.

Should you need any ammunition, you can get some facts and figures concerning women's employment records during their childbearing years from the Equal Opportunities Commission. Most of these show working mothers in a very positive light and may assist you in breaking down ridiculous prejudices. Remember also that men are changing too, since many now have working wives and young children and have needed flexibility from their employer on occasions.

> *When I adopted a baby, I was outraged when my personnel department told me I wasn't eligible for the standard company maternity package. I did something extraordinary. I wrote a confidential letter to the MD's wife. I'd only met her once but I thought that*

since they'd got three children and probably had friends who'd adopted children, she'd understand. Within a couple of weeks the company policy had changed, although my letter was never acknowledged and nobody ever explained the reasons for the change. ❜

Another woman, perversely, discovered that refusing to take no for an answer was actually good for her career. She was working as a litigation clerk when she was told she would have to resign if she wanted an extended maternity leave. She won her case when she had the temerity to point out that the court clerks and secretaries were permitted to take longer leave entitlements. She was given credit for pleading on the basis of similar cases.

KEEPING YOUR JOB ALIVE DURING YOUR ABSENCE

Your boss will have much more confidence in you (and in your intention to return with the same level of commitment as before you got pregnant) if you leave in place a coherently written, properly thought-through strategy for covering your work whilst you're on maternity leave. Make sure that you have consulted all the people whose jobs will be affected by your absence before you put your strategy on general release.

Of course, the consultation process cuts both ways. Ask to be sent the organisation newsletter, department reports or other relevant documentation so that you can keep appraised of what is going on whilst you are away.

Ensure that the people who will be covering your responsibilities are properly briefed. Withholding information only serves to make their lives difficult and makes you seem irresponsible – it will not make you indispensable.

If you deal with a lot of external people, take positive steps to keep your network warm. If you are happy with the idea, you could make it clear that you will welcome calls at home to discuss issues. Schedule these for a certain time each day to suit your routine with the baby, or leave an answering machine on all the time and return the calls when it suits you. You may be able to make a case for your employer paying for some of your phone bill.

After a few weeks, when you're feeling more like yourself, take the baby into work to say hello. People love to see a new baby and you needn't stay very long. If you are definite about your decision to return to work it is worth continually reinforcing the message that you plan to return and that, when you do, you will be as effective as before you left. There are also certain legal requirements (such as sending letters confirming your intention to return) which you must comply with in order to protect your rights.

RETURNING TO WORK

Deciding whether or not to return to work can be difficult.

For some mothers, there is no decision to make. Some of us know from the start that we will return because there is no other way that the family will survive. For a lot of us, we need to return to affirm our own identity separate from the baby and to resume our hard-worked-for career path. For some women, however, the choice is a lot less clear cut – particularly when they take into account the expense and anxiety of finding quality childcare.

If your decision is to return to work, you may find that your overriding feeling is one of gratitude to be going back to some adult company and intellectual stimulation. Or you may find that you have major anxieties about the possibility of jeopardising your relationship with your baby and disturbing the rhythm of the child's life. Most of us experience both of these feelings and many more. Be aware that your first few weeks will be quite tough.

> *What a mass of conflicting emotions on my first day! On the one hand, I was just so relieved to get back to the office for a rest. The pace of my job is very much dictated by me, unlike motherhood which is utterly dominated by the needs of someone else. I couldn't believe that I was once more master of my own destiny. On the other hand I was also very scared about having left her and very uncomfortable with massive hard, leaky breasts. I called home every half-hour to check everything was OK. Of course it always was.*

Rest assured that it is highly unlikely that your relationship with your baby will be damaged. Of course, your relationship will change but do bear in mind that it has to evolve all the time if either of you are going to survive or grow.

Much publicity has been given to the need for mothers to be ever-present during the first months of children's lives in order to establish a strong emotional bond between them. Since the early 1950s many psychiatrists and paediatricians have peddled the notion that the disruption of this bonding would result in later emotional problems. Though this has never been established, it is little wonder that many mothers feel a tremendous burden of guilt if they leave their child to go to back to work. They have inherited a legacy of baggage which suggests that this bond will be damaged and their children will pay a long-term price.

In other words, mothers have been put under pressure needlessly, made to feel guilty without cause and given an added burden at a time when they are already overloaded. In reality there is no likelihood of serious problems arising provided that certain simple precautions are taken to maintain healthy, happy babies who are properly attached to their parents. The following are some guidelines to consider:

▶ **Stick to a consistent routine.** The routine that has been built up throughout your baby's short life, for feeding, changing and exercise, must be maintained. Usually these routines involve lots of cuddles and happy contact. Sometimes they also involve little games or songs or some other consistent behaviour from one or other parent which becomes firmly associated with the activity. These routines help the baby to feel secure and comforted and should be worked on in the morning and the evenings. Remove this continuity and there is likely to be distress for both baby and mother.

▶ **Continue your feeding routine.** If you are breast feeding, there is no reason why you should not continue to do so. You may find you can use a hand-operated or battery-powered breast pump to express your milk, or that you would get on better with a full-scale electric pump which can be hired from your local health authority, the National Childbirth Trust or major chemist. If you plan in advance, you can build up reserves before you return (breast milk freezes well) and express some at lunchtime each day at work in order to ease the discomfort and to keep your supply going. It is worth persevering if your feeding is working well and suits you both but if you find it is adding unduly to your burden, be sensible and switch to the bottle.

▶ **Work on cutting down stress.** You will find out how long it takes to complete even the simplest preparations when there is a baby involved. By the time you have finished, you may well be in a tearing hurry to get off to work. This is a potential stress time for the baby, who also has to adjust to separation. Unfortunately, you can transmit stress to your children no matter how young they are. It is important therefore to make the preparations for going to work as calm as possible. This can be very difficult as everything seems to go wrong – buttons will not fasten, nappies will get soiled at the last moment, and so on. The trick is to do anything you can (such as preparing feeds) the night before and try and make these leaving for work times an opportunity for fun.

▶ **Make time for play.** Play is a vital part of early child development. It is largely responsible for the growth of thinking and reasoning skills, co-ordination, strength and stamina. Play with parents is also an essential ingredient of a child's social development. Set aside time for play, preferably after everyone has returned home. It is a good idea if the fun people a baby spends her time with before going to sleep are her parents. On no account should this early social play be stifled or left solely to others such as nursery staff or childminders (although obviously the odd evening will not make any difference).

Being a relaxed working mother is easier said than done but work at it – it will cause less disturbance of the relationship between mother and child in the long run. Remember also that a little stress is better than a lot of stress. For example, if money is a major problem and no other solution can be found, a return to work by the mother will ultimately be better for the baby's quality of life. Simple measures such as those outlined here can usually help to prevent this from causing additional stress. A little forward planning to meet the basic needs of your baby will be well rewarded by continued happy relationships and healthy development.

> For the first six months after my child was born, I could safely say that I was floundering – just about keeping things under control. But it was taking its toll – I was exhausted all the time, I wasn't performing well as a worker, a mother or a partner. So, I sat down and worked out a timetable and strategy for all the activities in my life and (after a few teething problems), I feel able to cope with it all and actually have some time to myself as well. It did wonders for me at work. I felt so confident

that I could turn the situation around and I seldom feel daunted by anything they throw at me now.

ALTERNATIVES TO THE NINE-TO-FIVE

There are a number of alternatives to full-time working that women pursue in order to have the flexibility to care for their young children (or their dependent parents) and to carry on working. These include part-time working (the most common), flexible working, job-sharing and home-working.

My mother was the original superwoman, she always worked nine-to five, and she had five children. On top of that, she was very famous in her professional field. But I knew that I could never emulate her energy. I needed to work part-time.

With 80% of part time workers being women, part-time status has, until recently, suffered from poor conditions of service. However, conditions are improving and skills shortages mean that the range and status of jobs being offered on a part time basis is increasing.

It was the perfect solution for me. The nature of my work makes it easy to compartmentalise. When I'm at work, I'm happy to be there. But on Thursday and Friday, I'm delighted to be in the playground.

Whilst working part-time may be the answer to making it all hang together right now, there is little doubt that a part-time schedule will slow your career. That fact can be frustrating at times but it's important to remember that you don't have to be at the peak of your career your whole life. You will make compromises during certain phases. So will organisations.

In some organisations, flexitime schedules permit women to tailor the working day to suit their family commitments without losing productivity. Flexitime allows employees to choose, within set limits, the times they start and finish work. Most organisations have core hours when employees must be at work. It also permits the carry-over of any excess or deficit of hours beyond the end of the accounting period, usually a month. In most schemes, excess hours may be taken as leave. The main benefit to women is that it allows them greater freedom to organise their working lives to suit their needs.

Job sharing is a somewhat more radical approach than flexitime. In this scheme two or more people voluntarily share the responsibilities of one full-time job and divide the money, holidays and so forth according to the number of hours worked. This means that employees can pursue professional careers on a part-time basis. For the employers the results are higher productivity, reduced absenteeism and a reduction in staff turnover. If you and a colleague wish to investigate this route, a good source of advice and assistance is from New Ways to Work, who can also advise on other types of flexible working.

> *Myself and a colleague decided we wanted to share one job so we wrote a proposal and presented it to senior management. Eventually, we were given the go-ahead for six months. At the end of the trial period, we reported back on how much revenue we had generated and the feedback from our clients and colleagues. We now work permanently on a job-share basis. To be honest, I think the company is getting a slightly better deal. But it's a no-lose situation. The clients are happy, the boss is pleased and we both have more time to spend with our children.*

Home-working (or teleworking) provides the ultimate in flexible lifestyles. On top of the satisfaction and self-esteem that comes from doing a job well, you get the creative space to do it your way and the chance to break out of the routine of the nine-to-five. However, you will need the physical space in your home to establish a permanent work station.

Although teleworking is not yet that prevalent, there have been definite moves towards a more flexible work force. Many more people are now self-employed or working temporarily or part-time and large, centralised offices are being ditched in favour of smaller, satellite offices. If you are considering home-working, you must first work out whether you really are an independent, self-starting sort of person. Be honest. Secondly, you need to ask how much you depend on people at work for your social life. Would you miss the fun of being part of a team or department?

You may also lose out on pay and conditions (there are no paid holidays or sick leave if you are self-employed) and on promotion prospects too – out of sight may well mean out of mind. Will you miss the status your job brings? You may find the outside world takes you less seriously as a home-worker.

As with most big steps, get as much advice and information as you can before you take any decisions that bind you in to a mode of working that may not suit you. If at all possible, negotiate a trial period for the package that you have in mind. That way you can both test whether it serves your mutual interests without committing yourselves.

CHILDCARE PROVISION FOR THE UNDER-FIVES

Returning to work after having a baby (especially if it is your first baby) is unbelievably stressful. The additional anxiety of finding the right childcare to suit you and your baby is immense.

However you tackle your search for the right childcare for your family, you will discover that the provision is very hit-and-miss.

A good starting point is your local authority which is required to monitor standards and to make information available to parents. They usually publish a booklet or brochure on childcare in the borough. In certain locations a computer-based pilot known as Child Care Links has been pioneered. This provides an excellent service to any parent who, by making one phone call, can give all their individual requirements and will receive a tailor-made print-out of childcare options that will meet their needs.

If you are looking for care within the home there are some excellent books available that will guide you through the minefield of nannies, childminders and au-pairs (see Further Reading on pages 351–352). Obviously, if you can afford it, can bear to share your privacy and have the space, a live-in nanny is the least stressful option for women with demanding careers.

A nanny will command some of your management skills: you need to find the right person, agree terms and conditions, set up PAYE/National Insurance systems, negotiate times and overtime and so on. Many women enjoy this extra management challenge, but for others it is just an added chore. There are some agencies who will undertake this work for you or you could use services such as the Chiltern Nursery Training College Nanny Scheme. This scheme will find you the right nanny and support her in place for up to a year if required, with contracts, systems for PAYE and so forth thrown in. The fee is £1,000. A conventional nanny recruitment agency will cost you anything from £400 to £1,500 just to find a nanny in the first place.

Another way to find a trained nanny is to approach any local colleges which run nursery nursing courses. However, you may find it better to recruit a nanny who has already had at least one position. Not only will she be more experienced generally, she will also be very much clearer about the employer/employee relationship and will not need as much spoon-feeding (or have as many false expectations) as someone in their first job.

> ❛ Since the birth of our first child, a live-in nanny has enabled me to be at the hospital at 7.00 a.m. and on call. I have the flexibility to stay late if I'm needed. This is important to my relations with my colleagues. I sometimes say, "You go home and rest. I'll take over." I don't have to watch the clock or run out the door at 5.00 p.m. That relieves a lot of stresses. ❜

For many women, a nanny is prohibitively expensive (as there is no tax relief for you on childcare expenses, you have to earn something of the order of £13,500 gross per annum in order to pay your nanny £8,500, taking into account things like National Insurance contributions). Many of us just would not be able to afford to go to work unless there were other options available.

Employing a childminder (someone who will look after your child in her home) is a more cost-effective option and can cost anything from £40 to £70 a week. If you are considering a childminder, make sure she is registered with the local authority.

Choosing a childminder has the advantage that your child is still in a home environment and the disadvantage that you have to ferry child together with immense quantities of baby paraphernalia backwards and forwards from the minder's. As anyone who has ever tried to get out of a house in the morning with a toddler will tell you: it's no joke. There are a few things that you can do to ease the strain a little. Deliver enough frozen meals into your childminder's freezer together with a sufficient quantity of fruit on a Monday to last your child through the week. If she has room, buy nappies in bulk or have them delivered and let her have enough for a month's supply. It may also be worth the expense to keep a second supply of bottles and a steriliser at her house if she is amenable.

Since childminders have their own family responsibilities, they will to expect you to stick to the hours agreed and will not be best pleased if you are late to pick baby up. There isn't normally much flexibility in the system. Try to pre-empt any potential problems by being totally honest when you first interview the minder, resisting the temptation to make the deal seem more attractive than it is in order to make sure of her. You may get the childminder to agree to take on your child this way but it is not a recipe for long-term success and harmony.

> ❛ I never fail to be impressed by my childminder. The number of different transactions she carries out in a day and the organisational skills she needs take my breath away. That's not to mention her extraordinary stamina. She has a whole skills base that I never could emulate. Her job would exhaust me. ❜

If you decide that the best solution is for your child to attend a nursery (or day-care centre), you need to research carefully what is available in your area and what the cost will be. If you are looking for publicly funded day care, don't hold your breath. The UK comes bottom of the league in terms of publicly funded nurseries. If you enjoy a reasonable level of support within a two-parent family, it is unlikely that you will be able to procure a place for your child in a state-funded nursery. Private-sector places are normally very much more expensive (anything up to £160 a week) but still cheaper than paying a nanny, and your child may stand to gain from exposure to other children and the facilities available.

In any circumstances, one-on-one care is the best deal for your child but since this is always expensive, aim for the lowest carer-to-child ratio you can afford in whatever situation you are looking at.

CHILDCARE PROVISION FOR THE OVER-FIVES

Some women experience more of a barrier to their continuing career once their children reach school than they ever suffered during the pre-school years. Much childcare for the under-fives is geared to the working day, whereas school times just are not. Contrary to popular perception, women often go on to part-time hours at this stage, rather than on their immediate return to work. Life is further complicated by the need to arrange cover for the whole day during the long school holidays.

> **'** *When they talk about childcare and work, they seem to think that it comes to an end when they start school. There's a perception that you don't need childcare after that, but you do. My daughter is ten but I still need someone to look after her after school and during the holidays. I've been very lucky because I've found a child minder who will look after her for those times. But it's difficult to find someone who will.* **'**

The general picture of after-school care in this country is worse than the provision for under-fives. To make matters worse, a lot of nannies and trained childminders tend to find older children too boisterous and difficult to control to be enthusiastic about taking them on. There is plenty of anecdotal evidence of well-to-do and career-minded women producing babies at regular intervals to keep their nanny on board.

For those of us who are less well-to-do, there is an enormous problem. This is borne out by the shocking facts that less than 1% of school-age children have access to an out-of-school supervised group care scheme and more than 20% of five-to-ten-year-olds are left alone during school holidays, with 15% being left alone after school.

Some splendid work on the pioneering of after-school care has been done by the National Out of School Alliance who can provide advice to parents on how to find facilities in their area. There are three hundred out-of-school schemes currently operating in the UK but estimates show that there is an unfulfilled demand for eight thousand. The Kids Club Network, also works to extend care and play provision for school-age children.

Most women rely on a tenuous web of friends and relations, neighbours and au pairs to bridge the gap in care. Really clever mothers can activate an emergency support network at a moment's notice but most of us have witnessed at least one slip-up when a child has been left stranded at the school gate for twenty minutes as we dashed from work to get them. It is at times like these that women come to understand the value of the extended family, as anyone with a mother (or their partner's mother) living nearby will testify.

> *I'm really lucky to have my mother living nearby to take the children to school and to pick them up again. If she weren't with them, I would never have peace of mind. Until we moved back here, for four and a half years I took them to a childminder. I was up until 1.00 a.m. every night making bottles and getting their clothes ready. Every morning I had to haul two kids and a pushchair up and down stairs. Then there was the added stress of picking them up by 5.45 p.m. to avoid paying overtime. I never want to go back to that.*

COPING WITH A SICK CHILD

No matter how well organised you are, crises do occur from time to time. You can't always anticipate them but you can have good contingency plans to help you cope. The most testing of these is a sick child, nanny or childminder or an epidemic at the nursery.

> *I love my boss. He says to me, "If your children get ill, you can work at home but don't tell me you couldn't get an assignment in on time because your children were ill." That's the sort of straight relationship we have. Mind you, I have worked for him for eleven years.*

Many working women are just not able to postpone or cancel meetings or miss a day's work at a moment's notice. If you are one of these then you need to keep a list of other people who can help you in such a crisis. Ask around and find out who could support you in the eventuality of something going wrong.

If the child is sick and you have a nanny, a mother's help or an au pair, your problems are easily solved because there is someone with a meaningful relationship to your child in the house. If you have a reliable daily who has a relationship with the children, she might also be used as a stopgap.

Nurseries, however, will not accept a child who is poorly and it is unfair to try to leave your child in school when she is coughing and spluttering and liable to infect the other children. If your child becomes ill in the middle of the day, the school will call you and expect you to collect her. They will not take kindly to any prevarications such as asking the school to hold on for a few more hours until the presentation to the key client is over. They expect someone to come as soon as possible to collect an unwell child both for the child's sake and for the sake of the other children.

A minder will not accept an unwell child for the same reasons and will also call the responsible parent if there is any sign that the child is unwell.

This is one of those crises where the development of your own extended family or friends is crucial. The Working Mothers Association, with its seventy branches up and down the country, was set up to function in exactly that way, as a large extended family of working mothers prepared to help each other out. However, with a sick child who is also infectious, you are not going to find it easy to get someone to come round and sit with your child, particularly if it involves bringing her own children with her.

Take a critical look at you own support network. If you find it wanting then you must develop some contingency plans now rather than wait for the day when something goes wrong. You could develop a relationship with an agency which you know can provide you with help at a moment's notice. Some run an emergency service to cover just such crises.

RETURNING AFTER BRINGING UP YOUR CHILDREN

If you have taken a few years out of your career, you may need some support and assistance to relaunch yourself in the job market. Over 200,000 of us will return to work this year, many after taking some years out to bring up a family. A lot of us will not know how to deal with the new technology or even how to go about re-entering the world of work.

A good first stop is the Women Returners Network which offers practical advice and assistance with retraining and upgrading of skills. They also publish a very useful annual directory called Returning to Work. There is a wide range of return to work courses aimed at helping women build their confidence and reassess their skills before they re-enter the employment market. Your local job centre, TEC office, community centre or library may also have information on return-to-work courses. If you are a single parent, you may be able to benefit from the return-to-work programme run by the National Council for One-Parent Families. You may also find the Gingerbread organisation useful. This is a national network of self-help groups for single parents which, amongst other things, provides training and personal development opportunities. They also have advice centres and childcare facilities within the network.

It is important that your CV does not stop with the day you left paid employment. Your life has not stopped: you have gone on to do a whole range of other things – looking after children or older people is no mean feat and it is important to be able to indicate the kind of things you have been involved in whilst out of paid employment. Being a full-time mother and housewife involves managing many complex matters.

If you have organised the baby-sitting circle then you have organisational skills; if you have been actively involved in a Parent Teachers' Association you may have the ability to speak up at meetings. If you have been involved in voluntary work of any kind, or part-time employment – these things show you are a person who is active, involved and doing things.

HOW MOTHERHOOD AFFECTS YOU

Contrary to the general perception, many women find that the perspective gained by motherhood fosters the wisdom needed for making many of the tough decisions that management requires. It is true that there are other pursuits and interests that can serve the same function, but motherhood imposes a fairly relentless discipline on women which provides a great challenge. It is often the detours that people take on the road to career success which are the biggest learning experiences of all. One-track minds don't necessarily always move in the right direction.

> *Having children keeps you very humble. You come home and you're just Mummy. You realise your job is not the centre of the universe. It keeps things in perspective.*

Office crises suddenly seem simple and mundane compared to the skill and sense of humour it takes to juggle a full-time job, two pre-school children (or even at-school children) and a dual-career household.

Possibly the toughest problem for you as a working mother is finding the time you need. Not time for the baby, but time for you and time for you to spend with your partner if you have one. Most career women find every twenty-four hours crowded enough. With a child as well, something has to give. It is probably unnecessary to say that time management (see Chapter 6) is of even more importance to a working mother than to a childless woman.

To find a solution that will work for you, you need to think about priorities and you need to find support. It may sound harsh but you need to start thinking about your priorities as a mother which put you first, your partner second and your child or children third.

This goes against the grain of our biological urges (and the powerful conditioning we have all unwittingly received) but unless you start thinking in these terms you will find that your own needs will get submerged. This is not selfish: it makes sense. If you are exhausted, overworked and depressed, constantly trying to juggle an impossible set of demands, then you are not going to be a good mother. Neither are you going to be any good at work. You need sleep, time for yourself and emotional support. You need time with your partner, to keep your relationship alive and growing.

> *I could have coped with all of it – my double life as mother and personnel manager – if he'd just slept through the night even once a week. It was the lack of sleep that was the last straw. For the whole of the first year I was like the walking dead. Roland would be awake every night between two and four and there was nothing I could do to induce him to sleep. Liam took his turn every second night but the chances were that the baby's screaming would wake us both anyway. We finally got some really good advice: it transpires we have quite a bright baby who just wanted to spend some time with his parents! We implemented a new regime of intensive playing and stories and activities until ten o'clock each evening and he now sleeps*

through with no bother. It's tough to have to do this after we've both had a hard day at the office but it's a hell of a sight less tough than being woken every night.

If you suffer with a sleepless child, you deserve all the sympathy in the world. It is not that uncommon and there are some very good books available and support groups established to help parents deal with this terrible burden. You and your partner (or another helper) must take the sleepless nights turn and turn about: research shows that six hours of uninterrupted sleep is a lot more restorative than eight hours of disturbed sleep. You must get some uninterrupted sleep at least one night in two or else you will go under.

Examine all the demands on your time and decide what matters to you most. It helps to write down roughly how much time each activity takes. In the same way as your organisation would do an audit on its accounts, do a time audit to sort out your real priorities. The more detailed you make your time audit the easier it is to see where you are overdoing it.

You will learn to live with being tired and even learn to accept it with resignation. Most parents get by on less sleep than they are used to but do try not to sacrifice your sleep in order to keep up with everything else you did previously. Remember, this phase in your life will end.

▶ ▶ ▶ ▶ ▶ Further Reading and Useful Contacts

Chapter 1: Firm Foundations

FURTHER READING

Charles Handy, *The Age of Unreason*, Random House

Mike Pedler and Tom Boydell, *Managing Yourself*, Fontana, (1985)

Liz Willis and Jenny Daisley, *Women's Development Workbook Springboard*, Hawthorne Press

Jane Skinner and Rennie Fritchie, *Working Choices*, J.M. Dent & Sons Ltd., (1988)

Anne Dickson, *A Woman in Your Own Right*, Quartet, (1982)

Manuel Smith, *When I Say No, I Feel Guilty*, Bantam, (1981)

Beverley Hare, *Be Assertive*, Optima, (1988)

Ken and Kate Black, *Assertiveness at Work*, McGraw Hill, (1982)

Chapter 2: Your Career Strategy

FURTHER READING

Dave Francis, *Managing Your Own Career*, Fontana, (1985)

Natasha Josefowitz, *Paths to Power*, Columbus Books, (1980)

Ian Bryce, *The Influential Woman*, Piatkus

Sue Slipman, *Helping Ourselves to Power*, Pergamon Press, (1986)

Judith Bardwick, *The Plateauing Trap*, Bantham Books, (1986)

Marie Jennings, *10 Steps To The Top*, Piatkus

Marilyn Davidson, *Reach For The Top*, Piatkus

Bridget Wright, *Which Way Now?*, Piatkus

Dan Finn and Lucy Ball,
Unemployment & Training Rights Handbook

Just the Job (A booklet on all the schemes available to unemployed people published by the Employment Department. Available from your local Jobcentre or Unemployment Benefit Office)

USEFUL CONTACTS:

Training & Enterprise Councils (TECs) (England & Wales)
Local Enterprise Companies (LECs) (Scotland)
(These are responsible for ensuring that there is vocational training available and can give advice and information on vocational guidance and training. Look in your local phone directory.)

Jobcentres
Employment Service Head
Office
St Vincent's House
30 Orange Street
London WC2H 7HT
Tel: 071 839 5600
(Each area has its own office.
Check your local phone
directory.)

UK Volunteering Centre
International Voluntary
Service (IVS)
Old Hall, East Bergholt
Colchester CO7 6TQ

**Community Service
Volunteers (CSV)**
237 Pentonville Road
London N1 9NJ
Tel: 071 278 6601

**National Association of
Volunteer Bureaux**
St Peter's College
College Road
Saltley
Birmingham B8 3TE
Tel: 021 327 0265

**REACH (Retired Executives
Action Clearing House)**
89 Southwark Street
London SE1 0HD
Tel: 071 928 0452

Chapter 3: Changing Your Job

FURTHER READING

Occupations '89, Careers and Occupational Information
Centre (COIC)

Career In .. series, Kogan Page

Anna Alston, *Equal Opportunities: A Careers Guide*,
Penguin, (1987)

Diane Burston (ed.), *An A-Z of Careers*, Kogan Page

Leslie Morphy, *Career Change*, CRAC, (1987)

Rebecca Cornfield, *Preparing Your Own CV*, Kogan Page

Yvonne Sarch, *How to Write A Winning CV*, Century Business

Susan Clemie and Dr John Nicholson, *The Good Interview Guide*, Rosters

Job Hunting Made Easy, Kogan Page

CHAPTER 4 : ACTIVATING SUPPORT SYSTEMS

FURTHER READING

Dr Peck, *Mentoring and Networking*, Piatkus

Susie Orbach and Luise Eichenbaum, *Between Women*, Arrow, (1994)

M Scott Peck, *The Road Less Travelled* Rider, (1987)

David Clutterbuck, *Everyone Needs a Mentor*, Institute of Personnel Management, (1985)

Judi Marshall, *Women Managers – Travellers in a Male World*, Wiley, (1984)

Joel Kovel, *A Complete Guide to Therapy*, Penguin

Peter Firebrace and Sandra Hill, *A Guide to Acupuncture*, Paul Hamlyn, (1989)

J R Worsley, *Is Acupuncture for You?*, Element Books

Peter Mole, *Acupuncture: Energy Balancing for Body, Mind and Spirit*, Element Books

Gloria Steinem, *Revolution from Within: a Book of Self Esteem*, Bloomsbury

USEFUL CONTACTS

Women in Management
64 Marryat Road
Wimbledon
London SW19 5BN
Tel: 081 944 6332
(Network of women
managers and those aspiring
to be. Offers training and
development activities.)

Women's Therapy Centre
6 Manor Gardens
London N7
Tel: 071 263 6200
(Provides psychotherapy for
women from a feminist
perspective. Offers courses
and publications.)

**General Council and
Register of Osteopaths**
56 London Street
Reading
Berks RG1 4SQ
Tel: 0734 576585
(Provides a list of registered
osteopaths in your area.)

**British Association of
Counselling**
37A Sheep Street
Rugby
Warks CV2 1 3BX
Tel: 0788 578328

**The Society of Teachers of
the Alexander Technique**
10 London House
266 Fulham Road
London SW 6 9EL
Tel: 071 351 0828

Council for Acupuncture
179 Gloucester Place
London NW1 6DX
Tel: 071 724 5756
(Accreditation and co-
ordination body for
acupuncturists in the UK.
Will provide a list of
practitioners in your area.)

**Council for Complementary
and Alternative Medicine**
179 Gloucester Place
London NW1 6DX
Tel: 071 724 9103

CHAPTER 5 : YOUR TRAINING STRATEGY

FURTHER READING

Helen Bridge and Heather Salt, *Access and Delivery in Continuing Education and Training*, Publications Unit, Department of Adult Education, Education Building, University Park, Nottingham NG7 2RD. Tel 0602 514427.

DOFE Directory of Further and Many Higher Education Courses in the United Kingdom, CRAC,

Directory of Grant-Making Trusts, Charities Aid Foundation (1987)

Open Learning Directory Training Agency, (1989)

Andrew Pates and Martin Good,
Second Chances : A National Guide to Adult Education and Training Opportunities, COIC, (1989)

Fred Orr, *How to Succeed at Part-Time Study*, Unwin, (1988)

Joan Perkin, *It's Never Too Late*, Impact Books, (1984)

Floodlight, ALA/LBA

Grants to Students: A Brief Guide, Department of Education and Science (DES), Despatch Centre, Honepot Lane, Canons Park Stanmore, Middlesex HA7 1AZ

USEFUL CONTACTS

The Council for the Accreditation of Correspondence Colleges
27 Marylebone Road
London NW1 5JS
Tel: 071 935 5391

The Women Returners Network
8 John Adam Street
London WC2H 6EL
Tel: 071 839 8188

The Open College
FREEPOST TK 1006
Brentford
Middlesex TW8 8BR
Tel: 0800 300 760

EI Office, Open University (OU)
PO Box 71
Milton Keynes MK7 6AG
Tel: 0908 274066
(Will provide the address of your nearest OU Regional Office.)

National Extension College (NEC)
18 Brooklands Avenue
Cambridge CB2 2HN
Tel: 0223 316644

Women & Training Ltd
Hewmar House
120 London Road
Gloucester GL1 3PL
Tel: 0452 309330
(Women's training newsletter, workshops, regional network and resources bank.)

The Industrial Society
The Pepperell Unit
Robert Hyde House
48 Bryanstone Square
London W1H 7LN
Tel: 071 262 2401
(The Industrial Society's Pepperell Unit run regular training courses designed to improve working skills for women.)

Scottish Education Department
New St Andrews House
Edinburgh EH1 3TG
Tel: 031 244 4806

Career Development Loans
Freephone 0800 585505

CHAPTER 6: YOUR TIME, YOUR CHOICE

FURTHER READING

E. Bliss, *Getting Things Done*, Bantam Books, New York (1976)

S. F. Love, *Mastery and Management of Time*, Prentice-Hall, New York (1978)

Me, My Time, My Life, Time Manager International, (1981)

Alan Lakein, *How to Get Control of Your Time and Your Life*, McKay, New York (1973)/New American Library (1974, paperback)

Winston Stephanie, *Getting Organized*, Norton, New York, (1978)/Warner Books (1878, paperback)

Sally Garratt, *Managing your Time*, Fontana, (1985)

Marjorie Shaevitz, *The Superwoman Syndrome*, Fontana, (1984)

USEFUL CONTACTS

Time Manager International
50 High Street
Henley in Arden
Solihull
West Midlands B95 5AN

CHAPTER 7: EFFECTIVE COMMUNICATIONS

FURTHER READING

Michael Gelb, *Present Yourself*, Aurum Press, (1988)

Christina Stuart, *Effective Speaking*, Pan, (1988)

Genie Z Laborde, *Influencing with Integrity*, Syntony Publishing

CHAPTER 8 : WORKING RELATIONSHIPS

FURTHER READING

Janice La Rouche and Regina Ryan, *Strategies for Women at Work*, Counterpoint, (1984)

CHAPTER 9 : RESOLVING CONFLICT

FURTHER READING

Natalie Hadjifotiou, *Women and Harassment at Work*, Pluto Press, (1983)

Andrea Adams, *Bullying At Work*, Virago

Statement on Harassment at Work, Institute of Personnel Management, IPM House, Camp Road, Wimbledon, London SW19 4UX (Tel: 081 946 9100)

Sexual Harassment in the Workplace – The Facts Employees Should Know, Employment Department, ISCO 5, The Paddock, Frizinghall, Bradford BD9 4HD

USEFUL CONTACTS

ACAS (Advisory Conciliation and Arbitration Service)
(For advice contact your regional office. The number will be in your phone book.)

The Equal Opportunities Commission
Overseas House
Quay Street
Manchester M3 3HN

National Harassment Network
Vicki Merchant
Tel: 0772 892512
(For an annual membership of £35, members receive a quarterly newsletter and an opportunity to attend network meetings. The network also provides training and consultancy services on harassment at work.)

Trades Union Council (TUC)
Congress House
23–28 Great Russell Street
London WC1B 3LS
Tel: 071 636 4030

Women Against Sexual Harassment (WASH)
242 Pentonville Road
London N1 9UN
Tel: 071 837 7509
(Provides support and advice for women who have been sexually abused at work.)

CHAPTER 10 : HARNESSING YOUR STRESS

FURTHER READING

Ursula Markham, *Women Under Pressure*, Element, (1990)

Jacqueline Alkenson, *Coping with Stress at Work*, Thorsons, (1988) (Good all-round book on work related stress and how to cope with it.)

Dr Herbert Freudenberger, *Burn Out*, Arrow, (1980)

Rachel Charles, *Mind, Body and Immunity*, Cedar

CHAPTER 11 : MANAGING YOUR HEALTH

FURTHER READING

Directive 90/270/EEC May 1990,
(available from the Health and Safety Commission (tel: 071 243 6000). European Community Directive on the legal responsibility of your employer to make the office a safer and more comfortable place to work. Binding from December 1992.)

Sick Building Syndrome, LHS Centre, (1990)

Peggy Bentham, *VDU: Terminal Sickness* 1992, (Green Print)

Susan Curtis and Romy Fraser, *Natural Healing for Women*, Pandora Books

Alan Carr, *Easy Way to Stop Smoking*, Penguin

Gillian Riley, *How to Stop Smoking and Stay Stopped for Good*, Vermillion

Boston Women's Collective, *Our Bodies Ourselves*, Penguin

Xandria Williams, *Choosing Health*, Letts

Xandria Williams, *Choosing Weight*, Letts

C Haddon, *Women and Tranquillizers*, Sheldon Press, (1984)

Louise Hay, *You can Heal your Life*, Eden Grove Publications, (1984)

Dr Margery Morgan, *The Well Woman*, BBC Books, (1992)

Dr Dean Ornish, *Reversing Health Diseases*, Century

USEFUL CONTACTS

Alcoholics Anonymous
General Office
PO Box 1
Stonebow House
Stonebow
York YO1 2NJ
Tel: 071 352 3001
    0904 644 026

Women's Alcohol Centre
66 Drayton Park
London N5
Tel: 071 226 4581
(Offers free confidential advice to all women who are concerned about alcohol affecting their lives. Local groups.)

National Association Pre-menstrual Syndrome
PO Box 72
Sevenoaks
Kent TN13 3PS
(Write with SAE for membership details. Support groups and information.)

Women's Sports Foundation
London Women's Centre
Wesley House
4 Wild Court
London WC2B 5AU
Tel: 071 831 7863
(A voluntary network for women committed to improving the opportunities for women in sport at all levels. Encourages women to get/keep fit and healthy.)

TRANX (UK) Ltd
National Tranquillizer Advice Centre
25a Masons Avenue
Wealdstone
Harrow
Middlesex HA3 5AH
Tel: 081 427 2065 (clients)
081 427 2827 (24 hours)
(Offers support and advice to people wanting to shop taking tranquillisers.)

London Hazards Centre Trust (LHCT)
Tel: 071 837 5605
(A specialist charity for office health and safety. Will assist in building a good case for office environment improvements on health grounds.)

Action on Smoking and Health (ASH)
Tel: 071 935 3519
(Can supply a health pack on how to introduce a no-smoking policy at work.)

QUIT
Tel: 071 487 2858
(Can come into your workplace and do presentations on the inadvisability of smoking at work and help you maintain any no-smoking policies you may set up.)

RSI Association
Tel: 0895 238663
(Can supply an information pack and a list of specialists. Will also suggest likely solicitors if you are seeking compensation for RSI as a work-related injury.)

CHAPTER 13 : HOME AND CASH

FURTHER READING

Redundancy Handling, Advisory Booklet No. 12 (Free), ACAS, 27 Wilton Street, London SW1X 7AZ

Phil Laut, *Money is my Friend*, Trinity Publications, (1978)

Marie Jennings, *Women and Money – The Midland Bank Guide*, Penguin, (1988)

Colette Dowling, *The Cinderella Complex*, Fontana, (1981)

Anthea Massey, *How to Become a Woman of Substance*, Piatkus, (1987)

Stuart Wilde, *The Trick to Money is Having Some*, White Dove International, (1989)

Ray Proctor, *Finance for the Perplexed Executive*, Fontana, (1986)

Anne Bottomley *The Cohabitation Handbook*, et al., Pluto Press, (1981)

Penny Pinchers' Guide, 14 Wardens Lodge, North Street, Daventry, Northants NN11 5PN

USEFUL CONTACTS:

**Redundancy Payments
Service**
Tel: 088 848489
(Free advice line.)

**Citizens Advice Bureau
(CAB)**
Tel: 071 833 2181 (head
office)
(There is a CAB in most
areas. They give free,
confidential advice and
information on just about
anything, including
employment matters.)

FIMBRA
(Financial Intermediaries,
Managers and Brokers
Regulatory Association)
22 Great Tower Street
London EC3R 5AQ
Tel: 071 929 2711

Fiona Price and Partners
33 Great Queen Street
London WC2B 5AA
Tel: 071 430 0366

CHAPTER 14: BABIES?

FURTHER READING:

I Need A Childminder, National Childminding Association

Jill Black, *Working Mothers Survival Guide,* Simon and
Schuster

Judith M. Steiner, *How to Survive as a Working Mother,*
Kogan Page

Andrew Bibby, *Home is Where the Office Is,* Hodder &
Staunton

Working from Home, BT information pack. Available free
by calling 0800 800845.

Job-Sharing: Improving the Quality and Availability of Part-Time Work, Equal Opportunities Commission

Francis Kinsman, *The Telecommuters*, John Wiley and Sons, (1987)

Elizabeth Dobbie, *Returners*, National Advisory Centre on Careers for Women, (1982)

Caroline Bailey, *Beginning in the Middle*, Quartet, (1989)

Maggie Steel and Zita Thornton, *Women Can Return to Work*, Grapevine , (1988)

Women Returners Network, *Returning to Work*, Longman, (1987)

David Clutterbuck (ed.), *New Patterns of Work*, Gower, (1986)

Amanda Cutbertand Angela Holford, *The Baby and the Briefcase*, Mandarin

Robin Skynner and John Cleese, *Life and How to Survive It*

Pamela Anderson, *Simple Steps for Returners*, Poland Street Publications

Tess Gill and Larry Whitty, *Women's Rights in the Workplace*, Pelican, (1983)

USEFUL CONTACTS

Maternity Alliance
15 Britannia Street
London WC1X 9JP
Tel: 071 837 1265
(Offers support and
information service about
maternity rights and benefits
and campaigns on maternity
issues.)

Daycare Trust
Wesley House
4 Wild Court
London WC2B 5AU
(Campaigns for free
nurseries and properly
organised childcare facilities
for the under-fives. Has an
information service for
parents.)

**National Council for One
Parent Families**
255 Kentish Town Road
London NW5 2LX
Tel: 071 267 1361
(Offers help and advice for
single parents on any
problem and campaigns on
behalf of them and their
children for better facilities
and support. Runs a return-
to-work programme.)

**Gingerbread National
Office**
35 Wellington Street
London WC2E 7BN
Tel: 071 240 0953
(Offers support, training and
childcare facilities to single
parents.)

**Practical Alternatives for
Mums, Dads and Under
Fives (PRAM)**
c/o 162 Holland Road
Hurst Green
Oxted
Surrey RH8 9BQ
(Promotes facilities for
young families and
publicises information on
local facilities.)

**Working Mothers
Association**
77 Holloway Road
London N7 8JX
Tel: 071 700 5771
(A self-help organisation set
up to support working
mothers and their children
with information and advice
as well as local groups.)

Chiltern Nursery Training College
16 Peppard Road
Caversham
Reading RG4 8JZ

National Out of School Alliance
(The Kids Club Network)
279–281 Whitechapel Road
London E1 1BY
Tel: 071 247 3009
(Has lists of after-school and holiday playschemes. Advises on setting up schemes.)

CRY-SIS Support Group
B.M.CRY-SIS
London WC1N 3XX
Tel: 071 404 5011
(Help and support for parents of babies who cry excessively or who have sleep problems.)

National Childbirth Trust (NCT)
Alexandra House
Oldham Terrace
Acton
London W3 6NH
Tel : 081 992 8637
(Gives practical help before and after baby is born.)

Carers National Association
29 Chilworth Mews
London W2 3RG
Tel: 071 724 7776
(Charity to support those whose lives are restricted by caring for others. Provides support, information and advice. Also lobbies government and other policy-makers.)

National Childminding Association
8 Masons Hill
Bromley
Kent BR2 9EY
Tel: 081 464 6164
(To enhance the image and status of childminding. To improve conditions for childminders, parents and children. To encourage higher standards of childcare.)

Company Kids
28 High Street
Bidford-on-Avon
Warwickshire B50 4AA
Tel: 0789 773785
(Assists and advises employers in the establishment and management of childcare facilities.)

Luncheon Vouchers Ltd
50 Vauxhall Bridge Road
London SW1V 2RS
Tel: 071 834 6666
(Setting up a childcare
voucher scheme. Freephone
0800 289307 for advice on
childcare facilities and costs,
by area.)

**Pre-School Playgroups
Association (PPA)**
63 Kings Cross Road
London WC1
Tel: 071 700 5771
(A charitable organisation
providing preschool
childcare.)

New Ways to Work
309 Upper Street
London N1 0PD
Tel: 071 226 4026